BLESSED ARE THE ACTIVISTS

Father Stanley Rother's truck, San Lucas Tolimán, Guatemala, where it ended up after his murder. In 2015, I rode in this truck to conduct interviews with genocide survivors, unaware that the truck purportedly had once belonged to Rother. (Michael J. Cangemi.)

BLESSED
ARE THE
ACTIVISTS

Catholic Advocacy, Human Rights, and Genocide in Guatemala

Michael J. Cangemi

THE UNIVERSITY OF ALABAMA PRESS
Tuscaloosa

The University of Alabama Press
Tuscaloosa, Alabama 35487–0380
uapress.ua.edu

Copyright © 2024 by the University of Alabama Press
All rights reserved.

Inquiries about reproducing material from this work should
be addressed to the University of Alabama Press.

Typeface: Arno Pro

Cover image: Girl in front of pictures of murdered Catholic
missionaries at the tomb of Bishop Juan Gerardi, Guatemala City,
2004; photograph by REUTERS/Daniel LeClair DNL/HB
Cover design: Sandy Turner Jr.

Cataloging-in-Publication data is available from the Library of Congress.
ISBN: 978–0–8173–2178–9 (cloth)
ISBN: 978–0–8173–6126–6 (paper)
E-ISBN: 978–0–8173–9477–6

FOR JEAN QUATAERT, WITH GRATITUDE

CONTENTS

List of Illustrations   ix

Acknowledgments   xi

Abbreviations   xv

Introduction: When the Wolves Attack   1

1. "A Group of Soldiers Shot Down a Small Plane"   11

2. "Our Policy Is Designed to Serve Mankind"   32

3. The Parochial Nationalist and the Wily Manipulator   52

4. The Worst Possible Outcome   71

5. "We Need the Closest Possible Cooperation with the Church"   87

6. "In More Than One Office a Picture of Che Guevara"   116

7. Burning the Devil   142

Conclusion: "Aquí no lloró nadie"   165

Notes   173

Bibliography   209

Index   219

ILLUSTRATIONS

Figures

Frontispiece. Father Stanley Rother's truck, San Lucas Tolimán, Guatemala

I.1. Iglesia Santiago Apóstol, Santiago Atitlán, Guatemala   2

1.1. Archbishop Mariano Rossell y Arellano, Guatemala City, Guatemala, 1954   15

1.2. Catholic priest population in Guatemala, 1934–1966   20

2.1. Writ of habeas corpus for Robin Mayro García, 1977   42

2.2. *Prensa Libre* headline, June 1, 1978   48

3.1. Bodies inside the Spanish Embassy, Guatemala City, 1980   63

4.1. United States ambassador Frank V. Ortiz Jr. and Brigadier General Fernando Romeo Lucas Garcia, 1979   76

5.1. Father Stanley Rother   99

5.2. Quic family photo   102

6.1. President Ronald Reagan and General José Efraín Ríos Montt, San Pedro Sula, Honduras, December 1982   135

7.1. Catédral de San José, Antigua, Guatemala   147

7.2. Inscription by Ambassador Ortiz on back of the photograph shown in Figure 4.1   153

Tables

2.1. United States Department of Defense arms sales to El Salvador, Guatemala, and Honduras, 1960–1976   38

2.2. United States Military Assistance Program expenditures to El Salvador, Guatemala, and Honduras, 1960–1976   38

2.3. Selected Munitions Control Export License approvals to Guatemala, 1977–1978   45

2.4. Guatemalan election results, 1978   47

5.1. Catholic priests murdered or abducted in Guatemala, 1981   97

6.1. Guatemalan electoral polling data, November 1981 to February 1982   120

7.1. Guatemalan presidential election, first-round results, November 3, 1985   161

7.2. Guatemalan presidential election runoff results, December 8, 1985   161

ACKNOWLEDGMENTS

Neil Peart, drummer and lyricist for the legendary Canadian rock band Rush, once wrote that "nothing can survive in a vacuum, no one can exist all alone." Neither can history books. This book simply would never have happened without the assistance, encouragement, and support of scores of friends, family, mentors, and people I met along the way. I would first like to thank Penelope Cray, Claire Lewis Evans, and Wendi Schnaufer at the University of Alabama Press for their enthusiasm and help in making this book a reality. I am grateful for their support and patience.

At Binghamton University, I was blessed with a multitude of people who pushed me to be the best scholar, teacher, and writer I can be. Steve Ortiz was the best mentor I could have ever hoped for. He encouraged me to dig deeper, to think big, and to find a way through the problem when I could not find a way around it. I thank him for his advice, patience, and support. Nancy Appelbaum challenged me to reconsider what I thought I knew about Latin America and its relationship with the United States. I am grateful to her, and to Howard Brown, Sandra Casanova-Vizcaino, Heather DeHaan, Ben Fordham, Gerald Kadish, Diane Miller Sommerville, Rob Parkinson, Kent Schull, Wendy Wall, and Michael West for their guidance and time. I also thank Don Frysinger, Kim Hewitt, Dan Katz, Anastasia Pratt, Mark Soderstrom, and Chris Whann for their advice and mentorship and, in many ways, for being responsible for all of this in the first place.

I am also grateful to Jean Quataert for sparking my interest in activism and human rights history. Jean was as exacting as she was insightful, and her excitement for this book or its topics never waned. Like so many of Jean's students, I am a better scholar, thinker, and person for her guidance and kindness. This book is dedicated to her memory in gratitude for her advice, knowledge, and mentorship. I wish she could have read it in its completed form.

I completed this book while serving as a postdoctoral fellow at the United States Military Academy. During my time at West Point, I was part of an incredible team that truly reflected and lived the idea of wisdom through history. I would like to thank David Frey, Mike Geheran, Kirsten Cooper, Rick Anderson, Greta Bucher, Mak Campbell, Carolyn Corrigan, Shelley-Anne Douglas, Brian Drohan, Jess Engel, Bryan Gibby, Jeff Goldberg, Krista Hennen, Rose Horswill, Claudio Innocenti, Holly Mayer, Eric Muirhead, Anil Mukerjee, Phil Murray, Tom Nimmick, Mandi Rollinson, Lou Roberts, Nadine Ross, Jess Rudo, Sam Watson, Romyer Witten, and Gail Yoshitani for their advice, collegiality, patience, and friendship. I would also like to thank Seth Bolden, Alexis Bradstreet, Sam Eden, Dahlia Flores, Ryan Griffin, Joe Holland, Mason Hutchins, Leo Martinez, Ramsey Rouhabia, Jovani Sierra, Ian Tjelta, Caroline Vincent, and all the cadets whom I was privileged to teach at West Point. I am eternally grateful for my time there.

I am also grateful to the many archivists and librarians who helped me make this book a reality. I would like to thank Mary Ahenekew, Herbert Cáceres, Jessica DiSilvestro, Elaine McConnell, Reyna Pérez, Thelma Porres Morfin, Jesse Reneau, Susan Sizemore, Elise Thornley, the Archivo Histórico de la Policía Nacional, Center for Research Libraries, Centro de Investigaciones Regionales de Mesoamérica, the Fray Angélico Chávez History Library, Jimmy Carter and Ronald Reagan Libraries, Maryknoll Mission Archive, National Security Archive, and the Ralph Bunche Library at the US State Department for their assistance, hospitality, and expertise. Likewise, I thank Arch Mrvicka for helping me rescue this book. When I worried that this project was at a dead end before it had even begun, Arch, who had never met or even spoken to me, not only opened his home to me so that I could read scores of archived mission documents and papers but also arranged the interviews that I conducted for this book. Arch also offered advice and encouragement at a critical moment in this book's final stages that pushed it to the finish line. I would like to thank Arch, Chris Clancy, Bill Peterson, and Terri Wong at the Friends of San Lucas Mission and Diocese of New Ulm for their kindness and trust. In San Lucas Tolimán, Father John Goggin, Katie Wallyn, and all the mission's staff and volunteers welcomed me and made me feel as though I was an old friend. I would also like to thank all those who trusted me with their stories. Finally, George Rigazzi offered invaluable assistance and friendship in Oklahoma City as we talked about Guatemala, Stan Rother, and baseball. I thank him, Archbishop Paul Coakley, and the entire archdiocese staff for their warm welcome.

I would like to thank my family and friends as well. My mother taught me to be part of the solution, and my father taught me to express myself. I hope I have made them proud. I also appreciate my friends for their encouragement and for giving me the chance to disconnect myself from writing about genocide and other horrors. I thank Mobashar Ahmad, Rahil Ahmad, Mayra Alejandro, Joanna Allen, Erin Annis, Chris Battaglia, Jason Becker, Geoff Beekle, Gary Belfour, Ben Beranek, Lindsey Brown, Edgar Chivilu, Hubert Cook, Stacey Costabile

Wenslauskis, Cassie Drogose, Aaron Dumas, Andrew Fagal, the FBSN, Brigitte Fielder, Paul Fikentscher, Rob Frías, Cindy, Gerry, Tim, Danica and Dylan Greenfield, Michelle Hickenbottom, Matt Hollis, Aaron Huff, Jessica Hudnall, Cindy Husband, Jason Iacona, Dane Imrie, Alex Jablonski, Tim Kerswell, Kelly Krohn, Aurora Landers, Ken Lane, Bryant Little, Dan MacRae, Dave and Nannette McCormick, Joe Mangi, Jason Mellor, Mike Miceli, Joe Miczensin, Dan Pearson, Trinisa Pitts, Alysa Pomer, Leonard Reese, John Riley, Shelley Rose, Danielle St. Julien, the Semo family, Will T. F. Shawburg, Julia Smith, Katie Stankiewicz, Stephen Sutherland, Adolfo Tapia, Lauren Turek, Kevin Vrevich, and Becky Weidman-Winter for their friendship, patience, and, in some cases, absolute lack of interest in this book and its contents when I needed it. I am grateful to all of them.

I am most grateful, though, to my wife, Laura. Her encouragement and support made this possible. She believed in this book—and me—when I no longer could and helped me find the will to finish what I had started. She is the true cornerstone of this project and so much more. I could not have done any of this without her.

Portions of chapter 4 were originally published in Michael J. Cangemi, "Ambassador Frank Ortiz and Guatemala's 'Killer President,' 1976–1980," *Diplomatic History* 42, no. 4 (September 2018): 613–39. Portions of chapter 5 were originally published in Michael J. Cangemi, "'We Need the Closest Possible Cooperation with the Church': Catholic Activists, Central America, and the Reagan Administration, 1981–1982," *U.S. Catholic Historian* 37, no. 1 (Winter 2019): 167–91.

ABBREVIATIONS

ARA—Bureau of Inter-American Affairs, US Department of State
CACIF—Comité Coordinador de Asociaciones Agrícolas, Comerciales, Industriales y Financieras
CAN—Central Auténtica Nacionalista party
CEDAC—Consejo Permanente Episcopal Centro Américano
CEG—Conferencia Episcopal de Guatemala
CEH—Comisión para el Esclarecimiento Histórico
CELAM—Consejo Episcopal Latinoamericano
CERJ—Consejo de Comunidades Etnicas Runujel Junam
CNA—Catholic News Agency
CNT—Central Nacional de Trabajadores
CUC—Comité de Unidad Campesina
DCG—Democracia Cristiana Guatemalteca party
DIA—Defense Intelligence Agency
EGP—Ejército Guerrillero de los Pobres
EOS—Escuela de Orientación Sindical
ESA—Ejército Secreto Anticomunista
FAR—Fuerzas Armadas Rebeldes
FMLN—Frente Farabundo Martí para la Liberación Nacional
FSLN—Frente Sandinista de Liberación Nacional
FUR—Frente Unido de la Revolución
GHRC—Guatemala Human Rights Commission
GNIB—Guatemala News and Information Bureau
GOG—Government of Guatemala
HA—Human Rights and Humanitarian Affairs bureau, US Department of State
MAP—Military Assistance Program
MLN—Movimiento de Liberación Nacional
MR-13—Movimiento Revolucionario 13 de Noviembre
NISGUA—Network in Solidarity with the People of Guatemala

ORPA—Organización Revolucionaria del Pueblo en Armas
PAC—Patrullas de Autodefensa Civil
PGT—Partido Guatemalteco del Trabajo
PMA—Policia Militar Ambulante
PN—Policia Nacional
PRC—Presidential Review Committee
RNS—Religious News Service
TAN—Transnational Advocacy Network
URNG—Unidad Revolucionaria Nacional Guatemalteca
USAC—Universidad de San Carlos
USCC—United States Catholic Conference

BLESSED ARE THE ACTIVISTS

Introduction

WHEN THE WOLVES ATTACK

In a letter to Oklahoma City archbishop Charles A. Salatka dated November 4, 1980, Father Stanley Rother, a native of Okarche, Oklahoma, recounted a series of recent events in the town of Santiago Atitlán, Sololá, Guatemala, where he had served as a parish priest at a local mission sponsored by the Archdiocese of Oklahoma City. Rother reported that "several hundred" soldiers had established a camp in the area and committed a wave of kidnappings, death threats, and other human rights abuses in recent days, including the kidnapping of two parishioners from their homes on the evening of October 23. According to Rother, neither man had been seen since. The next night, the patrols abducted Gaspar Culán, the director of mission radio station Voz de Atitlán, from his home after reportedly beating him unconscious and robbing the radio station's offices. Rother also noted that several priests and parishioners had fled the area in fear for their lives while hundreds of others slept communally inside the Saint James the Apostle Church for their protection.[1] Acknowledging the immediate danger in the area, Rother included legal forms granting the archdiocese power of attorney over his estate while the otherwise-typed letter included the handwritten message "they may be coming here tonight" on the first page.

Although repression and violence had seemingly paralyzed Santiago Atitlán, Rother's letter also offered glimpses of ordinary life amid extraordinary violence. He shared updates on the mission's medical program, a recent automobile accident that left Rother's truck at the bottom of Lake Atitlán courtesy of a drunk driver, and news of the mission nuns' annual retreat. He also took a defiant stance against the immediate danger that both he and the parish faced and told Salatka, "I am a little tense tonight about where to sleep and whether to have someone stay here with me. . . . The group that broke into the radio station last night may be coming here tonight. I have just about decided to leave all the doors open to avoid breaking them in, and sleep where they won't find me. There won't be much danger from ordinary thieves because people just aren't found on the streets anymore at night." Rother punctuated his letter with a stirring reaffirmation of his faith and commitment to the people of Santiago Atitlán. He informed Salatka that he and other area priests were attempting to secure a visa for his associate priest, Pedro Bocel, to leave the area for his safety. He also asserted his own intention to remain in Santiago Atitlán and stated, "I still don't want to abandon my flock when the wolves are making random attacks."[2] Eight months later, the wolves attacked again and murdered Rother in the church rectory (Figure I.1).

Figure I.1 Father Stanley Rother's church, Iglesia Santiago Apóstol, Santiago Atitlán, Guatemala. (Courtesy Edgar Chiviliú.)

Stanley Rother was one of the thousands of priests, nuns, and lay Catholics from the United States to serve as a missionary in Guatemala and across Central America during the Cold War. These Catholics served their parishioners in ways that extended beyond the spiritual. Just nine miles east of Santiago Atitlán, for example, Rother's fellow priest and friend Father Gregory Schaffer helped lead an ambitious mission program in the town of San Lucas Tolimán that offered vocational training to help alleviate the area's poverty, worked with numerous groups to expand access to clean drinking water and cooking stoves, and spearheaded multiple public health initiatives for San Lucas Tolimán's residents.[3] Similarly, Maryknoll Father Bill Woods, a trained pilot, routinely flew timber and other building supplies to the department of Quiché to construct homes for some of the region's poorest citizens. Elsewhere, Christian Brother James Miller oversaw the order's schools in Guatemala and Nicaragua, and priests like Father Ronald Hennessey and Father Bernard Survil consistently provided Catholics in the United States with firsthand accounts and thoughtful analyses of Central America's inequality, poverty, and violence during the 1970s and early 1980s. Their actions came with a tragic cost, as Woods, Rother, and Miller were all murdered between 1976 and 1982, and other clergy, nuns, and missionaries were abducted, tortured, or threatened by a dictatorship that viewed them as Marxist-inspired political subversives. Similar violence occurred in El Salvador and Nicaragua, as Catholic clergy, missionaries, and prelates in those countries also suffered similar reprisals for their advocacy.

Missionaries like Rother, Schaffer, and Woods were part of a broader coalition of Catholic activists who brought Guatemala's inequality, poverty, and violence to greater public attention in the United States during the bloodiest years of the country's lengthy civil war (1960–1996). This coalition was remarkable for its diversity and included Catholics from numerous ethnicities, nationalities, and economic classes and counted cardinals, bishops, priests, nuns, and lay Catholics among its ranks. Its members attributed Guatemala's crises to the country's long-entrenched military dictatorship for protracting its historical economic, political, and social inequities, which Catholic activists understood as human rights abuses. They also used a variety of methods to press US and Guatemalan policymakers to help end the war and, just as importantly, to bring increased attention to Guatemala's poverty and social inequity. Many individual activists within this coalition also worked with other like-minded Catholics who sought to halt similar crises in neighboring El Salvador and Nicaragua. For these activists, their understanding of how power and poverty intersected in places like Guatemala, alongside their methods of activism, linked them to a longer tradition of Catholic social activism that had originated in Italy during the late nineteenth century and exploded in Guatemala by the mid-twentieth.

That variety is also at the heart of this book's primary questions: How and why did Catholic activists of different backgrounds use different types of activism to try halting Guatemala's rampant violence and human rights abuses and bring those abuses to greater public attention? How and why did Catholic activists bring political pressure to bear on US policymaking decisions on Guatemala? How did the US Catholic press facilitate greater grassroots actions on Guatemala and Central America as a whole? Finally, how did this multifaceted, multipronged type of Catholic activism contribute to the Jimmy Carter and Ronald Reagan administrations' policy debates on Guatemala and Central America?

To answer these questions, this book explores Catholic activists' methods and objectives in Guatemala and makes four arguments. First, Catholic activists in the United States and Guatemala were among the most prominent voices to condemn Guatemala's inequality, poverty, and violence during the late 1970s and early 1980s, the most violent period of the country's civil war. They were also some of the most prominent critics of the Carter and Reagan administrations' anemic responses to Guatemala's crises. This book shows how different types of Catholic activism contributed to the movement's prominence during this period. These included reportage, political action, local facilitation, and rescuing children from combat zones and offering shelter to refugees and those targeted for death by the dictatorship. This breadth made Catholic activism more visible and simultaneously offered individual Catholics multiple local options for participating in the larger movement.

Second, although Catholic activists failed to help end the war during this period, they were successful in other ways. Importantly, missionaries like Rother, Schaffer, and Woods helped build and strengthen ties between their home dioceses and missions in the United States and the parishes and communities they served in Guatemala. These ties yielded mission projects like agricultural programs in San Lucas Tolimán and Santiago Atitlán and cooperative markets and housing projects in the Ixcán. Additionally, Catholic activism's breadth of action brought greater public attention to conditions in Guatemala, as Rother, Hennessey, and visiting prelates like Bishop Lawrence Welsh of Spokane, Washington, shared firsthand accounts of Guatemala with their home dioceses in the United States. These accounts offered US Catholics local context for understanding Guatemala and its crises and, at times, excoriated US policies toward the country. They also often focused on Guatemala's racial and class inequities as much as they did on the war itself—a connection clear and indivisible in the minds of many Catholic activists. Although that indivisibility unsurprisingly placed Catholic activists and US policymakers at cross-purposes on many occasions, Carter and Reagan administration officials alike considered Catholic activists' positions and their influence within their policymaking calculus on Central America, including Guatemala.

Third, while cities like Spokane, Pittsburgh, and Dubuque were smaller than cities like New York, Los Angeles, and Chicago, they were nevertheless critical to Catholic activism and its successes. Across the country, diocesan newspapers like the *Pittsburgh Catholic* and Dubuque's the *Witness* routinely published news and commentary about Guatemala and US support for the country's dictatorship, at times better and more frequently than nationally circulated religious and secular newspapers like the *National Catholic Reporter* or the *New York Times* did. These cities' dioceses also sponsored mission projects in places like San Lucas Tolimán, Santiago Atitlán, and many other municipalities across Guatemala. Additionally, dioceses from Ogdensburg, New York, to Portland, Oregon, hosted speaking engagements and teach-ins, letter-writing campaigns, food and clothing drives, and a host of other events focused on Guatemala. The breadth and consistency of these events underscore the importance of smaller cities and dioceses within Catholic activism during this period.

Finally, the men and women whom this book examines were part of a transnational advocacy network (TAN) that aimed to promote and protect Guatemalans' human rights. TANs, as defined by scholars, including Margaret Keck and Kathryn Sikkink, are networks of activists "working internationally on an issue, who are bound together by shared values, a common discourse, and dense exchanges of information and services."[4] As the following chapters show, these activists' values were shaped by a shared faith, built connections between places like New Ulm and San Lucas Tolimán and Oklahoma City and Santiago Atitlán, and were critical sources of information on conditions in Guatemala. Examining them as a TAN gives their advocacy a deeper context and, as historian Jean Quataert has noted, keeps local and international settings in simultaneous focus.[5]

This book also offers a different perspective on Guatemala's lengthy, brutal civil war, which left more than two hundred thousand people dead and disappeared and displaced an estimated one million people within the country and across Central America, Mexico, and the United States as refugees.[6] While these totals reflect the enormity of the war's violence, they can also depersonalize historical accounts of the war by obscuring individual accounts from victims and survivors. Nor do they distinguish between different *types* of violence like torture, death threats, malnutrition, or rape, among others. Thus, I have utilized the UN-backed Comisión para el Esclarecimiento Histórico's (CEH) mammoth twelve-volume, four-thousand-page postwar report on the causes of the conflict and the nature, sources, and individual instances of human rights abuses committed during the war. I have also used testimonies collected by the CEH and interviews I have conducted with some of the war's victims and Catholic activists to show how acts of rape, torture, public intimidation, and religious persecution in Guatemala contributed to the country's abysmal human rights record during the late 1970s and early 1980s.

These accounts highlight just how personal and relentless the war's abuses were. For example, the CEH concluded that the department of Quiché—an area the size of the city of Juneau, Alaska—was the site of more than seven hundred known human rights abuses in 1981 and more than eleven hundred in 1982, an average of two and a half abuses committed per day during that period. The CEH's reporting also includes recorded instances of abuses like rape, torture, and war-related deaths from malnutrition and forced displacement, among a host of other categories. Accounting for these types of abuses offers a more comprehensive perspective not only on the scale of the war's violence but also on its breadth. These testimonies are also a reminder that not all the war's victims perished from the abuses that they suffered, and, for many, the war's traumas are still obstacles to reconciliation and reconstruction.

Diocesan newspapers also captured how individual Catholics, their parishes, and dioceses learned about and understood Guatemala's violence and upheaval during the 1970s and 1980s. As historian Edward Brett has shown, nationally circulated newspapers like the *National Catholic Reporter* and wire services like the Catholic News Service and Religious News Service offered coverage and analysis of Central America's multiple, simultaneous wars and widespread repression that equaled and, at times, surpassed that of the *New York Times, Washington Post,* or *Los Angeles Times.*[7] Diocesan newspapers, however, have been comparatively understudied. Newspapers like the *Pittsburgh Catholic*, Portland, Oregon's *Catholic Sentinel*, and Dubuque's the *Witness* were also a critical component of US Catholic press coverage of Central America because they were able to emphasize parochial and diocesan connections to events in Guatemala or Central America in ways that national newspapers could not. Stories about local nuns, priests, and lay Catholics serving as missionaries in Guatemala routinely appeared in diocesan newspapers alongside reports about food and clothing drives for Guatemalan Mayans, parish or diocesan-hosted events focused on Guatemala, news on the country's horrific violence, and impassioned editorials calling for an end to the war. This local focus made diocesan newspapers a vital part of the US Catholic press and an equally vital tool for Catholic activists in the United States.

Guatemala's civil war was one of the many crises that shaped the Carter and Reagan administrations' relationships with Central America and its governments. Wars in El Salvador and Nicaragua killed tens of thousands of men, women, and children, and the region's violence exacerbated its poverty and social inequality. As conditions across the region grew worse in the early 1980s, US policymakers attempted and, at times, struggled to balance their bilateral and regional goals for Central America against political and public criticism. Historians have likewise examined those struggles from national, bilateral, and regional perspectives.[8] *Blessed Are the Activists* contributes to this work by examining US-Guatemalan relations with an emphasis on the diplomatic "middle," that is, on the ambassadors, diplomats, and other mid-level bureaucrats who struggled to find this balance in a country that neither US administration could afford to be too close to or too far from.[9]

This book also explores understudied moments in US-Guatemalan relations. Historians have typically emphasized two critical events in Guatemala's Cold War history: Árbenz's overthrow and Brigadier General José Efraín Ríos Montt's genocidal dictatorship.[10] That emphasis has overshadowed other critical historical moments, especially during the Carter and Reagan administrations. *Blessed Are the*

Activists addresses this lacuna by examining how Guatemala's human rights abuses left US-Guatemalan relations at a diplomatic impasse by the late 1970s, and how this impasse exposed the practical limits of the Carter administration's human rights–based foreign policy.[11] It also examines the Reagan administration's relationship with the General Óscar Humberto Mejía Victores regime following Ríos Montt's overthrow in August 1983. Taking these events into consideration allows a more comprehensive image of US-Guatemalan relations to emerge from the long historical shadows cast by Árbenz and Ríos Montt.

Religion occupies a central place within that more comprehensive image. In some ways this is unsurprising, as religion and religious groups exerted significant influence over US policymaking during the Cold War.[12] This was especially true in Central America, where foreign missionaries, politically active religious figures like Salvadoran Óscar Romero and Nicaraguan archbishop Miguel Obando y Bravo and a growing marketplace of faith all further complicated the region's historically complex church-state relationships. This book broadens the already rich literature on the intersections of diplomacy, faith, and politics by highlighting the impressively broad array of tools that Catholic activists used to safeguard Guatemalans' human rights, disseminate news and information about conditions in Guatemala on a parochial and diocesan level across the United States, and press policymakers in both countries to act. In this respect, *Blessed Are the Activists* recenters Catholicism and Catholic activists within a body of literature that has often emphasized evangelical Protestantism.

Blessed Are the Activists navigates this political and religious terrain and foregrounds some of the ways that Catholic activists brought Guatemala's human rights abuses to greater global attention and that Catholic activism contributed to US policymaking decisions on Guatemala. Chapter 1 offers the historical context for the book's arguments by summarizing important developments in Guatemalan politics, the country's war, and the Roman Catholic Church pre-1976 and how these developments contributed to US relations with Guatemala.

The relationship between the Guatemalan government and Catholic activists took a violent turn beginning with the Woods's murder in 1976. Chapter 2 examines how and why Guatemala's human rights abuses grew in frequency and intensity following Father Bill Woods's murder in 1976. The chapter also recounts human rights' central role in the Carter administration's foreign policy model, along with the administration's goals for Central America and the ways that the administration's diplomatic clashes with the Kjell Eugenio Laugerud García regime emphasized critical flaws in the Carter administration's human rights–based foreign policy.

Chapters 3, 4, and 5 examine the human rights abuses of the Fernando Romeo Lucas García regime and its relationship with the United States. Chapter 3 examines the Lucas regime's human rights abuses following his ascent to power in July 1978 and how Catholic activists responded to the increased violence and repression through direct intervention and reportage. It also explains how foundational shifts within Catholic doctrine following the Latin American Episcopal Conference (CELAM) meeting in Puebla, Mexico, in 1979 contributed to increased tensions between the Lucas regime and the Guatemalan church, as well as the consequences of those tensions.

Chapter 4 is a respite from the previous chapter's violence and focuses on how conditions in Guatemala affected the country's diplomatic relationship with the United States. It explains how Guatemala's human rights abuses affected internal policy discussions within the State Department as different bureaus within the organization, most notably the Bureaus of Inter-American Affairs and Human Rights and Humanitarian Affairs, disagreed on how to engage with Lucas on human rights issues and how simultaneous crises in El Salvador and Nicaragua forced State Department and Carter administration officials to prioritize resources and attention away from Guatemala. These problems hamstrung Frank V. Ortiz Jr. during his brief tenure as US ambassador to Guatemala in 1979 and 1980. Ortiz's challenges as ambassador and his personal antipathy for Lucas refute claims from Ortiz's critics that he had been too politically conservative and close to the Lucas regime to secure meaningful human rights reforms. Instead, as Ortiz repeatedly noted, the administration's human rights–based foreign policy had left him without any meaningful diplomatic leverage, particularly military assistance, to use with Lucas in human rights discussions. While Ortiz was ultimately proven correct, his recall highlights the fraught nature of US-Guatemalan relations by 1980. The chapter also examines the ideological and practical challenges to the Carter administration's foreign policies and how these challenges effectively ground US-Guatemalan relations to a halt as the Lucas regime's human rights abuses increased.

The Reagan administration's relationship with Catholic activists was contentious and uneven. Chapter 5 shows how Catholic activists' persistent criticism of the Reagan administration's foreign policy goals for Central America contributed to the administration's decision to forego reviving military assistance to Guatemala in 1981 and how Catholic activists pressed both countries' governments to respond to Rother's murder in 1981. Activists' pressure fostered additional tensions between US and Guatemalan policymakers, and by 1982 these tensions had led some State Department and White House officials to conclude that the Reagan administration needed to change its policy approaches to Guatemala, Central America, and Catholics alike. They argued that as Catholic activists became more inextricably entangled in Central America's multiple crises, they also had the potential to foment anti-US sentiment among fellow Catholics in the United States, especially in parishes and dioceses with large Latino populations across the country. In response, apprehensive policymakers advised the Reagan administration to secure "the closest possible cooperation" with the church to mitigate and, if possible, undercut this potential threat to its domestic and foreign agendas.

Chapter 6 examines how Guatemala's 1982 presidential election and subsequent coup affected the war and the country's domestic politics and relationship with the United States. The chapter follows US-Guatemalan relations during Ríos Montt's prodigiously violent dictatorship from March 1982 to August 1983. Although US policymakers and Catholic leaders initially hoped that Ríos Montt's reputation for integrity, strong leadership, and deep Pentecostal faith were encouraging signs that the country's violence would subside under his rule, Ríos Montt's fervent millenarianism and rigid autocracy plunged the country deeper into violence and genocide. This, in turn, fueled withering criticism from Catholic activists and further complicated the Reagan administration's policy goals for Guatemala. The chapter examines the forms Catholic activism took in the United States during this period, especially the role Catholic newspapers played in reporting on Guatemala and Central America during the early 1980s. It also recounts the horrors of the Ríos Montt regime and how Catholic churches themselves became sites of human rights abuses.

After Ríos Montt's overthrow in 1983, his successor, General Óscar Mejia Victores, immediately announced his intention to hold legislative and presidential elections and a return to civil government by 1985. Despite this, his regime's violence and thorny relationship with the Guatemalan church raised concerns among Catholic activists that Mejia would be no different than his predecessors. The final chapter explores the Mejia regime's turbulent relationship with the Guatemalan church and the Guatemalan church's role in the country's 1985 presidential elections. It shows how in 1983, a wave of anti-Catholic violence and rhetoric in Guatemala deepened the country's church-state tensions and led US ambassador to Guatemala Frederic Chapin to characterize these tensions as a considerable impediment to peace and improved bilateral relations. It also recounts how Chapin acted as an intermediary between the Mejia regime and the Conferencia Episcopal de Guatemala (CEG) during 1983 and early 1984 as the two sides attempted to reconcile. Church-state relations improved enough that in late July 1984, the country's National Assembly asked Archbishop Prospero Penados del Barrio to celebrate a special mass to bless their inaugural legislative session, a previously unthinkable development. Pope John Paul II also recognized Guatemala's slow but perceptible progress in a special pastoral letter that year in which he encouraged continued cooperation and offered his prayers for reconciliation. With the Guatemalan church's endorsement and collaboration, the National Assembly ratified a new constitution in May 1985 and the CEG exhorted all Guatemalans to vote in the November presidential election as a matter of Christian obligation. Christian Democratic Party candidate Marco Vinicio Cerezo Arévalo's victory signaled a new era in Guatemalan politics and society, as the military ceded its hold on the presidency and the country began its slow transition to peace.

Rother's letter is a window into the challenging territory that Catholic activists negotiated in Guatemala. In Santiago Atitlán, Rother helped improve access to medical care and legal assistance for parishioners, reported the army's local occupation and crimes like Culán's abduction and Voz de Atitlán's robbery, and worked to secure Bocel's safe exit from the area. He also spearheaded agricultural initiatives that increased local production, led funeral masses for parishioners murdered by both the army and guerrillas, consoled families of the disappeared, and welcomed dozens of visiting mission volunteers from the United States. Further, Rother's love for Santiago Atitlán and its people never waned, despite the very real danger that he faced as a priest. Rother and Bocel were forced to leave Guatemala for Oklahoma in January 1981 after their lives were threatened, just two months after his letter to Salatka. Both men nevertheless returned to Santiago Atitlán in May of that year to serve the parishioners they could not abandon. Likewise, Schaffer, Miller, and many other priests, nuns, and missionaries remained in Guatemala and sought equitable, peaceful solutions to Guatemala's crises of violence, poverty, and inequality. Working together with like-minded allies in the United States, Catholic activists in Guatemala were a prominent voice in US policymaking decisions during the Carter and Reagan administrations, advocated for the poor and powerless, and shielded their flocks from Guatemala's wolves.

1

"A Group of Soldiers Shot Down a Small Plane"

In an airgram to the State Department dated May 4, 1976, US ambassador to Guatemala Francis Meloy updated officials in Washington on clashes between the Kjell Eugenio Laugerud García regime and the armed Marxist group Ejército Guerrillero de los Pobres (EGP) in the department of Quiché, where EGP forces had concentrated their activity near the towns of Nebaj, Chajul, and San Juan Cotzal, an area familiarly known as the Ixil Triangle. Meloy reported on a series of airstrikes and bombings in the region that had begun in 1975 and forced thousands of rural, indigenous Guatemala campesinos to flee to the surrounding mountains. The airstrikes unsettled Meloy because "the less-than-pinpoint accuracy of Guatemalan Air Force pilots" killed more civilians than guerrillas, and he was concerned about US missionaries and clergy in the region. Meloy also reported that Guatemalan army officers were "convinced an American Maryknoll priest who works with a large agricultural cooperative in northwestern Quiché is helping the guerrillas. [He] denies the charges, and the Embassy has no information to substantiate them."[1] Although he was not identified by name, the priest was Father Bill Woods, a Houston, Texas, native who joined the New York–based Maryknoll order in 1958.

Woods arrived in the Ixcán region of Quiché in 1969 to replace Father Edward Doheny, a fellow Maryknoll priest who had helped to coordinate indigenous groups' settling of the area's uninhabited jungle since 1966. "Padre Guillermo" helped the settlers, known as *parcelistas*, form the Ixcán Grande Cooperative in 1970. According to former Jesuit priest Ricardo Falla, the cooperative took ownership of the land, formed credit and savings unions for *parcelistas*, established a common market to sell crops, and "provided a forum for organizational learning for this multiethnic, multilingual" group that included Chuj, Jakalteko, Mam, and Q'anjob'al Guatemalans.[2] The cooperative worked with Maryknoll missionaries to establish five cooperatives by the mid-1970s with each *parcelista* receiving approximately forty-three acres of land to tend and live on; by 1975, the Xalbal cooperative alone was home to 256 *parcelistas*.[3] Woods, a pilot with more than two thousand hours of flight time since arriving in Guatemala, also flew supplies into the area from Guatemala City in his Cessna airplane. On the morning of November 20, 1976, witnesses saw Woods's airplane plunge out of the sky and crash into the Chuchumatanes mountains near San Juan Cotzal, killing all on board.

Multiple accounts blamed the army for Woods's death. According to one *pareclista* (smallholder), "The people working in San Juan Cotzal . . . said that a group of soldiers shot down a small plane . . . and that the soldiers refused to let them look at" it.[4] Another reported that in 1978, "Colonel Fernando Castillo admitted the army's complicity, and stated 'I am not guilty, but other colonels planned [Woods's] death.'" Further, Woods himself had stated prior to his death that should the army ever wish to shoot down his airplane, a clearing near the Chuchumatanes—precisely where he was shot down—provided an ideal line of sight.[5]

Guatemalan officials did little to investigate the crash. In one of the few published accounts of Woods's death, journalist Ron Chernow noted that Guatemalan civil aviation officials flew via helicopter to the crash site, "hovered over the spot, then whirled back to the capital to file their report. . . . When Bill Woods's associates pointed out that their report erroneously claimed that [Woods's airplane's] engine had burned up, the investigators rushed to delete this information." Finally, regime officials refused to allow Armand Edwards, a US National Transportation Safety Board investigator, to inspect the crash site out of concern for guerrillas in the area and because "all the helicopters in Guatemala were grounded for maintenance" at the time of his visit.[6] No legitimate investigation into the crash or the army's involvement was ever made.

Woods's murder was a pivotal moment in the relationship between Guatemala's dictatorship and many of the country's Catholic priests, nuns, and catechists. Although many Guatemalan Catholics like Archbishop Mariano Rossell y Arellano had initially welcomed the right-wing dictatorship that had ruled the country virtually uninterrupted since 1954, a series of foundational changes within Catholicism eroded Guatemala's church-state relationship and by the mid-1970s had placed the institutions at cross-purposes. The Second Vatican Council (Vatican II) examined the church's relationship with a rapidly changing temporal world, while landmark papal encyclicals like Saint John XXIII's *Mater et Magistra* and *Pacem in Terris* and Paul VI's *Populorum Progressio* articulated the church's positions on human dignity, socioeconomic rights, and industrialized nations' obligations to the world's poor. Additionally, liberation theology's emergence in Latin America from the Catholic Action movement saw many priests, nuns, and laity interpret those positions in a regional context and criticized Latin America's dictatorships for their repression and violence during the late 1960s and through the 1970s. In Guatemala, these developments coincided with the war's escalation and Woods's murder.

This chapter explores Guatemala's church-state rupture during the late 1960s and early 1970s. It traces Catholic activism's roots to the late nineteenth century, when Europe's nascent Catholic Action movement challenged lay Catholics to take a greater, more direct role in combatting poverty and social inequalities. Catholic Action had spread to Latin America by the interwar period and resonated with many of the region's faithful, especially in Peru, where the movement was bolstered by the Great Depression and a desire to distance the church from the recently deposed Augusto Leguía regime. It also resonated with John XXIII, who had been influenced by Catholic Action as a young priest and introduced many of its tenets into church doctrine during his papacy. This chapter examines those connections, their importance to liberation theology's emergence in the late 1960s, and how these events contributed to Woods's murder.

On April 4, 1954, the archbishop of Guatemala, Mariano Rossell y Arellano, issued a pastoral letter denouncing the ambitious economic, legal, and political reforms introduced by President Juan José Arévalo Bermejo and his successor, Jacobo Árbenz Guzmán, over the preceding decade.[7] These reforms included expanding suffrage to women and working-class men, legalizing unions and political parties, including the communist Partido Guatemalteco del Trabajo in 1951, and, most notably, implementing a sweeping agrarian reform plan known as Decree 900 in which the Árbenz government nationalized tracts of unused land owned by companies like the United States–based United Fruit Company and redistributed it to landless rural workers.[8] Rossell, alongside many conservative Guatemalans and Americans, perceived these reforms as part of a larger effort to turn the country into a Soviet-allied Marxist state. In his letter, the archbishop warned that "the 'Soviet paradise' is a concentration camp where, behind the force of tanks and cannons, all are forced to work for the Master State."[9] He also called upon Catholics to "fight against communism" as a matter of religious obligation.

Two months after Rossell issued his letter, on June 17, a force of approximately 150 CIA-trained fighters loyal to Colonel Carlos Castillo Armas, the US government's preferred choice to replace Árbenz, invaded Guatemala's eastern Zacapa department from neighboring Honduras, as another one hundred men entered the country at Puerto Barrios on the Caribbean coast. The invasion, known as Operation PBSUCCESS, faced what historian Piero Gleijeses has described as "hardly an impressive war machine" of approximately 6,200 poorly trained and ill-equipped soldiers and combined naval and air forces of 500 additional men.[10] They quickly capitulated to the invading force, and by June 25, Árbenz's advisers informed him that the army had no desire to fight off the invasion. Defenseless and demoralized, Árbenz resigned the presidency to Armas two days later.[11]

Some of Guatemala's Catholics welcomed the coup. For example, Sister

Mary Martina Bridgeman, a Maryknoll Mission sister in Guatemala City, wrote a lengthy letter to the mission's Mother Superior and founder, Mother Mary Columba, that described conditions in the capital during the invasion and coup. In one vivid passage, Bridgeman reported that while driving to church on June 19, she and another nun, Sister Anna Maria, had been caught in a shootout in front of the Escuela Politécnica, which she described as "the West Point of Guatemala." Bridgeman also noted that on June 24, one of the teachers at the mission's school, the Colegio Monte María, told the sisters of reports that Castillo Armas had dedicated his army to the *Cristo Negro de Esquipulas*, a sixteenth-century carving of Jesus's crucifixion and Guatemala's most revered Catholic icon.[12] For Armas, the association reaped clear benefits: according to Bridgeman, "when Castillo Armas arrived [in Esquipulas] the whole city went over to his side. A High Mass was offered at the shrine with all the people of the village in attendance and God's blessing was invoked upon his undertaking. With this knowledge we feel assured that God will be with him and that his cause will succeed."[13]

The US Catholic press reported on Árbenz's overthrow in mostly positive terms. *Pittsburgh Catholic* editor John Collins opined that while both Arévalo and Árbenz had intended to introduce meaningful reforms designed to "loosen the grip of the United Fruit Company" in the country, "the Communists offered their 'help' to the [Arévalo and Árbenz] administration[s] which [were] foolish enough to accept it and to try to 'co-operate' with the Reds."[14] Likewise, an essay printed in the Rochester, New York, *Courier-Journal* reported that although the Árbenz government denied any support for Marxism, Guatemala had become "a police state as terrifying as Red China" where Catholics were persecuted for their faith, a stance that was echoed in an opinion column by the Reverend John B. Ebel in the Wichita, Kansas, *Catholic Advance*.[15] Philadelphia's *Catholic Standard and Times* also ran two separate stories on Guatemala's purported anti-Catholicism and three alleged plots to exile Rossell, and Cincinnati's *Telegraph-Register* warned ominously that "the Guatemala situation ought to teach us that Communism flourishes best where (1) religion has grown weak and (2) social justice is not practiced."[16] One notable exception was Richard Pattee's analysis in his *St. Louis Register* column. Pattee asserted that the invasion had violated Guatemala's domestic sovereignty, an argument that Laugerud would later make when he rejected US military assistance predicated on Guatemala's human rights record. In a strikingly prescient conclusion, Pattee asked, "Is the sanctity of absolute sovereignty so great that even the installation of Communism must be tolerated, because to do anything about it would violate that sovereignty? If this were true, then everything that is going on in Southeast Asia—among other places—makes no sense."[17]

As Castillo Armas praised the Lord and the United States for his triumph,

Rossell publicly lauded the new regime. On July 7, the archbishop held a funeral mass for pro-Castillo Armas forces killed during the coup and cast Árbenz's overthrow in biblical terms. During his remarks, Rossell cited the Vision of the Dry Bones, a passage from the book of Ezekiel that describes God's creation of a new Israel from the ruins of the old: "Thus says the Lord God, Look! I am going to open your graves; I will make you come up out of your graves, my people, and bring you back to the land of Israel."[18] Eleven days later, Rossell attended a mass honoring his sixtieth birthday in front of Guatemala City's Metropolitan Cathedral, where, according to a report in the newspaper *El Imparcial*, he declared that he had "faith in the liberation movement's triumph" and had been ready to "give his blood" during the coup (Figure 1.1).[19]

Figure 1.1. Archbishop Mariano Rossell y Arellano, Guatemala City, Guatemala, 1954. (Courtesy Centro de Investigaciones Regionales de Mesoamérica, GT-CIRMA-AH-001-001. This work does not represent the opinions of CIRMA. Responsibility for the content and execution lies with the author.)

Castillo Armas faced multiple crises during his presidency, including coup attempts in August 1954 and January 1955, as clashes between pro– and anti–Castillo Armas factions became increasingly frequent. These clashes were often fatal: in one notable example, Guatemala City police fatally shot several demonstrators outside the Palacio Nacional on June 25, 1956, after two days of anti–Castillo Armas protests. The shootings prompted Castillo Armas to declare a state of siege and suspend the country's constitution until the crisis had passed. The violence pushed Castillo Armas and his government further to the political right, which garnered support from the army, the country's wealthy conservatives and elite, and, importantly, the Eisenhower administration. As a State Department report noted, this shift came "at the expense . . . of his prestige with middle class and labor elements."[20] As the country's politics grew increasingly polarized, so too did its violence and intrafactional tensions, which US policymakers struggled to understand fully: when Castillo Armas was assassinated in July 1957, State Department officials could not initially determine whether the assassin was affiliated with the country's extreme left or with one of Armas's rivals on the far right.[21]

On November 13, 1960, a group of eight junior army officers led an unsuccessful coup attempt against Castillo Armas's successor, General José Miguel Ramón Ydígoras Fuentes. US Embassy officials in Guatemala City reported that the coup had been driven in large part by Minister of Defense Rubén González Siguí's unpopularity with army officers and Ydígoras's small "circle of favored Army officers" but also took care to note that "it was in no way influenced by Communists or political parties, at least in the beginning."[22] Additionally, historian Carlos Sabino has argued that the attempt was also partially rooted in Ydígoras's decision to use Guatemala as a training ground for Cuban exiles who would attempt to overthrow Fidel Castro during the Bay of Pigs fiasco the following year.[23] The revolt, which lasted three days, left thirteen dead and sixty injured, and fifty-two government and military officials fled the country and obtained political asylum in Honduras.[24] The remaining conspirators regrouped along the Guatemala-Honduras border and formed the group Movimiento Revolucionario 13 de Noviembre (MR-13). By 1962, MR-13 had allied with the remnants of Guatemala's communist party, the Partido Guatemalteco del Trabajo (PGT), and other smaller leftist groups to form the Fuerzas Armadas Rebeldes (FAR), who would go on to assassinate political figures during the 1960s.

As Guatemala began its descent into lengthy civil war, the Catholic Action movement spurred thousands of Catholics across Latin America to bring greater economic and social equity to the region. Catholic Action emerged during the late nineteenth century in response to what Pope Leo XIII saw as the negative consequences of Europe's increasing urbanization and industrialization. He believed that economic and social classes across the continent had become more rigid as production modernized and that relations between capitalists and laborers were dangerously strained. He also lamented "the misery and wretchedness pressing so unjustly on the majority of the working class" and Marxism's potential to disrupt

European politics and society.[25] He articulated these concerns emphatically in his 1891 encyclical *Rerum Novarum*, which called for a more equitable relationship between the capital and working classes, affirmed that while all people had a right to private goods and property, they were spiritually obligated to share their possessions with the poor, and declared that the state's primary function as an entity was to ensure that laws and institutions served the common good, to protect all people's well-being and prosperity, and to maintain peace among its citizens.

Rerum Novarum's themes were also central to Catholic Action, which sociologist Milagros Peña has described as "an international movement concerned with the plight of workers and the living conditions produced by capitalism."[26] Its most crucial component was the laity: lay Catholics organized and oversaw Catholic Action programs with relatively minimal intercession from church hierarchy. In this sense, Catholic Action preceded liberation theology's Comunidades Eclesiales de Base (Ecclesiastical Base Communities), local reformist organizations led by lay Catholics with a clerical advisory.

One of Catholic Action's earliest success stories was Bergamo, Italy, a historically poor area in the country's Lombardy region. Through Catholic Action's auspices, by the late 1800s Bergamo's laity had organized and maintained approximately one hundred Catholic social groups, credit and labor unions, health clinics, and schools, with around forty-two thousand men and women involved in at least one of these groups. Catholic Action's influence in Bergamo led *l'Osservatore Romano*, the Vatican's daily newspaper, to declare it "*la Catholicissima Città*," or the most Catholic of cities.[27]

One notable Bergamo resident was Angelo Giuseppe Roncalli, a young priest ordained in the town in 1904 who would later become known to the world as John XXIII. As a parish priest in Bergamo, Roncalli worked under the tutelage of Bishop Giacomo Maria Radini-Tedeschi, a devout adherent to Catholic Action who initiated a sweeping public works scheme to update churches that had fallen into disrepair within the episcopate. As Lawrence Elliott has noted, Roncalli's priesthood and, later, his papacy as John XXIII, reflected Catholic Action's core tenets. His belief that "we must all . . . live good lives and try consistently to do our duty without meddling in politics" was apparent in his work with Bulgarian laity to help coordinate refugee relief efforts following World War I and, later, his personal intervention to spare European Jews from the Holocaust as Apostolic Delegate to Turkey and Greece in the 1930s.[28]

Catholic Action's success in Bergamo prompted Pope Pius XI to laud it as a bulwark against Marxism and modern secularism in his 1922 encyclical *Ubi Arcano Dei Consilio*. The encyclical praised "that whole group of movements, organizations, and works so dear to Our fatherly heart which passes under the name of 'Catholic Action,' and in which We have been so intensely interested. All these organizations and movements ought not only to continue in existence, but ought to be developed more and more. . . . It is without question an essential part of our Christian life and of the sacred ministry."[29] The Pope also instructed Catholic cardinals to "tell your faithful children of the laity that when, united with their pastors and their bishops . . . they are more than ever united with Us and with Christ, and become great factors in bringing about world peace."[30]

Some Catholic Action members served as missionaries in Latin America, where the movement had gained traction by the 1930s. According to Peña, the Great Depression facilitated Catholic Action's spread through the region because "proponents of Catholic Action pressed to be more actively involved in poor people's movements [and] university reform, rural unionizing, agrarian reform, and literacy programs."[31] These efforts were particularly successful in Peru, where priests like Father Jorge Calderón and Archbishops Mariano Holguín and Pedro Farfán lent critical support to a broad array of lay organizations dedicated to economic and social reform; another Peruvian priest, Gustavo Gutierrez, was later central to liberation theology's development.

Catholic Action moved closer to the church's doctrinal core following Roncalli's election to the papacy in October 1958. The new pontiff immediately informed his secretary, Monsignor Loris Capovilla, of his intention to convene an ecumenical council that would reexamine the church's relationship with the modern world.[32] The Pope announced his decision to convene the council to a group of cardinals at the Basilica of Saint Paul Outside the Walls on January 25, 1959, where he told the attendant prelates that the church was falling out of phase with the modern world and needed *aggiornamento* ("updating") to fulfill its spiritual mission. He also stated that one of the council's tasks would be to find reconciliation and common ground with other Christian and non-Christian faiths to facilitate peace and global communion while a Vatican Press Office statement issued that day noted that the forthcoming council was "intended to be an invitation to the separated communities to search for the unity for which so many souls in all parts of the world yearn today."[33]

The council, familiarly known as Vatican II, opened on October 11, 1962.[34] More than 2,800 bishops from around the globe participated in at least one of its four sessions between 1962 and 1965, more than quadruple the number that had attended the First Vatican Council, which met in 1869 and 1870.[35] During the council's sessions, its members produced two dogmatic constitutions, two pastoral constitutions, three declarations, and nine decrees that allowed priests to celebrate Mass in the local vernacular instead of Latin, encouraged ecumenical harmony between Catholics and other Christian sects, and called on missionaries to adapt their work to meet "the necessities of the apostolate, the demands of culture, and social and economic circumstances."[36]

Vatican II also lauded missionary work. For example, the decree *Ad Gentes* called missionary activity "nothing else and nothing less than an epiphany, or a manifesting of God's decree."[37] This was, in some ways, unsurprising: the 1959 encyclical *Princeps Pastorum* had praised lay missionaries for answering the world's spiritual "cry for help," especially among the world's poor.[38] Similarly, *Ad Gentes* specifically recognized the need for missionaries to work in "the poorer portions of the globe" and called on clergy and lay Catholics alike to work closely with local pastors and bishops in those areas to fortify and expand the church's outreach.[39]

Dignity, reconciliation, and activism were also central themes for John XXIII's two landmark encyclicals. The first, *Mater et Magistra*, was issued in May 1961 and addressed the world's poor and working classes, proclaiming "both workers and employers should regulate their mutual relations in accordance with the principle of solidarity and Christian brotherhood."[40] Like *Rerum Novarum*, *Mater et Magistra* argued that greater respect for human dignity was central to securing economic equality for the world's poor and workers. *Mater et Magistra* also noted that technological progress had allowed industrialized nations to impose "a new form of colonialism" upon the developing world and threatened world peace.[41] *Mater et Magistra* called for greater consideration to "those values which concern man's dignity generally, and the immense worth of each individual human life" and for engaging in "a fruitful and well-regulated interchange of useful knowledge, capital and manpower" to facilitate that consideration within temporal law.[42]

The second encyclical, *Pacem in Terris*, was issued in April 1963. In it, John XXIII noted that temporal governments had historically ignored a litany of natural rights, including rights to food, medical care, "necessary social services," freedom of religious association and political conscience, and migration.[43] These rights framed what he described as a "natural law . . . that governs all moral conduct."[44] Peace, the Pope argued, was impossible if temporal governments ignored this natural law. Instead, lasting peace stemmed from the temporal world's adherence to the natural rights enumerated in the encyclical. *Pacem in Terris* also differed from previous encyclicals because it did not condemn Marxism to the extent that previous encyclicals like Pope Leo XIII's *Custodi di Quella Fede* and Pius XI's *Quadragesimo Anno* and *Divini Redemptoris* had.[45] Instead, *Pacem in Terris* decreed that "a man who has fallen into error [communism] does not cease to be a man. He never forfeits his personal dignity; and that is something that must always be taken into account."[46]

Additionally, John XXIII's Ten Percent Plan, announced in 1962, called for Catholic orders in the United States to commit 10 percent of their members to performing mission work in Latin America.⁴⁷ Although the plan never came to fruition, thousands of United States–born Catholics, many of whom were coming of spiritual age in the wake of Vatican II and John XXIII's papacy, streamed into Guatemala throughout the 1960s. This was a critical development, as Guatemala had historically suffered from a drastic shortage of priests: historian Bruce Calder has noted that there were only eighty priests to serve approximately three million Guatemalan Catholics in 1934. The priest shortage was worst in the Huehuetenango diocese, which Calder notes had two priests to serve more than 176,000 people at the time.⁴⁸ By 1966, an influx of foreign missionaries increased the country's priest population to 531, an almost sevenfold increase in thirty years (Figure 1.2). Moreover, 82 percent of priests and 88 percent of nuns serving in Guatemala by 1966 were foreign born, with a disproportionate number from Spain, the United States, and South America.⁴⁹

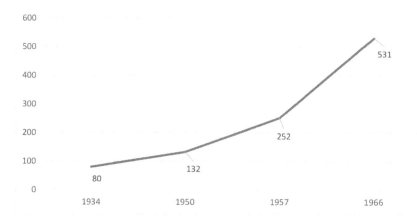

Figure 1.2. Catholic priest population in Guatemala, 1934–1966. (Michael J. Cangemi)

Father Gregory Schaffer was one of the many US-born Catholics to arrive in Guatemala during the 1960s. He arrived in San Lucas Tolimán on March 21, 1964, to assist parish priest Father Stanley Martinka with his pastoral and missionary duties. Schaffer and Martinka had both volunteered to serve as missionaries in San Lucas Tolimán as part of a pledge made by Bishop Alphonse Schladweiler of the New Ulm, Minnesota, diocese to "staff and finance" a parish and mission within the Sololá diocese, which had lacked a resident priest for some sixty years.⁵⁰ Three weeks after Schaffer's arrival in San Lucas, Martinka was called to active duty by the Minnesota Air National Guard to serve as a chaplain in Vietnam, leaving Schaffer to lead the mission until his death in 2008.⁵¹

The parish's poverty troubled Schaffer. By late 1964, he noted that "it became gradually evident that a people living in such misery, need, and emptiness needed a simultaneous thrust that would gradually help them to trust, to want to improve, to want to become positively productive. In the kind of evolutionary process born of much thought, discussion, disagreement and advice, we found ourselves pretty well involved in a threefold project of doctrine, education and socio-economic development."[52] These projects included building schools and a health clinic, and volunteer physicians and nurses from Minnesota made regular visits to the parish and worked alongside Luqueños (San Lucas Tolimán residents) to treat patients suffering from malnutrition and tuberculosis. Additionally, parish volunteers devised a local animal husbandry program that increased local access to meat, and, importantly, the parish opened Casa Feliz, a home for sick and orphaned children that also served as a haven for refugee children during the 1970s and 1980s.

The parish's various programs relied heavily on volunteers. The programs were also led and managed by Luqueños because, as Schaffer noted, "we came to see that as foreigners we will never be able to affect real change in the attitudes of the people. It will be up to them to provide an opportunity for growth and change to take place."[53] Ultimately, mission projects helped decrease the area's infant mortality rate from 65 percent in 1964 to 50 percent in 1971, tripled the number of children enrolled in school, increased literacy rates from 2.7 percent to 29.5 percent in five years, and increased the area's daily minimum wage from 50 cents per day to 60 cents per day during this period. Luqueños led all mission projects by 1971, and two-thirds of all mission-generated income remained local, stimulating the area's economy.[54] Together, the mission's projects had a transformative effect on San Lucas Toliman. According to Schaffer, by 1971 "about 3/4 of [mission] workers [were] Indian; they have been gradually becoming more economically secure, their children are in school . . . most of them have their names on a waiting list for the land development and model home projects; and any man holding a leadership position has been the recipient of professional instruction in San Lucas as well as other parts of the country."[55]

The mission's growth was concurrent with ongoing foundational shifts within the church. Following John XXIII's death in June 1963, his successor, Paul VI, oversaw the rest of the council, which met annually from 1963 to 1965. The council's landmark pastoral constitution, *Gaudium et Spes*, articulated the church's professed commitment to protecting human rights. Issued in December 1965, *Gaudium et Spes* analyzed what its authors described as "anxious questions about the current trend of the world, about the place and role of man in the universe, and about the ultimate destiny of reality and of humanity."[56] It declared that all people are born with a common, God-given dignity that is repudiated when a person's rights are violated and that "the equal dignity of persons demands that a more human and just condition of life be brought about. For excessive economic and social differences between the members of one human family or population groups cause scandal, and militate against social justice, equity, the dignity of the human person, as well as social and international peace."[57]

Gaudium et Spes also referred to global poverty, exploitation of the working class, authoritarian political systems, and nuclear proliferation as "problems of special urgency." To address these problems, it stated that "Christians should cooperate willingly and wholeheartedly in establishing an international order that includes a genuine respect for all freedoms and amicable brotherhood between all. . . . The greater part of the world is still suffering from so much poverty that it is as if Christ Himself were crying out in these poor to beg the charity of the disciples. . . . It is the duty of the whole People of God . . . to alleviate as far as they are able the sufferings of the modern age."[58] This was *Gaudium et Spes*'s essence, as well as that of Vatican II and the reforms championed by the Catholic Action movement, John XXIII, and Paul VI: economic and social justice were inextricably linked to temporal power, and authentic progress was possible only when it lifted all people out of poverty. It was an appropriate capstone to the council, which formally closed the day after *Gaudium et Spes* was promulgated.

These sentiments also underpinned Paul VI's 1967 encyclical, *Populorum Progressio*. In it, the Pope reflected on his visits to Latin America, Africa, Palestine, and India and lamented that "the hungry nations of the world cry out to the peoples blessed with abundance." He identified this circumstance as the legacy of colonialism and declared that "individual and group effort within these countries is no longer enough. The world situation requires the concerted effort of everyone, a thorough examination of every facet of the problem—social, economic, cultural, and spiritual."[59] For Paul VI, this effort included equitable access to land and natural resources for all people, rejecting "unbridled liberalism," and advocating for reform instead of revolution. Additionally, the Pope decreed that wealthy, industrial nations were morally obligated to provide economic assistance and fair trade with the developing world and to build "a human community where . . . the needy Lazarus can sit down with the rich man at the same banquet table."[60] *Populorum Progressio* also praised missionaries for their efforts in advocating dignity around the globe. The Pope rejoiced in the "ever increasing number" of Catholics serving mission but warned that "the people of a country soon discover whether their new helpers are motivated by good will or not. . . . The expert's message will surely be rejected by these people if it is not inspired by brotherly love."[61]

Populorum Progressio was especially resonant in Latin America, where the church's council of Latin American bishops, the Consejo Episcopal

Latinoamericano (CELAM), sponsored a seminar for priests in Santiago, Chile, in 1967 that drew clergy from fourteen countries.[62] The seminar was dedicated to analyzing *Populorum Progressio*'s substance and its meaning for Latin America. The attendant priests and bishops produced a document titled "*Populorum Progressio* and Latin American Realities" that lauded the encyclical's spirit and pronouncements but also worried that the region's economic and political leaders had ignored its message. This, they feared, would leave the encyclical "shelved in the recesses of some dusty archive instead of becoming a prophetic clarion call to restore justice and freedom to the peoples who are working for their own betterment."[63] The document also praised and encouraged lay individuals' and groups' mobilization in the temporal sphere and chastised Latin America's rightist dictatorships for characterizing all popular protest as communist machinations and not as the rejection of systemic inequality.

The Santiago seminar was a prelude to CELAM's conference in Medellín, Colombia, during August and September 1968. The conference, which was organized under the title "The Church in the Present-Day Transformation of Latin America in the Light of the Council," included 130 bishops from across Latin America and was a watershed moment for Latin America's Catholics and church. Theologian Rafael Luciani has described the Medellín conference as providing "a contextualized reception of Vatican II and thereby gave substance to what had previously been marginal concepts: the church of the poor, and a church committed to the liberation and full flourishing of the needy and the abandoned."[64] During the conference, CELAM's bishops crafted sixteen documents that addressed temporal suffering, evangelizing, and the church's institutional and structural realities. All three groups of documents, with titles like "Justice" and "Peace," shared an emphasis on delivering the poor from poverty and indignity and bringing the Gospel to the marginalized and called on the Latin American church to take a greater role in helping the poor realize their liberation, which, CELAM argued, was central to authentic Christianity. This more encompassing view, known as liberation theology, was not only a specifically Latin American interpretation of Vatican II but a singular event: no comparable meeting or conference of church hierarchy took place on any other continent in Vatican II's wake.

In Guatemala, liberation theology strained the country's church-state relations in the wake of the Melville affair, a diplomatic crisis involving Maryknoll Father Arthur Melville, his brother and fellow Maryknoll Father, Thomas Melville, and Maryknoll nun Marjorie Bradford. In the mission's official report of the affair, Maryknoll Regional Superior Father John M. Breen remarked that the missionaries had struggled with personal crises of faith during the mid-1960s. According to Breen, Thomas Melville "seemed to be looking for a utopia. . . . He had a real hang up on authority and . . . always wanted to be noticed and thought of as a real 'tough guy.'" Breen also noted that Bradford was "greatly bothered by poverty" in Guatemala and exhibited "growing hatred . . . of the rich."[65] In September 1967, the three missionaries attended the Latin American Sociology Congress in San Salvador, El Salvador, where Antonio García, a UN-affiliated expert on agrarian reform, delivered the meeting's keynote address. In his remarks, García argued that government-sponsored colonization of Guatemala's northern Petén department was undesirable because it mitigated the need for broader, more radical land redistribution schemes across the country. Breen characterized the meeting as a turning point for the three missionaries, as they began to discuss violence as a solution to Guatemala's political and socioeconomic problems.[66]

On December 2, 1967, Father Luis Gurriarán, a Franciscan priest from Quiché, informed Breen that four Maryknoll missionaries had helped organize a clandestine meeting of students, clergy, and leftists affiliated with the FAR three weeks earlier.[67] According to Gurriarán, the meeting was to discuss creating a camp in Huehuetenango for purportedly training guerrillas in combat techniques. Breen reported that Gurriarán "repeated insistently that it was definitely a planning session, not just speculation about violent revolution, and that [the four missioners] were fully committed to the action and would not be swayed from their resolve."[68] The Maryknoll missionaries also discussed using a mission-owned airplane to transport people and arms from Cuba and Mexico to the proposed camp. The meeting adjourned with a projected start date for the scheme of February or March 1968.[69]

Breen and Gurriarán met with US ambassador to Guatemala John Mein at the US Embassy in Guatemala City on December 12. Mein informed them that he was already aware of the plot and expressed his desire for the mission to resolve the matter internally.[70] Mein agreed to discuss the matter with an unnamed "high-ranking" Guatemalan government official and hoped the missionaries would leave the country voluntarily. Mein met with Bradford and the Melvilles at the embassy the following evening and admitted to the plan but refused to leave Guatemala. The missionaries, however, met privately with Breen later that night and offered to give Breen a full account of their plot in exchange for the identity of the informant. They also asked Breen to join their group. Breen refused both overtures. After a lengthy discussion, the trio agreed to leave Guatemala on December 21. Breen accepted their departure date but threatened to inform the Policia Nacional (PN) of the plot if they did not leave that day.[71] Bradford and the Melville brothers left on the agreed date and subsequently left the order altogether.[72]

The Melville Affair almost destroyed Maryknoll's mission in Guatemala entirely. The national daily newspaper *El Imparcial* first reported on the plot in

January 1968 and, as Breen later recalled, "we never left the front page of the newspapers. . . . The Archbishop and [Papal] Nuncio were personally sore at me and continuously bothering me instead of helping." The mission also faced increased harassment from police and military forces in the wake of the *El Imparcial* story. In his diary, Breen wrote that PN members monitored the Maryknoll convent house in Huehuetenango and interrogated its sisters for an extended period. Elsewhere, gunmen opened fire on a Maryknoll-run student center in Guatemala City.[73] At the same time, the affair alienated Maryknoll missionaries from other mission groups in the country. In her history of Maryknoll, Penny Lernoux noted that other mission groups "were horrified" by the incident and rumors circulated that Maryknoll's mission work was a front for Marxist subversives. At one point, Mission superiors in New York considered abandoning the mission's work in Guatemala altogether, as they believed that the Melville Affair "severely impeded" any potential good that the mission could accomplish there.[74] Press coverage of the affair and its fallout continued until March, when members of the right-wing death squad Mano Blanca kidnapped Rossell's successor, Archbishop Mario Casariego y Acevedo, and pushed the affair out of the news.[75]

Shortly after the furor surrounding the Melville affair subsided, Mein was assassinated, on August 28, 1968. According to Mein's chauffeur, Dr. Salvador Ortega, the ambassador's limousine was overtaken by "a green car, possibly a '64 Buick," on Avenida Reforma between Calle 12 and 13 in the city's Zona 10, approximately one mile north of the US Embassy.[76] A red truck stopped behind the limousine to block it, and a "youth" dressed in fatigues stepped out of the car and ordered Mein out of his limousine. Mein attempted to flee south on Avenida Reforma and was shot between five and eight times as the green car's driver yelled "shoot him, kill him!"[77] According to Ortega, Mein was likely killed instantly when one of the bullets severed his aorta.[78] The FAR claimed responsibility for the murder on August 29 and stated that Mein was killed in reprisal for the Guatemalan government's arrest of FAR leader Camilo Sánchez on the night of August 24–25.[79]

The Guatemalan government reacted swiftly. President Julio César Méndez Montenegro declared a state of siege on August 28 in which a curfew was instituted in Guatemala City while authorities conducted a house-to-house search for the shooters and all national borders were sealed.[80] US Embassy officials in Guatemala City reported that they were "satisfied [that the] Government of Guatemala [are] actually making every effort within its power [to] apprehend [the] culprits." Relatedly, US officials did not view assassination as a danger to the Méndez government's stability: in a White House briefing on September 9, Secretary of State Dean Rusk informed President Lyndon B. Johnson and congressional leaders that the military remained loyal to Méndez and that "despite the danger to some of our own people, we're not basically disturbed about the possibility the Communists could take over Guatemala."[81]

The Melville Affair and Mein's assassination were part of the war's escalation throughout the 1960s. In 1964, for example, the country's National Assembly approved Decree 283, which allowed finca owners, their administrators, and auxiliary military commissioners to carry arms without a license. The Archdiocese of Guatemala's Human Rights Office later noted that this effectively made these groups "the equivalent of salaried security agents" as they took a more prominent role in local security and surveillance operations around the country.[82] At the same time, paramilitary death squads like Mano Blanca and the Nueva Organización Anticomunista kidnapped, tortured, and murdered Guatemalans at the regime's behest. Death squads counted soldiers and police among their ranks: as the archdiocese's report noted, Mano Blanca "was one of the squads directed by the Army General Headquarters," while the ultraconservative, army-supported Movimiento de Liberación Nacional (MLN) organized funding and operations for the Nueva Organización Anticomunista.[83] The army's grip on national politics was strong enough that in May 1966 its commanding officers signed an agreement pledging to not overthrow Méndez Montenegro, who had been elected president just two months earlier, in exchange for total autonomy in its war against the FAR. The agreement was mutually beneficial, as the army was able to operate with impunity, and Méndez, the country's first civilian president since Arévalo, received assurances that he would be allowed to serve—and survive—his presidency.[84] Unsurprisingly, the war grew more violent in the wake of this agreement. Susanne Jonas has estimated that approximately eight thousand Guatemalans were killed in the war between 1966 and 1970.[85] Additionally, the Committee for the Defense of Human Rights, a Guatemalan group composed of families of some of the war's victims, provided the United Nations with a list of almost one thousand people kidnapped and murdered by death squads during this period.[86]

Amid the violence, General Carlos Arana Osorio won the 1970 election on a platform of law and order that pledged to halt disappearances and political murders.[87] Arana's victory troubled US officials because he had been removed from command in Zacapa in 1968 after what a CIA National Intelligence Estimate described as "Arana's use of terrorist attacks." According to the CIA, Arana had routinely murdered and tortured "individuals known or suspected of being even remotely involved with the guerrillas . . . until he and other similarly minded military officers were transferred to other duties."[88] Arana's predilection for violence, combined with his purported ties to death squads and role in a pair of coup plots against Méndez in 1966 and 1968, left the Richard Nixon administration apprehensive over the prospects of an Arana presidency.[89]

Arana declared a national state of siege on November 13, 1970, at the insistence of the country's extreme right-wing political groups and asked the Nixon administration for emergency military assistance. The administration approved an assistance package to the Arana regime that included twelve million dollars in arms and munitions and eight Cessna A-37B light attack aircraft, which Arana used to launch an offensive against the FAR and other leftists that recalled his extreme actions in Zacapa. The Arana regime also authorized the formation of additional death squads like Orden and Ojo por Ojo that abducted, tortured, and murdered alleged leftists and subversives in Guatemala City. This violence alarmed US officials: an undated CIA intelligence summary from the period characterized the regime's abductions and torture as counterproductive because security forces and death squads habitually destroyed evidence and kept no useful records of information extracted from their victims.[90] The summary also noted the CIA's concern that Major Elias Osmundo Ramírez Cervantes, Arana's first cousin, was head of the Guatemalan Government Security Service and that Ramírez "has said he never interrogated a prisoner without killing him. He has claimed, on his return from visits to Arana's office, that the President personally prepared lists of persons for him to eliminate."[91]

The regime's offensives had left the FAR and PGT reeling by the early 1970s. However, two new groups emerged during the period that compelled the regime to expand the war deeper into the country's rural areas. First, on January 19, 1972, a group of fifteen guerrillas led by former FAR members Ricardo Ramírez, César Montes, and Mario Payeras smuggled weapons, ammunition, and supplies into the Quiché department's northern Ixcán region from Mexico.[92] The group, which called itself the Ejercito Guerrillero de los Pobres (EGP), believed that greater coordination with the country's rural campesinos was critical for victory. After establishing a base of operations in the Ixcán, the EGP successfully appealed to local campesinos to join them. Payeras boasted that the EGP kept order among the Ixcán's villages and towns and was the region's "only authority."[93]

In 1973, FAR member Rodrigo Asturias, the son of one of Guatemala's most acclaimed authors, Nobel laureate Miguel Ángel Asturias, broke away from the group to form the Organización Revolucionaria del Pueblo en Armas (ORPA). As Sabino has noted, "ORPA was not an orthodox Marxist Leninist organization like the FAR, but a revolutionary structure [intended] to generate a 'people's war,' in the style of China or Vietnam, where the peasants, especially the indigenous people, would [become] a key social force."[94] This was also reflected in Asturias's *nom de guerre* Gaspar Ilóm, a fictional Mayan leader and martyr from his father's 1949 novel *Hombres de Maíz*. Asturias developed a long-term three-stage strategy for ORPA. In the first stage, the group obtained weapons and trained new recruits.

In the second, ORPA would formally enter the war alongside the EGP and FAR, ultimately culminating in victory and establishing a Marxist government during stage three. According to Sabino, ORPA eventually established a network of approximately five hundred members primarily located in Guatemala City and San Marcos.[95]

As ORPA slowly formed, the EGP launched its first offensive in 1975. On June 7, four EGP members entered the office of La Perla, a massive fifteen-thousand-acre finca in Quiché, and shot owner José Luis Arenas Barrera in the head. Arenas had founded the far-right Partido Unificación Anticomunista party during the early 1950s and was known locally as "the Tiger of the Ixcán" for his private army and brutal treatment of the indigenous campesinos that harvested the plantation's coffee crop. Payeras later claimed that the EGP chose that date because it was payday for La Perla's workers, which allowed the shooters to enter the office without arousing suspicion. After shooting Arenas, the EGP members led workers in a chant of "death to the rich!" before fleeing the scene.[96] In retaliation for the murder, military forces tortured and disappeared at least thirty people in the area in six separate incidents between June 1975 and early 1976.[97]

As the war intensified during the early 1970s, so too did Catholic activism. In an episcopal message issued in 1971, the country's conference of Catholic bishops, the Conferencia Episcopal de Guatemala (CEG), condemned the ongoing violence and lamented the poverty and misery that many Guatemalans struggled to overcome. The bishops criticized "the violence of terror imposed by brute force or threats of any kind [and] organized violence of any ideology, whose methods include sabotage, kidnapping, and assassination," and echoed Paul VI's admonition that violence of any sort was not Christian.[98] The bishops also declared that any effort to end the war had to be undertaken "without demagoguery and without sowing hatred" and had to include labor unions and grassroots organizations. Relatedly, the CEG also lauded the Maryknoll Mission and Woods by name in a 1974 statement for their pastoral work in the Ixcán and Huehuetenango diocese.[99]

Additionally, some missions helped finance the creation of cooperatives around the country. In San Lucas Tolimán, for example, Schaffer helped raise more than three hundred thousand dollars between 1964 and 1971 that funded housing projects, health clinics, and schools and, most importantly, purchased parcels of land that were subdivided and sold to landless campesinos to build homes and small farms. As Schaffer explained, "if [a man] has no land, not even a small peace [sic], and this is the common situation, we help him purchase a piece. He sets [sic] us . . . a small monthly payment at no interest, over a long period of time. Any problem causing stoppage of payment will be absorbed by the program."[100] This program received support from several religious organizations across Minnesota, organizations like the Washington, DC–based American Freedom from Hunger Foundation, private donations, and Schaffer himself, who donated six thousand dollars of an inheritance to fund mission activities in San Lucas Tolimán. Similarly, Woods and Maryknoll missionaries had helped develop areas of the Ixcán by the mid-1970s. As Donna Whitson Brett and Edward Brett have noted, by 1976 the Maryknoll Ixcán project had created five towns, each with a school and medical clinic, and the project's farms produced beef, coffee, maize, and beans to be sold by the towns' cooperatives. Unsold crops were flown to Guatemala City and Huehuetenango for sale in local markets; Woods often transported these goods himself using one of the project's four airplanes.[101] The Arana regime responded to projects like these with suspicion: in 1974, the Arana regime deported five "communist priests" from the Huehuetenango, Quiché, and Quetzaltenango dioceses on the eve of the country's presidential election. The CEG expressed their indignation over the expulsions in a telegram to Arana and demanded he intervene to facilitate the priests' readmission to the country.

Relations were no better under Arana's successor, General Kjell Eugenio Laugerud García. In early 1976, US ambassador to Guatemala Francis Meloy warned Woods that some members of Laugerud's cabinet suspected the priest was receiving illicit support from the Cuban government and accused the priest of stealing from his parishioners.[102] The Laugerud regime also revoked Woods's aviation license in May 1976, except for flying from his home in Huehuetenango to the Ixcán to fulfil his religious obligations. On May 17, Woods wrote a letter to Laugerud in which he sharply denied any connection with ORPA, the EGP, reaffirmed that he had "no political ideals," and personally appealed to Laugerud for support. "Mr. President," Woods wrote, "the Ixcán Project and I need the help of the Guatemalan government and especially yours. . . . I am sure that if you could personally see the achievements the project has made, you would agree that it cannot be abandoned, and therefore, I extend a most sincere and cordial invitation to honor us with your visit to the Ixcán Project."[103] Laugerud never responded, and Woods left the country in September.

Woods returned to Guatemala in November after having his license reinstated and clashed with the Laugerud regime almost immediately. Shortly after resuming his supply flights, Woods flew to the site of an airplane crash in the Ixcán without authorization. Woods's rescue flight reignited the Laugerud regime's antipathy for the priest, culminating in his murder on November 20. That morning, Woods departed from Guatemala City's La Aurora Airport for the Ixcán, accompanied by passengers John Gauker, Selwyn Puig, Ann Krendt, and physician Michael Okado. In one of the few published accounts of the flight, *Mother Jones* magazine correspondent Ron Chernow reported that Woods's airplane "twisted and spun back into the mountain at a speed of 150 miles per hour. It shattered under the impact; Bill Woods and his four passengers were killed instantly."[104]

Woods's murder underscores how thoroughly the Guatemalan church's relationship with the country's dictatorship had crumbled by the mid-1970s. Following Árbenz's overthrow in 1954, Rossell had declared that he had been willing to die during the coup. Just two decades later, the Laugerud regime had seemingly authorized the murder of a US-born Catholic priest. This change was, to some extent, a consequence of the church's epochal shift during that period. Shortly after Árbenz's overthrow, Vatican II's reforms compelled many Catholics to view economic and social conditions in places like Guatemala with a more critical eye. Subsequently, liberation theology built on Catholic Action's ideas and methods and challenged many Catholics in Latin America to take more direct action to ameliorate those conditions. In Guatemala, these changes were further compounded by the actions of US missionaries like Schaffer, the Melvilles, and Woods, whose activism took multiple forms with varying degrees of success.

Those successes came with a cost. Laugerud, like his predecessors, perceived calls for reforms as a grave threat to a lethally anti-communist status quo and speculated that the church had been infiltrated and corrupted by Marxists. This was especially resonant in Guatemala, where the Melville Affair had caused a diplomatic and political crisis a decade earlier. The reality, however, was quite different. Many priests in Guatemala sidestepped political discussion, and, more broadly, liberation theology, as best they could. In his letter to Laugerud, for example, Woods flatly denied holding any interest in the country's politics and simply wanted to continue his mission work while protecting those he served. Despite this, the country's repression and violence contributed to an increasingly polarized political climate in which the Laugerud regime's enemies, both real and perceived, grew to include the Guatemalan church and priests like Woods.

Woods's murder also underscores the profound shift in the relationship between the Maryknoll Mission and Guatemala's dictatorships after 1954. Like Rossell, Maryknoll missionaries like Mary Martina Bridgeman had welcomed the coup, but in the interim, events like the Melville Affair and the Ixcán project irrevocably changed the mission's relationship with the country's leaders. Although this relationship would improve in time, it never fully returned to its pre-Melville comity. A similar shift occurred in the US Catholic press, as the full-throated endorsements of Árbenz's overthrow that appeared in newspapers like the *Pittsburgh Catholic*, *Courier-Journal*, and *Catholic Telegraph-Register* had by the late 1970s given way to criticisms of Guatemala's poverty and violence. These criticisms would, in time, become a powerful organizational tool for Catholic activists.

Finally, Woods's murder portended Guatemala's bloody future, as violence and human rights abuses increased dramatically in the late 1970s and would claim tens of thousands of lives by decade's end. This violence was also, in some ways, explicitly anti-Catholic, as the army increasingly viewed indigenous Catholics as subversive Marxists, and soldiers desecrated churches through acts of vandalism and violence on multiple occasions. Further, Catholic priests and catechists were specifically murdered because of their faith, including the murder of more than a dozen priests between 1976 and 1984. As the following chapter shows, Guatemala's prodigious violence strained the country's relationship with the United States as the Carter administration attempted to place a greater emphasis on human rights concerns within its foreign policy calculus. The ensuing diplomatic impasse severely limited the Carter administration's responses to the unfolding horror in Guatemala while simultaneously making Catholic activism in both countries more important—and contentious.

2

"Our Policy Is Designed to Serve Mankind"

During his address at the University of Notre Dame's commencement ceremony on May 22, 1977, President Jimmy Carter repeatedly used fire as a metaphor for global human rights. In his opening remarks, Carter recalled a humorous story he had heard at the White House. "I was sitting on the Truman Balcony the other night with my good friend, Charles Kirbo," the president began, "who told me about a man arrested and taken to court for being drunk and setting the bed on fire. When the judge asked him how he pled, he said not guilty. He said, 'I was drunk, but the bed was on fire when I got in.'"[1] Carter also lauded the university's president, Father Theodore Hesburgh, as well as Bishop Donal Lamont and Cardinals Paulo Evaristo Arns and Stephen Kim, who, like the president, were being awarded honorary doctorates that afternoon for their human rights advocacy: Lamont was arrested and subsequently deported from Rhodesia in 1977 after his public criticism of Prime Minister Ian Smith's racist government, and Arns was tortured by the Brazilian military for condemning the Emílio Garrastazu Médici dictatorship's rampant human rights abuses, and Kim had routinely denounced South Korea's Park Chung-hee dictatorship for its repression.[2] Carter remarked, "Quite often, brave men like these are castigated and sometimes punished, sometimes even put to death, because they enter the realm where human rights is a struggle, and sometimes they are blamed for the very circumstance which they helped to dramatize." Carter also chided repressive regimes around the globe for their human rights abuses, noting that "the flames which they seek to extinguish concern us all and are increasingly visible around the world."[3]

Carter also chastised his predecessors' foreign policies, remarking that "for too many years, we have been willing to adopt the flawed and erroneous tactics of our adversaries, sometimes abandoning our own values for theirs. We have fought fire with fire, never thinking that fire is better quenched with water. This approach failed in Vietnam, the best example of its intellectual and moral poverty."[4] He acknowledged that the Vietnam War, decolonization, and détente with China and the Soviet Union had fundamentally reshaped the global geopolitical order in less than a generation and pledged that his administration's foreign policy would reflect these changes. Carter remarked, "Our policy is derived from a larger view of global change. Our policy is rooted in moral values, which never change. Our policy is reinforced by our material wealth and by our military power. Our policy is designed to serve mankind. It is a policy that I hope will make you proud to be Americans."[5]

Although the Carter administration emphasized human rights within its foreign policy, that policy was largely a failure in Central America, where decades of repression inflamed the region, culminating in widespread violence by the late 1970s.[6] In Nicaragua, the Marxist Frente Sandinista de Liberación Nacional (FSLN) and its supporters would overthrow Anastasio Somoza DeBayle in 1979, ending the Somoza family's dynastic rule of the country. Likewise, generational oligarchic rule, economic and social injustice, and military dictatorship pushed El Salvador the country to the brink of full-fledged civil war and claimed the life of the country's archbishop, Óscar Romero, who was murdered while celebrating mass in March 1980.[7]

In Guatemala, the Carter administration's policies facilitated an increase in human rights abuses and hampered diplomatic relations with the United States. Brigadier General Kjell Eugenio Laugreud García rejected the Carter administration's foreign policy as interventionist, refused any US military assistance predicated on Guatemala's human rights practices, and secured alternative arms deals with both US allies and private manufacturers. Additionally, key Washington policymakers viewed the Carter administration's foreign policy as "fundamentally out of phase" with historic and contemporary political and social conditions in places like Guatemala and unsuccessfully pressed administration officials to avoid publicly criticizing human rights violators and instead to engage in quiet diplomacy to halt abuses. The result was a diplomatic impasse in which neither the Carter administration nor the State Department could authoritatively respond to the Laugerud regime's increased human rights abuses.

As Guatemala's human rights abuses increased under Laugerud, so too did his regime's antipathy for Catholic activists and, more broadly, a significant portion of the Guatemalan church itself. This antipathy took multiple forms: far-right politicians like Movimiento de Liberación Nacional (MLN) founder Mario Sandoval Alarcón publicly claimed that the church had been compromised by Marxists, while members of the Laugerud regime attempted to blame a 1978 massacre in Panzós, Alta Verapáz, on local priests, who, the regime claimed, supported the country's guerrillas. As events like these drove Guatemala into further disarray and eroded the country's relationship with the United States, Catholic activists in Guatemala and the United States continued advocating for dignity and called for a fresh approach to US-Guatemalan relations that prioritized economic and humanitarian assistance over military aid and support for dictators like Laugerud and his successor, General Fernando Romeo Lucas García, who assumed the presidency under fraudulent circumstances in July 1978.

This chapter explores why the Carter administration's desire to craft a human rights–based foreign policy model failed in Guatemala and left the United States unable to respond to increased Guatemalan violence beginning in 1977. Laugerud viewed the Carter administration's policy goals as another form of yanqui imperialism that infringed on Guatemala's political sovereignty and was able to obtain weapons from other sources, including private, US-based weapons manufacturers and US allies. This chapter also highlights the Laugerud regime's bilious relationship with the Guatemalan church, culminating in its initial response to the Panzós massacre in May 1978. These developments gave Catholic activists a more prominent voice and presence in debates surrounding US relations with Guatemala and, more broadly, all of Central America as the region's twin fires of violence and activism continued to burn.

The tensions that complicated US-Guatemalan relations during the Carter administration were rooted in US policymakers' increased interest in human rights throughout the 1970s. As historian Sarah Snyder has noted, four key House Foreign Affairs subcommittees received new chairmen following the 1970 midterm election.[8] The new leadership, including International Organizations and Social Movements Subcommittee chairman Donald Fraser and Foreign Economic Policy Subcommittee chairman John Culver, sought to incorporate human rights issues and greater congressional influence into US foreign policy in what the Washington-based magazine *National Journal* described as a "more critical appraisal of U.S. foreign policy from the House than anyone on Capitol Hill can recall."[9] The subcommittees' influence was most visible in the increased number of House Foreign Affairs Committee hearings on human rights, which, as historian Mary Stuckey has noted, jumped from just two in 1971 to more than thirty between 1973 and 1976.[10] Two pieces of legislation passed during the mid-1970s reflected congressional efforts to create a human rights–based foreign policy and made US military and economic assistance conditional on states' human rights records. First, Iowa representative Tom Harkin's amendment to the Foreign Assistance Act in 1975 prohibited US military assistance to governments deemed persistent human rights violators. Second, the International Financial Institutions Act of 1977 (IFIA) prohibited the United States from contributing to development loans issued by multinational institutions such as the Inter-American Development Bank and World Bank to states that violated human rights.[11]

Carter also tried using human rights language and ideals to unite the

Democratic Party's conservative cold warriors and pro-détente international-ists on the campaign trail. In March 1976, for example, Carter assailed the Soviet Union's disregard for human rights in an address to the Chicago Council on For-eign Relations. In his remarks, Carter alluded to the Soviet government's ongoing crackdown against human rights activists, dissidents, and other foes, which vio-lated the human rights provisions of the Helsinki Final Act, signed the previous year. Carter noted, "To the Soviet Union . . . having the Helsinki Accords without the requirement of living up to the human rights provisions which form an inte-gral part of it . . . is not the road to peace but the bitter deception of the American people."[12]

Carter also appealed to liberal Democrats by making human rights central to his foreign policy. During a speech to the Foreign Policy Association in New York in June, he stated, "We and our allies . . . can take the lead in establishing and pro-moting basic global standards of human rights. We respect the independence of all nations, but by our example . . . and by the various forms of economic and political persuasion available to us, we can quite surely lessen the injustice in this world." Carter also criticized covert and overt US interventions during the Cold War and noted in Chicago that "for years, we were the only free nation with the military ca-pacity to keep the peace. . . . But we also had the power to make or break regimes with adroit injections of money or arms, and we sometimes used this power in ways that [were] less commendable."[13]

Guatemala was one such regime. An Amnesty International report from 1976 estimated that more than twenty thousand Guatemalans had been murdered, tortured, or disappeared by "official and semi-official" forces between 1966 and 1976.[14] By the mid-1970s, this violence and US policymakers' resurgent interest in human rights complicated the two countries' relationship in two ways, both of which were evident in a statement that the Laugerud regime submitted to a House International Organization Subcommittee hearing on human rights in June 1976. First, the statement rejected out of hand US legislation like the Harkin Amend-ment as an infringement upon Guatemala's sovereignty and warned that, as a sov-ereign power, Guatemala could "never accept directives or allow interference in its national problems, since this domain belongs exclusively to the Guatemalans themselves."[15] The statement foreshadowed Laugerud's later, more forceful re-marks to Guatemala's legislators that the country was prepared "to make the high-est sacrifice . . . the defense and protection of national sovereignty" in response to foreign interventions.[16]

The statement also stipulated that "the Government [of Guatemala] not only respects but also guarantees universally respected human rights expressly men-tioned in the [Guatemalan] Constitution," including rights to free expression, assembly, religion, and labor unions, among others. It also claimed that "criminal acts by groups of extremist ideology" within the country jeopardized Guatemalan citizens' access to those rights and that the regime's repression was a "superhuman effort for the control and punishment of the terrorists" that purportedly included members of the country's political left.[17] Laugerud's foreign minister, Adolfo Molina-Orantes, further articulated this idea in an address to the United Nations General Assembly the following year, where he declared, "We must protect man against the brutal acts of terrorism, which are a threat to the personal integrity and freedom of innocent persons—whether citizens or government officials and diplomatic representatives. . . . Violence and lack of respect for human rights are the result of an interaction of abnormal social forces of which the consequences as well as the deep roots must be combatted."[18]

Human rights abuses and deteriorating conditions across Central America were thus a main concern for the Carter administration in early 1977. On January 26, Carter ordered a Presidential Review Committee (PRC) to perform a comprehensive analysis of US-Latin American relations. He directed committee members, which included ranking officials from the State Department, Defense Department, and CIA, to formulate a new diplomatic approach to the region predicated on, among other concerns, noninterventionist principles, respect for Latin American states' sovereignty, encouraging Latin America's greater political participation in multinational institutions, and a "fundamental concern" for protecting human rights and human rights activists in the region.[19] Indicative of its importance, Latin America was the only region in the world to undergo such a review during the Carter administration.

The PRC candidly assessed what it saw as deficiencies in US-Latin American relations. Its report characterized the United States' relationship with the region as "often intrinsically negative" and noted, "We want them *not* to aggravate East-West tensions; *not* to deny us access to . . . their raw materials; *not* to develop nuclear capabilities. In sum, we want sufficiently stable . . . growth *not* to weaken our security, create new global problems, or offend values" (emphasis in original). According to the committee, this approach, which dated to the mid-nineteenth century in various forms, fueled Latin American condemnations of US policies as interventionism, which the PRC characterized as having "cast a pall over our motives and aroused suspicions that may take years to overcome."[20]

The committee also concluded that the Carter administration's envisioned foreign policy model, with its emphasis on human rights, would be counterproductive and self-contradictory in Latin America. Their report noted that while the United States historically emphasized civil and political rights as human rights, Latin American governments emphasized economic and social rights, especially for the poor. According to the committee, this had created an ideological clash between "libertarians" in the United States and "egalitarians" in Latin America. Relatedly, the committee argued that legislation like the Harkin Amendment "symbolized to many our overriding stress on political as opposed to economic rights. . . . Our concern for fundamental political rights is thus out of phase with the appeals and ideologies of most of the developing world. Most simply, the poor . . . see life and survival as more important than liberty."[21] Here, the committee considered two potential solutions: either expand the Harkin Amendment's reach to include economic and social rights abuses or repeal it altogether.[22]

Instead, the PRC ultimately advised the administration to refrain from linking military assistance and arms sales to human rights records on logistical and strategic grounds. The committee noted there was "little left to cut" in terms of US military assistance after a steady decline in sales of sophisticated arms and weapons systems that had begun during the mid-1960s. Indeed, the United States had become the fourth-largest arms supplier to the region by 1977, behind Italy, the United Kingdom, the Soviet Union, Israel, and Western European states like West Germany and France—both US allies—were increasing their arms sales to the region.[23] This, coupled with improved weapons development and manufacturing programs in Argentina and Brazil, left the United States with a significantly smaller share of the Latin American weapons market: approximately one-seventh of total arms sales and assistance to the region. This, the committee argued, showed that the Harkin Amendment's provisions had little actual resonance and that further restrictions would hamper the United States' relationships with Latin America's numerous dictatorships. The report bluntly noted, "To [restrict military assistance] while increasing our attention to human rights could result in a virtual break with the critical institutions in Latin America—the military."[24]

On March 11, one day before the PRC submitted its final report to National Security Adviser Zbigniew Brzezinski, Laugerud directed the Guatemalan government to preemptively refuse any US military assistance that was contingent on his regime's human rights record, making Guatemala the fourth Latin American country and the first in Central America to do so.[25] The Laugerud regime's refusal was particularly significant, because although the United States' overall military assistance to Latin America had declined steadily over the previous decade, Guatemala had received the bulk of US assistance to Central America's Northern Triangle (El Salvador, Guatemala, and Honduras) during that period. Between 1960 and 1976, US arms sales and Military Assistance Program (MAP) expenditures to Guatemala totaled 35.4 million dollars, compared to 6.5 million for Honduras and just 2.8 million for El Salvador (Table 2.1, Table 2.2).

Table 2.1. US Department of Defense arms sales to El Salvador, Guatemala, and Honduras, 1960–1976						
	1960–1969	1970–1973	1974	1975	1976	**Total** (millions of US dollars)
El Salvador	0.8	0.2	0.1	0.3	0.3	1.7
Guatemala	2	11.5	1.5	3.4	1.4	19.8
Honduras	0.2	0.2	0.8	0.6	4.7	6.5

Source: "U.S. Military Assistance Deliveries to Foreign Governments, by Country," Foreign Military Sales and Military Assistance Facts (Washington, DC: Government Printing Office), 1976.

Table 2.2. US Military Assistance Program expenditures to El Salvador, Guatemala, and Honduras, 1960–1976						
	1960–1969	1970–1973	1974	1975	1975	**Total** (millions of US dollars)
El Salvador	0	0.8	0	0.1	0.2	1.1
Guatemala	9.6	3.9	1.5	0.3	0.3	15.6
Honduras	0	0	0	0	0	0

Source: "U.S. Military Assistance Deliveries to Foreign Governments, by Country," Foreign Military Sales and Military Assistance Facts (Washington, DC: Government Printing Office), 1976.

The Laugerud regime articulated its grievances in an official statement carried in the national newspaper *Prensa Libre* on March 18. The regime argued that the Carter administration's human rights policies were an intervention in Guatemala's political affairs, noting, "In the history of the inter-American system, the principle of nonintervention has been consecrated as one of the states' fundamental duties and any undue interference by one of them has always been rejected, even if the interference was for altruistic purposes."[26] Laugerud's successor, General Fernando Romeo Lucas Garcia, later did likewise and referred to Carter as "Jimmy Castro" when denouncing US policies.[27] Meanwhile, Guatemala's violence continued to worsen: according to the national newspaper *El Gráfico*, the country suffered 893 politically related murders between January and November 1977, with nearly one-third of those occurring in the departments of Guatemala, Chimaltenango, and Sacatepéquez.[28]

Laugerud's directive coincided with two striking condemnations of the Guatemalan church. In April, MLN founder and Laugerud's vice president, Mario Sandoval Alarcón, denounced the Guatemalan church during an address to the World Anti-Communist League in Taiwan. In a speech provocatively titled "God, Fatherland, and Liberty," Sandoval claimed that "our Catholic Church, which represents millions of people, has been, to this day, one of the most important vehicles with which Communism has reached our villages, natives, and common people. This happened after the Second Vatican Council."[29] Sandoval levied similar charges at the league's meeting the following year, where he declared that "revolutionary priests" and "intense Marxist penetration" were at the root of the church's greater attention to human rights.[30]

The CEG also faced dissension within its ranks following Father Rutilio Grande's murder in Aguilares, El Salvador, on March 12. Grande, an ardent supporter of liberation theology, had been central to the Jesuit Society's efforts to help organize campesinos and workers in Aguilares, where he served as a parish priest. Grande's murder was a galvanizing moment in El Salvador's lurch toward civil war during the late 1970s that solidified the Salvadoran church's break from the Colonel Arturo Armando Molina dictatorship, and several of the country's priests, including Óscar Romero, later described Grande's murder as a personally transformative moment.[31] Guatemala City archbishop Mario Casariego, however, denounced Grande as an example of "the sad rebellion of priests and religious . . . against Church authority for novelty's sake." He also chastised Catholic activists, remarking that "those who sow hatred are against Christ, even if they try to sell their actions under the label of social justice and struggle on behalf of the poor."[32]

The CEG responded in early May. In it, the bishops lamented that "it is unfortunate that some people see the activity of the Church as a vehicle of international communism and class warfare. Instead, it is the persistence of these abysmal inequalities and the absence of brave and urgent reforms to bring about a more human, fraternal, and just community that contribute to communism." They also chided "those who wish to see the Church's mission reduced to the abstract predication of the mysteries revealed by God, without any concrete reference to [Man's] problems today." According to the bishops, the Guatemalan church's Christian mission *required* it to defend human dignity, referring to *Gaudium et Spes* and the Gospels of Luke and Matthew, as they had in earlier statements, and they concluded with an expression of support for all men and women who were "motivated by a spirit of charity and justice" to eradicate Guatemala's economic and social inequalities and work for peace.[33]

In the United States, Catholics' support for Guatemala was relatively benign. In one notable example, Eddie Fischer, a Georgetown University student described by the *Pittsburgh Catholic* as "a church-going Catholic all his life," attempted to raise money for a water system in Baja Verapáz's Rabinal Valley by walking 4,100 miles from Rabinal to Philadelphia, Pennsylvania, during the year. Fischer said, "I went looking for the most needy people I could help. I found them in Rabinal, Guatemala."[34] Additionally, some missionaries, such as Father Francis W. Wright, returned from Guatemala and shared their experiences with their home parishes in the United States. Wright, who was also the national director of the Pittsburgh-based Holy Childhood Association, traveled to Guatemala earlier in the year "to study the needs of children there following the massive earthquake which struck the country" in 1976, according to the *Pittsburgh Catholic*. After returning to Pittsburgh, Wright told the newspaper that Guatemala "still [had] a long way to go in overcoming the serious physical and mental disabilities that are the result of malnutrition, contaminated water, widespread disease, and insufficient medical supplies."[35] Elsewhere, the New Ulm diocese's Saint Monica Society for Widows held an annual fundraiser to benefit mission projects in San Lucas Tolimán, and the Saint Meinrad's Parish Catholic Women's Union in Prairie View, Arkansas, held a clothing drive for Guatemalan infants.[36]

A series of high-profile murders in Guatemala during the summer of 1977 captured national headlines and alarmed US Embassy officials. The first occurred on June 8, when right-wing extremists murdered Mario López Larrave, a prominent labor lawyer and union organizer, in Guatemala City. From 1970 to 1974, López had been secretary of the Juridical and Social Sciences faculty at the Universidad de San Carlos (USAC) and cofounded the Escuela de Orientación Sindical (EOS), a Guatemala City–based unionist training program, with fellow labor leaders Manuel Andrade Roca and Santiago López Aguilar in 1975.[37] The EOS's mission reflected López's desire to "promote not trade unionism alone but a syndicalism that [leads] both to the defense of the working class's immediate interests and to [their] full rights as citizens."[38] By late 1976, López was receiving death threats attributed to the MLN, which had also publicly denounced USAC's labor and student activism.

On June 8, 1977, MLN-affiliated gunmen murdered López. Witnesses reported that as López walked out of his office, an automobile exited an adjacent parking lot onto Vía 7 and stopped "half in the street, half on the sidewalk."[39] Two men exited the automobile and opened fire on López with machine guns and shot him nine times before fleeing in a second automobile.[40] López died at Centro Médico hospital approximately an hour later.[41] Approximately twenty thousand Guatemalans marched in López's funeral procession, where USAC rector Roberto Valdeavellano eulogized the slain leader as a martyr, lauding "the beautiful and dignified example [of] . . . Mario López Larrave [that] strengthens and multiplies [with] his spilled blood."[42]

Members of Guatemala's extreme left attempted to kidnap Robert Fischer Sandhoff, the son of a Guatemala City automobile dealer, in retaliation on June 19. Although the kidnapping failed, Fischer and one of the would-be abductors died in a shootout with police. Guatemalan officials later claimed the dead abductor was a PGT/FAR member who had participated in US ambassador John Mein's assassination in 1968. Fischer's attempted kidnapping and death was front-page news, and numerous Guatemala City businesses and schools offered condolences in the press. The following day, a group of leading Guatemala City businessmen representing the Comité Coordinador de Asociaciones Agrícolas, Comerciales, Industriales y Financieras (Coordinating Committee of Agriculture, Commercial, Industrial, and Financial Associations, CACIF) met with Laugerud and directed him to create additional paramilitary groups and death squads to murder leftists and prevent kidnappings and murders like Fischer's. A US Embassy account of the meeting noted the delegation "warned [Laugerud] they were prepared to act on their own" if he refused to meet their demands.[43]

The delegation did not wait long. On June 22, a group known as the Ejército Secreto Anticomunista (Secret Anticommunist Army, or ESA) issued a press release announcing its formation and denounced the Laugerud regime's "inefficiency, apathy, [and] incompetence" in eradicating Guatemala's leftists. The press release also praised the MLN for its hard-line anticommunism and proposed an alliance between the two groups. MLN leaders publicly denounced the ESA the next day, when vice chairman Elizardo Urizar Leal stated, "The MLN has its own ideals and there is a difference between the struggle of ideals and the ESA's intended armed struggle. . . . There is no relation between the ESA and MLN; they contribute nothing to the national peace Guatemalans seek."[44] Although the MLN publicly distanced itself from the ESA and there was no demonstrable proof that the ESA actually existed beyond an anonymous press release, US ambassador Davis L. Boster warned the State Department that "some kind of illegal right-wing response" seemed imminent.[45]

Demonstrable proof came on August 4, when the mutilated corpse of USAC student Robin Mayro García Dávila was found alongside a rural highway outside of Palín, Escuintla, approximately thirty miles southeast of Guatemala City. Government forces abducted García, a known EGP member, and his friend, fellow USAC student union leader Aníbal Leonel Caballeros Ramírez, after the two attended a party on June 28. Caballeros's body was found tortured and strangled near the USAC campus on June 30. Subsequently, attorneys and citizens filed multiple writs of habeas corpus on García's behalf to compel the regime to produce him before the court, and an estimated ten thousand people demonstrated in front of the Palacio Nacional on August 1, many with banners that proclaimed "*QUEREMOS A ROBIN VIVO*" ("We want Robin alive") (Figure 2.1). When García's body was discovered, it contained a note from the ESA in his pocket that claimed responsibility for his torture and execution. More than fifty thousand people accompanied García's body to Guatemala City's Cementario General for his burial, and simultaneous demonstrations in Quetzaltenango, Huehuetenango, Jutiapa, Mazatenango, and Chimaltenango protested his murder.[46]

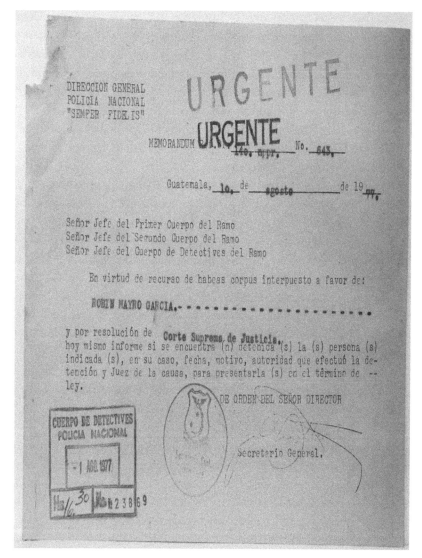

Figure 2.1. Writ of habeas corpus for Robin Mayro García, 1977. (Courtesy Archivo Historico de la Policia Nacional.)

The murders were a transformative moment for both the country and the war because all three victims, especially López, had attempted to bring students, factory workers, and farmers together in solidarity. Historically, USAC's student body had consisted primarily of children from Guatemala City's wealthy families. López, however, was a liaison between the academic elite and working classes through his simultaneous roles as academic, faculty leader, and union organizer. As labor historian Heather Vrana has observed, "Mario unified rural *campesinos* and urban unionized workers. His death was a priority for rightist forces, as he represented the greatest challenge to conservative political authority in Central America across the twentieth century—a meaningful alliance between workers and students."[47] Emblematic of this, López's book *Breve historia del movimiento syndical guatemalteco* was a bestseller at the USAC bookstore, alongside Amaru Barahona Portocarrero's history of Nicaraguan workers and biography of Nicaraguan revolutionary Augusto Caesar Sandino and analyses of Lenin and of Guatemalan land reform.[48]

López, Caballeros, and García's funerals were also part of this transformative moment. Tens of thousands of mourners, *ladinos* and *indigenas, universitarios, obreros,* and *campesinos* alike, lined the funerals' processional routes through Guatemala City. As Vrana has highlighted, each funeral also tellingly featured inclusive eulogies that specifically honored each man's dedication to the *pueblo*, rather than more narrow commemorations of their activism alone.[49] This inclusiveness removed class barriers and made the funerals, as well as their circumstances, evocative symbols of inclusion for all Guatemalans, irrespective of economic or racial background. Urban workers, students, and *campesinos'* growing coalescence facilitated what US Embassy officials later described as a "siege mentality" that fueled the war's increased violence beginning in 1978.

Policymakers in Washington recognized that Guatemala's violence was growing worse but also acknowledged their inability and disinclination to intercede. In a report dated July 13, 1977, the State Department's Bureau of Inter-American Affairs shared its views on Guatemala with embassy officials in Guatemala City. The report noted in part that "there are some indications that the present administration ordered at least several killings of suspected terrorists. It also used heavy-handed tactics in the rural areas of Northern Guatemala in 1976 in an effort to stamp out a guerrilla movement."[50] The report also noted what it described as Guatemala's "continuing failure" to safeguard economic and social rights following Árbenz's overthrow in 1954 and expressed concern that Laugerud would manipulate the 1978 election to keep the military in power.

The report also showed the State Department's mounting frustration with US-Guatemalan relations. In one particularly reflective passage, the report acknowledged that the Eisenhower administration had engineered Árbenz's overthrow and that "in many minds we are still seen as defending the status quo and propping up repressive regimes. However ... it is now clear that both our influence and leverage are declining."[51] The report also notified Embassy officials that the State Department was "no longer willing to intervene clandestinely to compel one political result over another" and reiterated that the Laugerud regime's arms refusals had substantially undercut US influence on human rights matters. The report concluded with a recommendation to at least partially reinstate military aid as a gesture of goodwill "to show that we . . . are not trying to isolate Guatemala" and that the State Department fully disclose its intentions in order to appease human rights advocates in Congress.

The bureau's recommendations highlight the State Department's lack of consensus on Guatemala. While the Laugerud regime had indeed undercut US influence on its human rights practices, private weapons manufacturers' transactions with the Laugerud regime weakened the State Department's position even further because the Harkin Amendment's provisions did not extend to commercial sales. Between August 1977 and December 1978, the Guatemalan government purchased 350 guns, more than three million rounds of ammunition, twenty-four thousand rounds of artillery shells, and seventeen hundred tear gas grenades in eight separate transactions from companies like Smith & Wesson, International Armament Corporation, and Aircraft Armaments, Inc. (Table 2.3). The State Department's Bureau of Human Rights and Humanitarian Affairs and White House reviewed and approved each sale before they were completed.[52]

Despite knowing about state links to death squads, military and police involvement in murders and kidnappings, and Guatemalan businessmen establishing their own mercenary army, US embassy officials in Guatemala City resisted holding the Laugerud regime accountable for its role in the country's violence. In an airgram to the State Department dated October 19, embassy officials demonstrated little concern for who had killed people like López, Caballeros, or García. Instead, the airgram dismissively explained that "a mutilated body found in a riverbed or on a roadside, after all, can be a manifestation of many things," ranging from terrorism, anti-union intimidation, or "simply a personal grudge carried, in a violence prone society, to a sadistic conclusion."[53]

Ultimately, 1977 was a transformative year in Guatemala. Domestically, the Laugerud regime endured challenges from both ends of the country's political spectrum. The ultimatum of CACIF and subsequent mustering of the ESA were potential threats from the far right like those that the Miguel Ydígoras Fuentes and Carlos Arana Osorio governments encountered in the 1960s and early 1970s. At the same time, broader solidarity between student activists, labor unions, and campesino farmers was a potentially significant challenge from the Left. Furthermore, it was precisely these three groups—students, workers, and farmers—that liberation theologians and, before them, Catholic Action's proponents believed played critical roles in reforming Latin America's economic, political, and social structures. At the same time, the Laugerud regime's rejection of the Carter administration's conditional foreign policy fostered tension with Guatemala's most powerful ally, largest trading partner, and a state that had historically shown little

Table 2.3. Selected munitions control export license approvals to Guatemala, 1977–1978

Company	Item	Date Requested	Date Approved
Hamilton Associates	500,000 rounds .22-caliber ammunition	July 6, 1977	August 23, 1977
Smith & Wesson	100,000 rounds .38-caliber ammunition	August 1, 1977	September 7, 1977
International Armament Corp.	150 .38-caliber pistols 6 riot control shotguns 100 tear gas grenades 20,000 rounds .38-caliber ammunition 10,000 rounds .45-caliber ammunition 10,000 rounds .30-caliber M-1 ammunition 10,000 rounds shotgun shells	August 29, 1977	September 16, 1977
Hamilton Associates	1,000,000 rounds .22-caliber ammunition	September 12, 1977	October 13, 1977
Polak, Winters and Company	200 .38-caliber revolvers	September 13, 1977	November 23, 1977
Olin Corporation	1,000,000 rounds 5.56-caliber ammunition	February 1, 1978	March 7, 1978
Aircaft Armaments, Inc.	1,600 tear gas grenades 500 practice cartridges 200 launcher cartridges	February 8, 1978	March 15, 1978
Kisco Company, Inc.	24,000 105-mm Howitzer shell cases	May 8, 1978	June 14, 1978
Polak, Winters and Company	200 .38-caliber revolvers	July 12, 1978	July 24, 1978
Unknown supplier	5,000 tear gas canisters	August 17, 1978	August 22, 1978
Polak, Winters and Company	200 .38-caliber revolvers	October 27, 1978	December 15, 1978

Source: Reprinted from Michael J. Cangemi, "Ambassador Frank Ortiz and Guatemala's 'Killer President,' 1976-1980," *Diplomatic History* 42, no. 4 (September 2018): 613–39; table 3.

hesitancy to invade its hemispheric neighbors. Thus, Laugerud had to balance the political capital he gained by clashing with the United States on sovereignty and human rights against risking economic sanctions and the loss of US assistance in other important diplomatic issues, including Guatemala's ongoing dispute with Great Britain over territorial claims to Belize.[54]

The year 1978 would prove to be just as fraught. In February, the country's bishops issued a catechesis that analyzed the country's political climate within an explicitly religious context. They lamented that "in Guatemala as in the rest of Latin America . . . large sectors of our society [do not have] . . . access to very important lifelines in society, such as education [and] health care . . . [and] live submerged in indifference and conformity and [are] thus marginalized, not only from civic life but also [made] incapable of developing adequate political consciousness."[55] The bishops argued that these conditions had led Guatemalans to associate politics with partisanship, violence, and corruption and acknowledged that it had become difficult to "free [politics] from this pejorative meaning."[56]

The bishops instead defined politics as an exercise of temporal power to create a stable, peaceful society predicated on a common good that ensured all people's rights to resources, goods, and dignity. This echoed sentiments in *Gaudium et Spes* and encyclicals like *Mater et Magistra* and *Populorum Progressio*, as well as Pope Leo XIII's encyclicals *Diuturnum* and *Rerum Novarum*, which had considered the nature of temporal authority and its relationship to Christianity during the nineteenth century. They also argued that protecting the common good was an obligation shared by governments and the governed alike, citing Paul VI's 1971 apostolic letter *Octogesima Adveniens*, which called on governments and political leaders to prioritize the common good over partisan political interests while calling on the country's bishops, priests, and laity to be a "critical conscience" in the country's politics.[57] They also urged all Guatemalans to vote in the following month's presidential election, noting that "no one is more obliged to do so than the true Catholic who knows what his faith demands. He can only be a true Christian if he is a good citizen."[58]

The bishops issued a press release on the eve of the election. In it, they bemoaned the election's expected low turnout and again urged all voting-aged Catholics to participate. They also chastised the country's political parties for "instrumentalizing" Catholicism for partisan gain and declared it "truly regrettable that, on many occasions, political parties have attempted to acquire more votes by taking advantage of the faith of our people, especially the simplest."[59] The bishops reiterated that the Guatemalan church was not bound to any political party, asked all Catholics "to act consciously" when voting, and prayed for a peaceful election.

The election was peaceful, but voters remained disillusioned after years of flagrantly fraudulent contests: according to Carlos Soto Rosales, just 638,000 votes were counted during the 1978 election, about a 5 percent decrease from the rigged 1974 contest that installed Laugerud.[60] Initial returns on March 7 showed MLN candidate and former president Colonel Enrique Peralta Azurdia leading over Lucas and Peralta's nephew, Ricardo Peralta Méndez. Election officials did not declare an official winner on election night, prompting many Guatemalans to suspect fraud. The US Embassy reported that the delayed result "severely injured [the] credibility of the result. Whichever candidate emerges . . . his legitimacy will be tainted in the eyes of everyone but his partisans."[61] Embassy officials also reported "blatant manipulation" in Guatemala City vote counts and that "some fraud, perhaps a great deal, doubtless occurred" elsewhere in the country. Lucas was declared the winner by fifty-eight thousand votes on March 10, but his failure to win 51 percent of the popular vote forced a runoff election among members of the national Congress, as mandated by Guatemalan law (Table 2.4). The congressional runoff took place on March 13, and Lucas won unopposed; only thirty-five of the country's sixty-one congressmen cast a ballot.

Table 2.4. Guatemalan election results, 1978		
Candidate	Vote Total	%
Fernando Romeo Lucas García (PR-PID)	269,973	42.31
Enrique Peralta Azurdia (MLN)	211,393	33.13
Ricardo Peralta Méndez (DC)	156,730	24.56
Totals	**636,096**	**100.00**

Source: Carlos Soto Rosales, *El sueño encadenado: El proceso político guatemalteco (1944–1999)* (Guatemala: Tipografia Nacional, 2002).

Church-state relations suffered further strain after an army massacre in Panzós, Alta Verapáz, on May 29. In one of the most detailed accounts to appear in the US press, the *Washington Post* described the massacre as "the climax to more than two years of tension, murders, and evictions in . . . Quiché and Alta Verapáz" following the discovery of oil and nickel deposits in the area. The land became coveted property for the country's elite and politically connected, who rushed to file claims to it and, in the process, rendered the area's Q'eqchi' Mayan campesinos squatters on land that they had communally held for generations. Q'eqchi' leaders sought a meeting with the town mayor in the days preceding the massacre and, according to the *Post*, "The mayor, not an Indian, reportedly told one of the [Q'eqchi'] leaders to come [on May 29] 'but come in a large group, otherwise you may be attacked.'" An estimated seven hundred Q'eqchi' men, women, and children met in Panzós on May 29, where they were met by a waiting army detachment. According to one survivor, "The shooting came from everywhere—from the rooftops, the windows and from the houses around the square."[62] Estimates of the number killed vary: the Laurgerud regime reported thirty-eight dead, while Catholic relief workers claimed 114 had lost their lives and another 300 had been wounded. Additionally, historian Greg Grandin has noted that "survivors then and now insist that the dead numbered in the hundreds."[63] Seven soldiers were also wounded in the massacre, which took place on the same day as similar violence in Panzós's Chichipate *barrio* and La Soledad on May 27, where soldiers killed one civilian and injured ten more.

On June 1, national daily newspaper *Prensa Libre* reported that Defense Minister General Otto Guillermo Spiegeler Noriega explicitly blamed the Guatemalan church and Marxists for the massacre (Figure 2.2). He denied that the army had been responsible for the massacre and said it was "stupid to blame either the president or myself for giving the orders for what occurred in Panzós" and blamed "guerrillas" for using women and children to provoke the military into shooting them.[64] Instead, Spiegeler claimed that the Alta Verapáz Diocese had conspired with the EGP to foment unrest by broadcasting anti-government propaganda in the Q'eqchi' language on the diocese-run radio station and had delivered incendiary homilies during mass. Spiegeler also refuted the Catholic workers' list of the dead and wounded and reiterated the regime's lower totals.

Figure 2.2. *Prensa Libre* headline, June 1, 1978. (Courtesy *Prensa Libre*.)

The CEG issued a press release the following day in which the bishops "condemn[ed] . . . the violent death of these *campesinos*" and affirmed their "solidarity with [those] . . . killed or wounded in circumstances that have not yet been fully clarified."[65] The bishops also called on the outgoing Laugerud regime to open a comprehensive, impartial investigation into the massacre and on Christians to demand meaningful and fair land reforms. Tellingly, the press release also characterized existing laws on land tenure—long viewed as the root cause of Guatemala's economic and social problems—as "anti-Christian," the first time that the CEG had used so strong of a term. They further articulated their thoughts on land reform in a longer statement on June 15, which stated in part that any solution to Guatemala's multiple crises had to include a "comprehensive, equitable and just agrarian policy" that recognized campesinos' right to land ownership.[66]

The Panzós massacre was international news. The bishop of the Alta Verapáz Diocese, Gerardo Flores Reyes, issued a statement on the massacre that was broadcast around the world on Radio Vaticana, the Holy See's global broadcasting service. Flores blamed Guatemala's violence on "the social structure that exists there, with very few people holding power over land and with hungry *campesinos* that have nothing."[67] He also proclaimed the Guatemalan church's solidarity with the country's poor and landless and that it would continue its efforts to raise awareness around the globe of Guatemala's economic and social inequality. The Holy See also took the unusual step of highlighting the Panzós massacre in the June 22 edition of its official newspaper, *l'Osservatore Romano*, which detailed the CEG's condemnation of the massacre and demanded a thorough, impartial investigation. United States Embassy officials in Rome viewed the article as indicative of the Holy See's specific concern with Guatemala's human rights crisis because it seldom reported on singular events like the Panzós massacre and typically did not call on individual episcopates like the CEG for local context when it did.[68] The massacre also garnered significant press attention in the United States from national papers, such as the *New York Times, Chicago Tribune,* and *Washington Post,* as well as smaller publications, such as Salem, Oregon's *Statesman Journal,* Billings, Montana's *Gazette,* and Oshkosh, Wisconsin's *Oshkosh Northwestern,* which printed wire reports from the Associated Press and United Press International on the killings in late May.[69] Likewise, the Catholic News Service and Religious News Service's reporting on the massacre was printed in diocesan newspapers across the country.[70]

The massacre also marked two critical shifts in the war. First, the locus of violence began to move farther away from Guatemala City and into the country's western and northwestern departments, ultimately accounting for most of the war's recorded human rights abuses. Quiché suffered the worst of the violence:

the CEH recorded more than 2,700 abuses in the department between 1978 and 1985—an average of one per day. Furthermore, these specific abuses account for 38 percent of the total human rights abuses recorded in their report. Second, as Grandin has noted, the demography of the violence shifted as the army increasingly targeted Mayan campesinos and rural communities after Panzós, leading to genocidal army campaigns under Lucas and his successor, Brigadier General José Efraín Ríos Montt.[71]

Violence spiked across the country during June. On June 14, the PGT's Special Combat Unit used a landmine to destroy a truck carrying twenty-five military policemen, killing seventeen of them. The unit claimed the attack was in retaliation for the massacre at Panzós.[72] Five days later, EGP members assassinated Colonel Samuel Humberto Ramírez Lima, director of the army's personnel division. The EGP also claimed responsibility for the murder of Calixto Hernández, a finca manager in the department of Escuintla, that month. In turn, Napoleón Torres, a campesino leader from Alta Verapáz and a purported leader of the Panzós demonstration, disappeared after his release from jail on June 21. The US Embassy reported that Torres was "returning to his home with his wife [when] his taxi was stopped by unknown persons. He was taken away and his wife, who tried to prevent his seizure, was beaten."[73] Torres was never seen again, and his body was never found. Finally, Father Hermógenes López Coachita, a priest from San José Pinula, was murdered in his parish on June 30. At the time of his murder, López led campesino communities near Guatemala City in their protests of the government's plan to divert drinking water away from some forty *barrios* for consumption in the capital. López was an outspoken critic of the army's impressment of indigenous campesinos into military service. He was the first priest murdered in Guatemala since Bill Woods in 1976, and, like Woods, López's killers were never officially identified.[74]

The Carter administration's foreign policy failed in Guatemala, where the Laugerud regime's violence and human rights abuses intensified in the year following Carter's Notre Dame speech. Mario López Larrave's and Robin Mayro García's murders were stark reminders of the Laugerud regime's antipathy for solidarity, even as tens of thousands of Guatemalans publicly denounced the killings. Likewise, CACIF's ultimatum to Laugerud and the ESA's subsequent formation highlights the far right's influence in Guatemalan politics during the regime's waning months. Additionally, the Panzós massacre marked a shift in the war to a genocidal, scorched-earth campaign under Laugerud's successors in what would become the war's most violent era. These escalations unfolded alongside rising violence in El Salvador and the ongoing Sandinista Revolution in Nicaragua and hamstrung the Carter administration's response to those crises in 1979 and beyond.

The Laugerud regime's rejections of US military aid also exposed the limits of the Carter administration's desire for a human rights–based foreign policy. Supporters of this policy shift believed that it was an opportunity to make fundamental changes to a foreign policy that had privileged containment and national security to virtual exclusion since the late 1940s. In contrast, Guatemalan leaders regarded it as little more than a contemporary version of the same interventionism that had dominated their relationship with the United States for decades. For them, rejecting the Carter administration and State Department's dictates was a patriotic act. Relatedly, the Laugerud regime's ability to secure arms from other sources demonstrated the limits of US influence over the region. Further, almost all the alternative suppliers were US allies that had sold large quantities of weapons to the regime prior to its rejection of US aid and would continue to do so afterward. Finally, private sales by US firms like Smith & Wesson and International Armament Corporation undercut the Carter administration's position even more. These events would pose a significant challenge for US-Guatemalan relations for the rest of the Carter administration, culminating with the recall of US ambassador Frank V. Ortiz Jr. in 1980.

The Guatemalan church also underwent an important transformation during this period. The CEG began to abandon its traditional modus vivendi of implicit, respectful critique of the country's economic, political, and social conditions in favor of more assertive criticism, culminating in the bishops' 1978 catechesis. This was in many ways a direct reflection of the ways that the bishops understood Vatican II and the Medellín Conference, particularly in terms of human dignity and the relationship between faith and politics. The CEG's shift, however, came at a considerable price. It left the bishops in direct opposition to the ardently conservative Casariego and created a fissure within the Guatemalan church's hierarchy. It also led to condemnations from Sandoval in Taiwan and Spiegler's post-massacre comments. Father López's murder, which US Embassy officials privately blamed on government forces, private mercenaries, or some combination of both, was a bloody confluence of the previous eighteen months' transformations. What came next under the Lucas regime, however, would prove even bloodier.

3

The Parochial Nationalist and the Wily Manipulator

General Fernando Romeo Lucas García assumed power as president of Guatemala on July 1, 1978. A career soldier, Lucas entered the Escuela Politécnica, the army's officer training school once described by Maryknoll Sister Mary Martina Bridgeman as "the West Point of Guatemala," in 1945 and had methodically risen to the rank of brigadier general by 1973. President Carlos Arana Osorio appointed Lucas as his minister of defense in 1974, a position he held until he announced his candidacy for president in 1977.[1] Lucas campaigned on a political platform of internal security and national development, particularly in the country's Northern Transversal Strip, a resource-rich area that spanned parts of the departments of Izabal, Alta Verapáz, Quiché, and Huehuetenango.

One month after Lucas assumed power, Pope Paul VI died on August 6. The pontiff's death sparked a worldwide outpouring of sympathy: President Carter lauded Paul VI as "a man whose life and works have served personally as a great source of moral inspiration," while both San Francisco archbishop John Quinn, president of the National Council of Catholic Bishops and United States Catholic Conference, and Philadelphia's Cardinal John Krol remembered Paul VI as one of "the greatest popes" in the church's history. Globally, Soviet newspaper *Izvestia* remarked that the pope had "declared many times in favor of consolidating peace [and] lessening international tensions," as world leaders like West Germany's Walter Scheel, Israel's Yitzhak Navon, Italy's Sandro Pertini, and United Nations Secretary General Kurt Waldheim, among many others, paid tribute to the late pontiff. Finally, the World Council of Churches remarked that Paul VI's pontificate had seen the "foundation . . . laid for a new and lasting communion among all Christian churches," and both the Greek and Russian Orthodox Churches praised his efforts to improve relations between Catholic and Orthodox Christian communities.[2]

Political and social upheaval elsewhere in Central America also had significant repercussions for Guatemala during the year. In El Salvador, the repression of General Carlos Humberto Romero's dictatorship worsened as many Salvadorans, most notably San Salvador archbishop Saint Óscar Romero, vociferously protested the regime's violence and the country's entrenched oligarchy, familiarly known as the Fourteen Families.[3] By 1980, El Salvador would plunge into a decade-long civil war that ultimately claimed one hundred thousand lives. Meanwhile, Nicaragua's Sandinista Revolution was poised to establish the hemisphere's third Marxist government by July 1979. As in El Salvador, influential Catholics like Archbishop Miguel Obando y Bravo and Father Miguel d'Escoto Brockmann were among that country's most prominent critics of the Somoza family dynasty, which had ruled Nicaragua with significant US support since 1937.

Guatemala's violence exploded during Lucas's first two years in power. The CEH reported that the number of recorded human rights abuses nationwide jumped from approximately fifty-five in 1978 to more than five hundred in 1980.[4] The nature of these abuses also changed, as massacres like Panzós became more frequent alongside brazen acts like the regime's burning of the Spanish Embassy in 1980, while rampant lawlessness within the army and PN plunged to new lows as leading officials openly ordered murders, massacres, and other depredations. Despite this, US policymakers subordinated Guatemala's rapidly deteriorating conditions to those in Nicaragua and El Salvador as Lucas upheld Laugerud's refusal of US military aid linked to Guatemala's human rights record and left US-Guatemalan relations at a diplomatic impasse. At the same time, Catholic activists in Guatemala and the United States continued to bring greater worldwide attention to Guatemala's worsening violence and inequality. This advocacy had tragic consequences, as the Lucas regime regarded Catholic activists and many Catholics more broadly as political foes during this period.

This chapter explores the intersections of politics, religion, and Catholic activism in Guatemala during Lucas's first two years in power. The regime's prodigious violence and concurrent foundational changes within the church placed even more ideological distance between the regime and Catholic activists during this period. These changes also widened the rift between the CEG and Archbishop Mario Casariego y Acevedo, who continued to acquiesce to the regime in the face of rising violence and anti-Catholic rhetoric. It also explores how priests, catechists, and laity, as well as grassroots organizations and the Catholic press, reported on Guatemala's human rights abuses and the Lucas regime's violent reprisal as the country descended deeper into civil war.

United States policymakers were dismissive of the new regime even before it took power. In a cable to the State Department on March 14, 1978, US ambassador Davis Boster reported, "We have the impression that dealing with Lucas (whose reputation is that of a rather parochial nationalist) . . . will be less congenial and straightforward than with the outgoing administration" and affirmed that Lucas's victory had been flagrantly fraudulent. Boster took a similarly derisive position on Lucas's vice president, Francisco Villagrán Kramer, who the ambassador described as "a wily manipulator" and a Machiavellian schemer with designs on the presidency.[5] Boster also noted in a subsequent cable that Lucas believed that he had dangerous political rivals on both the Left and the Right, an ominous warning of what Boster's successor, Frank V. Ortiz Jr., would describe as a "siege mentality" that fueled the regime's rampant violence.

The CEH testimonies and reports offer striking examples of that violence during the Lucas regime's earliest months. On September 15, soldiers and local military commissioners abducted and murdered Hilario Choc, a member of the Santa María cooperative in Cahaboncito, Alta Verapáz.[6] Later that month, Abelino Cuz Mo, who had previously been driven from his home in fear of being kidnapped, was abducted from the same area while bathing in the Cahabón River. The following month, area military commissioners abducted Pablo Cuz Mo, a member of a local land reform group, a catechist, and a relative of Abelino.[7] Neither Pablo nor Abelino were ever seen alive again.

Elsewhere, a September increase in bus fare led to widespread strikes and rioting in Guatemala City that the Lucas regime initially approached with uncharacteristic restraint before police actions restored order while leaving forty dead, three hundred injured, and 1,500 arrested.[8] Shortly after the crisis subsided, the PN and army murdered Oliverio Castañeda de León in October. Castañeda was president of the USAC student union, which had vigorously protested the Panzós massacre earlier in the year. He also helped coordinate the September bus fare strikes and was included on a list of thirty-eight people that the ESA threatened to kill in an announcement published in *Prensa Libre* on October 19. According to the group, those on the list were "cowards and traitors" and the "Oliverio Castañeda unit of the ESA would pick the time, place, and target for the first execution." Although most of those on the list were labor leaders and moderate or leftist politicians, Defense Minister Otto Guillermo Spiegeler, Interior Minister Donaldo Álvarez, and Police Chief Hernán Chupina were also named for their allegedly sluggish response to the bus fare protests.[9]

Castañeda was murdered the next day. According to witnesses, "a long turquoise sedan . . . with license plate P-109, a white Toyota Jeep [with] official [license] plates 0–8038 and a Bronco-type car [with] official [license] plates P-11716 . . . participated with the coordination of the Intelligence Directorate of the Army General Staff."[10] A PN officer later reported that the turquoise car belonged to the Regional Office of the Presidential General Staff, and the white Toyota belonged to the PN's Sixth Command Unit, an elite police squad that was responsible for a multitude of abductions and murders.[11] The ESA took credit for Castañeda's murder on October 26; the following day, brothers Fausto Enrique Fuentes and Mario Ventura Fuentes, who had been on the ESA death list, were shot to death in Nuevo Progreso, San Marcos.

These deaths were among an estimated five hundred political murders during the Lucas regime's first six months in power: according to Amnesty International, almost half the victims had been tortured.[12] Among these victims was Jorge Alfonso Lobo Dubón, a lawyer and social critic, who was murdered by PN agents in Guatemala City on December 5.[13] Additionally, hundreds of Guatemalan citizens disappeared during this period: in November 1978, for example, soldiers abducted Gaspar Chavez, Domingo Laynez, Gaspar Rivera, and Gaspar Puente in Chajul. Chavez was a local Catholic Action leader, and all four men had been members of a local agricultural cooperative. Likewise, members of the army and local military commission abducted four additional Catholic Action members from their homes in Chajul. None of the men were ever seen again.[14]

United States policymakers had mixed views of Lucas's first months in power. On the one hand, Boster noted that Lucas "ha[d] not made an impressive start," citing little progress in developing an economic or social policy, the bus fare protests, and the regime's initial sluggish, almost disinterested response to the protests. Boster also described Lucas as having "a flat public personapity" [sic] and his appearances as "leaden, and, maybe for that reason, infrequent. . . . Tellingly, the incessant 'Lucas jokes' of the electoral period have abated somewhat only to give way, during the October disorders, to ones casting doubt not on the chief of state's intellectual gifts, but on his very existence."[15] On the other hand, Boster hesitated to attribute the country's rising violence to either Lucas or the ESA entirely. In fact, he expressed doubt that the ESA even existed: after Castañeda's murder, Boster informed the State Department that "we are not persuaded that [the] ESA is an organization in its own right or that the now-famous list is more than an attempt by some sector or group to sow fear and confusion."[16] Instead, Boster noted, the list of responsible parties included the army, police, the MLN, the private sector, and, interestingly, the country's far left. This exemplified a broader pattern in US policymakers' contrary assessments of the Lucas regime's culpability in Guatemala's violence and severely hamstrung US-Guatemalan relations during this period.

Guatemala's turmoil intensified in 1979. In mid-January, EGP members launched an offensive in Nebaj, Quiché, and, according to a US Embassy report, took over the town "for several hours." Two weeks later, the group's Frente Luis Turcios Lima successfully occupied fincas near La Democracía, Escuintla, and Mazatenango, Suchitepéquez, where they destroyed sugarcane fields and farming equipment. In La Democracía, the finca's owner claimed losses of approximately 400,000 dollars.[17] Additionally, Lucas faced threats from within his regime, most notably from his vice president. Villagrán met with US charge d'affaires John T. Bennett in March 1979 and reported that Lucas's grip on power was "crumbling" and that two factions were preparing to launch coups. One group was led by Colonel Ricard Méndez Ruíz, Lucas's chief of security during the 1978 election campaign. According to Boster's account of the meeting with Villagrán, Méndez had warned the vice president of an assassination plot earlier in the year. The other group was led by General David Cancinos, who Lucas had publicly named as his personal choice for president in the 1982 election.[18] Cancinos was murdered three months later by unknown gunmen in Guatemala City.

Both plots unfolded against a larger wave of assassinations. On January 25, Alberto Fuentes Mohr, founder of the Partido Socialista Democratica political party, was murdered in Guatemala City. Fuentes had formerly served as Guatemala's foreign minister during Julio César Méndez Montenegro's presidency in the late 1960s and had been Brigadier General José Efraín Ríos Montt's running mate in the 1974 election. Fuentes was shot multiple times by gunmen as he waited at an intersection in the capital. United States intelligence sources believed the PN's Sixth Command was responsible for Fuentes's death.[19] Two months later, Frente Unido de la Revolución (FUR) party leader Manuel Colom Argueta was fatally shot to death near the US Embassy. Colom, a former mayor of Guatemala City, was one of the country's most prominent progressive political leaders and had officially registered the FUR as a national political party a week before his murder. According to US accounts, Colom's car was hit fifty times with machine gun fire, and, as had been in the case in Fuentes's murder, US intelligence believed the Sixth Command was responsible.[20] Elsewhere, soldiers murdered Domingo Mutzutz Jacobo, a purported FAR associate, in San Martín Jilotepeque, Chimaltenango, and Francisco Sisimit Par, a Democracia Cristiana party member and public education official, in the municipality of Santa Apolonia.[21] Additionally, members of the PN, in conjunction with the army's G-2 intelligence unit, murdered journalist Roberto Pensamiento in San Augustín Acasaguastlan, El Progreso.[22]

Amid these assassinations, the US House Foreign Affairs Committee voted on March 22 to eliminate a quarter million dollars in military training funds earmarked for Guatemala. Unlike federal foreign military sales, funding for training was not expressly linked to human rights metrics but was unsurprisingly voted down by the committee anyway, which cited the Panzós massacre, ongoing human rights abuses, and the Lucas regime's failure to investigate Fuentes's murder as reasons for eliminating the funding.[23] In response, Lucas defiantly told reporters in Tecpán, Chimaltenango, that the decision made no difference at all to him, and suggested that Congress send the money "to Apache Indian reservations," where it would do more good. According to reports published in the newspaper *Nuevo Diario*, Lucas also declared that he no longer wanted US military advisers in Guatemala.[24]

Robbery and theft were also tools of repression. In San Alfonso, Quiché, soldiers robbed and murdered five people before dumping the bodies in the Chixoy River. None of the dead were ever identified.[25] Similarly, soldiers in Nebaj, Quiché, participated in a house-to-house robbery spree on October 29, 1979. Among the victims was Antonio Chávez, who later testified to the CEH that soldiers stole 208 quetzales from him that he had borrowed to repair his home's roof. Another victim, Lucas Ajanel, likewise testified that soldiers robbed fifty-five quetzales from him, and Jacinto Brito had five quetzales stolen by soldiers.[26] On a larger scale, soldiers abducted and murdered German national Werner Kohler Bandhauer, owner of the El Naranjo finca in La Libertad, Petén. An Austrian citizen, Pedro Valerio, was also killed in the kidnapping, and Ovidio Oreallno Zaccarías, a Guatemalan, was abducted from the Santa Elena hospital and never seen again. Following the murders, Kohler's family received multiple death threats from the army to abandon the finca, which Kohler had owned.[27]

Unsurprisingly, Guatemala's violence had a profound impact on individual families. In one vivid example, a group of forty workers from the El Izotal finca and San Antonio textile factory in Sacatepéquez occupied the El Calvario church in Guatemala City on October 13, 1979. The men had been fired from their jobs eleven months earlier and hoped the occupation would bring greater attention to their firings. However, El Calvario's priest, Monsignor José Girón Parrone, supported the Lucas regime and allowed police to surreptitiously enter the church, whereupon they beat and arrested the forty men before using tear gas on a crowd of approximately one thousand people who had gathered outside the church in support of the men. The following day, the police murdered the group's suspected leader, Miguel Archila.[28]

On October 15, the police arrested high school students Fredy Valiente Contreras and Girón's niece, Yolanda de la Luz Aguilar Urizar, as they protested Archila's murder and distributed leaflets for the CNT labor union, for whom Aguilar's mother was an attorney. The police beat and tortured the teenagers, and Aguilar was raped by multiple officers while in custody. One of Aguilar's rapists was Manuel de Jesus Valiente, the head of the PN's detective squad. Aguilar was just sixteen years old at the time. Aguilar later wrote two scathing letters to her uncle, stating in the first, "I will never forget your attitude toward my people. . . . You go along with those who corrupt and kill us. I side with the persecuted people of my country." In the second, Aguilar wrote, "I was beaten, tortured, and raped but my will to struggle has survived. Today more than ever I am convinced of my duty to continue in the path I have chosen."[29]

As Guatemala descended deeper into violence, the church underwent historical changes of its own. Following Paul VI's death in August 1978, the College of Cardinals elevated Cardinal Alberto Luciani, the Patriarch of Venice, to the papacy on August 26 of that year. Luciani chose the name John Paul to honor his two predecessors and, on August 27, told an estimated fifty thousand people gathered in Saint Peter's Square that Paul VI had "extended himself to carry into effect the Second Vatican Council and to seek world peace, the tranquility of order. Our program will continue his; and his in turn [that] was ... drawn from the great heart of John XXIII."[30] He also offered praise "to the associations of Catholic Action [and] variously named movements which contribute with new energy to the renewal of society ... we are convinced that their work ... is indispensable for the Church today."[31] The Pope similarly instructed the Vatican diplomatic corps that their primary responsibility was to reinforce the rights to life, human dignity, and economic, social, and spiritual progress for all people—in their interactions with foreign states.

John Paul died five days after his homily at St. John Lateran. His thirty-three-day papacy was the shortest since Pope Leo XI's twenty-six-day reign in April 1605. John Paul was succeeded by Cardinal Karol Wojtyla, who assumed the papacy as John Paul II on October 18. As bishop of Krakow, Poland, Wojtyla had also participated in all four Second Vatican Council sessions and, like his predecessor, had enthusiastically supported its reforms and greater attention to the poor. By 1978, however, his personal theological orientation and episcopate under communist rule had placed him at odds with some aspects of liberation theology. The new pope believed that although political and social discrimination injured the world's poor, meaningful change was possible only through Christ's "transforming, peacemaking, pardoning, and reconciling love" instead of ongoing violent upheaval and some Catholic clergy's involvement in politics in places like Guatemala, El Salvador, and Nicaragua.[32]

These differences were evident during his visit to CELAM's third episcopal council in Puebla, Mexico, on January 28, 1979. In his remarks to Latin America's cardinals and bishops, he lauded CELAM's bishops for their conclusions on evangelism and spirituality at Medellín a decade earlier, "with all the elements that they contained, but without ignoring the incorrect interpretations at times made." He also subtly criticized liberation theology and its supporters by expressing his pleasure that CELAM delegates came to Puebla "not as a symposium of experts [or] a parliament of politicians ... but as a fraternal encounter of Pastors of the Church."[33] The pontiff then warned his audience that identifying Christ "as a political figure, a revolutionary, as the subversive of Nazareth does not tally with the Church's catechism" and moved them closer to Marxist apostasy. This perspective guided his papacy's approach to liberation theology and was most evident in the writings of Cardinal Joseph Ratzinger, who was named Prefect of the Sacred Congregation for the Doctrine of the Faith and would later succeed John Paul II as Pope Benedict XVI.[34]

The Pope's remarks to an audience of campesinos in Culiapán the following day seemingly contradicted his Puebla comments. In Culiapán, he pledged that "the present Pope wishes to be in solidarity with your cause, which is the cause of humble people, the poor . . . that are nearly always abandoned at an ignoble level of life and sometimes harshly treated and exploited."[35] He also denounced the industrialized world's exploitation of the poor and said, "It is not just, it is not human, it is not Christian to continue with certain situations that are clearly unjust. It is necessary to carry out real, effective measures at the local, national and international level. . . . It is clear that those who must collaborate most in this, are those who can do most."[36]

The Pope's visit to Mexico generated conflicting reactions around the Catholic world. The council published a statement that reinforced its belief that political activism was central to Christian action and described Latin America's entrenched inequality, extreme poverty, and human rights abuses as failures of Christian evangelization. The council's bishops stated they would continue their "mission to bring God to the people and the people to God" by pursuing higher living standards for the poor, more just distribution of resources, greater respect for human rights, and greater representation of the poor and indigenous in the region's political systems.[37] They also reminded Catholics that "Jesus was born and lived poor amid the people of Israel" and that consciousness of the poor was a spiritual prerequisite for a Christian life.[38]

The US Catholic press also debated the Puebla conference's ramifications for the church. In the February 9 edition of *Pittsburgh Catholic*, columnist Jerry Filteau reported that "three popes" had visited Mexico—the Marianist pilgrim, the "stern pastor" in Puebla, and the "pastor of the poor and disenfranchised" in Culiapán— and wondered if all three could coexist.[39] *Denver Catholic Register* reporter Frederic Lilly posed similar questions and wondered whether the Pope's visit would be troublesome for the Latin American church. Lilly asked whether the Pope's emphasis on spiritual renewal as a panacea for the region's woes was "naïve" and whether his remarks were "window dressing while trying to get clergy out of politics."[40] The National Conference of Catholic Bishops also issued a statement in late February that praised CELAM's emphasis on the poor as central to Christianity and pledged US bishops' support for their compatriots in Latin America while calling for the church "to become poor" to understand and eradicate poverty.[41]

The CEG had its own interpretation of the Puebla Conference. In a statement released on March 2, Guatemala's bishops declared that "liberating evangelism" was necessary for the country and that "the contradictions between the unjust social order and the Gospel's demands are evident. Our missions of denouncing these injustices and announcing Jesus [as] our savior are inseparable." They pointedly concluded that "murders, disappearances, acts of terrorism, kidnappings, torture and other degrading acts not only show a total disrespect for the dignity of the human person, but they also create in the survivors a climate of insecurity, pain, and fear, which makes the human and Christian fulfillment of Guatemalans impossible."[42] This blunt assessment underscored that Puebla had done little to close the burgeoning schism within the country's Catholic hierarchy. Despite the CEG's clear statement, Casariego continued to show open fealty to the army and far right: for example, Casariego maintained an amiable relationship with former vice president, MLN leader, and purported death squad organizer Mario Sandoval Alarcón, even after the latter had publicly stated that the church had been infiltrated by Marxist priests in the wake of Father Hermogenes López's murder the day before Lucas assumed power.[43]

Casariego also directed Guatemalan priests to avoid getting involved in national politics, as had happened in neighboring El Salvador, and announced that any priest expelled from that country for political activism would not be welcome in Guatemala.[44] According to Casariego, "had these priests not involved themselves in politics they would certainly be in their right place."[45] By 1979, the building tension between Casariego and more politically liberal members of the Guatemalan church's hierarchy were rumored to be the reason for the resignation of the Quetzaltenango Diocese's bishop, Luis Manera.[46] Finally, many parish priests in Guatemala also chafed against Casariego's conservatism and, at times, did so in novel ways. In one vivid example, the San Lucas Tolimán parish's priests adopted a stray cat that had routinely visited the rectory. After sending the cat to the town's veterinarian clinic to be neutered, the priests decided to name the cat Mario, after the archbishop.[47]

Lucas also feared the violence and instability that his regime had wrought. As Boster had previously noted, the dictator felt beset on all sides as the EGP's apparent gains and ORPA's emergence seemed by 1979 to signal a resurgent, growing militant left in the country. At the same time, coup rumors and the ever-present threat posed by ultrarightists like Sandoval remained a danger to Lucas's rule. Moreover, the police and death squads seemed even more predisposed to violence than Lucas. Further, US policymakers noted the very real—and potentially dangerous—differences between Lucas and Villagrán. Ortiz would later describe

Villagrán as "diametrically opposed" to the dictator, whom he referred to as "a slow-thinking, inarticulate, deliberative . . . country boy . . . ill-at-ease with cerebral schemes, foreign ideas, and grand designs."[48] In contrast, Ortiz characterized Villagrán as "one of the quickest and most facile minds in Guatemala . . . he enjoys fine food, choice wines, intellectual dialogue and smart company and is equally at home with the elites of Paris, Zurich, New York, or Quetzaltenango."[49]

Lucas regarded Catholic activists as another potential threat. Catholic activists had profoundly emphasized human dignity, solidarity, and economic and social reform in their words and deeds. This emphasis was especially resonant in Mayan communities, who had for centuries suffered under the country's non-Mayan and foreign elites. The EGP and ORPA recruited new members in indigenous communities using similar arguments and in the process created a Catholic-Mayan-Marxist mélange that, to Lucas, seemed a very dangerous threat to his rule. Catholic activists had also built impressive social networks that facilitated cooperative efforts across the country. For example, the Jesuit Society was able to coordinate projects simultaneously in Guatemala City, Quiché, and Chimaltenango, as well as with other orders and secular aid groups.[50] Finally, Catholic activists' international connections, particularly with individual parishes in the United States, continued to strengthen during the late 1970s. News from and about Guatemala appeared more frequently in the US Catholic press, and missionaries returning from their service often shared their impressions of Guatemala with Catholic groups and congregations across the United States. In Guatemala, these developments fueled Lucas's perception of Catholic activists as spiritual, racial, political, and diplomatic threats and contributed to what Ortiz referred to as the dictator's "siege mentality."[51]

Lucas predictably met these threats to his power with brutality, including one of the war's most brazen acts of violence in January 1980. Late that month, Máximo Cajal, the Spanish ambassador to Guatemala, visited Quiché and met with several local priests, who were Spanish citizens, to discuss the area's repression. During the meeting, Cajal offered the priests protection in the Spanish Embassy and told them that "if someone felt threatened, he could help take them out of the country."[52] Press outlets reported on Cajal's visit the following day, and the reports were read by members of the Comité de Unidad Campesina (CUC), who had, coincidentally, traveled to the capital to petition the government to open an investigation into an army massacre in Chajul the previous month.[53] After legislators refused to see the group, they asked multiple newspapers to publish their denunciations, which they refused to do. As a last-ditch effort, the group decided to occupy the Spanish Embassy, because they interpreted published reports on Cajal's offer of support for Spanish priests as a sign of solidarity.[54]

Twenty-seven members of CUC and the Frente Estudiantíl Robin García entered the embassy on the morning of January 31 and detailed for Cajal "all the army's injustice, evil, and cowardice [and their] persecution and threats" and the Guatemalan press's lack of reporting on the massacres in the countryside. Coincidentally, former vice president Eduardo Cáceres Lehnhoff, former Foreign Affairs Minister Adolfo Molina Orantes, and esteemed academic Mario Aguirre Godoy had also called on Cajal at the embassy that morning. This coincidence, according to Sabino, "gave the occupation of the embassy more resonance." At eleven o'clock, the group entered the embassy and, in Aguirre's recollection, "masked people in red handkerchiefs and straw hats began to swarm through the second floor."[55] Cajal seemed unperturbed by the intrusion and asked CUC members to stay as he listened to their denunciations.

The area outside the embassy compound soon filled with onlookers, reporters, and, ominously, a heavy police presence. Both Molina and Aguirre requested to no avail that the police leave the area. By one o'clock that afternoon, members of the Sixth Command prepared to storm the embassy in a flagrant violation of international law, as the embassy was legally recognized as sovereign Spanish territory. Police Chief Pedro García Arredondo ordered officers to set the embassy ablaze and refused to allow the fire department to respond. Television cameras captured the act, as well as the sight of firemen, eventually allowed to respond, removing dead bodies from the building.[56] In all, thirty-six people, including Cáceres, Molina, and all but one of the occupiers, were murdered. A Guatemala City mortuary worker testified, "I can't forget the titanic job of separating the cadavers from each other. . . . We separated them and they fell apart. Part of one body would be stuck in another, we found . . . it took almost fourteen hours to identify the bodies. . . . Almost none of them had a recognizable face" (Figure 3.1).[57] Cajál managed to escape the blaze and insisted that the lone surviving occupier, Gregorio Yujá Xona, be taken with him to the hospital to ensure his safety. Yujá was nevertheless kidnapped from his hospital bed that evening and murdered. Following the massacre, the Quiché Diocese issued a press release that stated, in part, "The regrettable events which took place in the Spanish Embassy are manifestations of the tension currently prevailing in the country and particularly in Quiché. Peasants seeking attention of fellow citizens and the authorities for a solution to their problems, problems which they had unsuccessfully tried to draw attention to through various means, today are added to the victims of the tragedy we are facing in our country."[58]

The Spanish Embassy Massacre was one of more than five hundred recorded human rights violations across the country during 1980, more than quadrupling the previous year's total. Some of these violations were particularly audacious.

Figure 3.1. Bodies inside the Spanish Embassy, Guatemala City, 1980. (Courtesy Archivo Historico de la Policia Nacional.)

On March 8, Julio César Lemus Martínez, a captain in the Guatemalan Navy, was murdered while investigating cattle thefts in Sipicate, Escuintla. One of the thieves was related to Manuel de Jesús Valiente Tellez, the chief of the National Corps of Detectives and one of Yolanda de la Luz Aguilar Urizar's rapists. According to a CIA report, the thief asked Valiente for assistance in the matter, who dispatched three detectives to kill Lemus. The army's G-2 investigative unit subsequently learned that Lemus's murderers were Valiente henchmen and gave him an ultimatum: either kill the three detectives responsible for killing Lemus or resign his position. The report noted that "the bodies of the three detectives were discovered on 11 March 1980 on the old road to Lake Atitlán."[59] Soldiers and civilian collaborators also murdered Alfredo Jalal and Roseado Crúz Juc, two workers at the Miramar finca in La Tinta, Alta Verapáz, on April 26 after the men complained that they had not been paid for two weeks.[60] In Guatemala City, thirty-two people were kidnapped from Parque Centenario during a May Day demonstration organized by the Comité Nacional de Unidad Sindical, and twenty-seven Central Nacional de Trabajadores (CNT) members were abducted on June 21; police abducted another seventeen CNT leaders from three factories in Escuintla on

August 24.[61] Elsewhere, a massacre in Pichec, Baja Verapáz, in September left one hundred dead, including multiple newborns.[62] Six days later, an army-led massacre killed twenty-one people in Panacal, approximately three miles north of Pichec.[63] Deaths related to forced displacement also increased during 1980, especially in Alta Verapáz and Quiché. In Alta Verapáz, over a dozen children died from hunger, illness, and exposure as their families fled into the mountains to escape the army. In Quiché, Juan Cardona Brito, age two, was one of five people to die from hunger and exposure.[64]

As atrocities like these spread across Guatemala, Catholic activism in Guatemala and the United States intensified and diversified. In some cases, priests, missionaries, and lay Catholics directly halted some human rights abuses. In San Lucas Tolimán, for example, Schaffer coordinated the rescue of a group of children after soldiers destroyed their homes. One of the children, Mariposa, recalled the journey she made with her brothers and sister to San Lucas Tolimán.[65] An army patrol "destroyed everything" in her community, arrested her parents, both of whom were catechists in the local parish, and killed her uncles and grandfather. "Some people came in the afternoon," she recalled. "They forced the children out of the house and told me they just wanted to talk to my mother. I never saw her again after that." Mariposa's younger brother, Pastor, noted that when the army abducted his mother, soldiers locked them and their younger sister inside a house and threatened to set it on fire. Mariposa was eight years old at the time; Pastor was seven, and her sister was still an infant. Mariposa then described what happened next:

> I went to look for my mother the next day. I saw a lot of dead people in the streets again, many young people and kids with their guts and intestines spilled out. . . . The military kept looking for more people because they said our community was full of guerrillas. They thought my parents were guerrillas. They wouldn't let us be in the Church. . . . After a week, [the army] forced us to leave or be killed, so we went to San Miguel Uspantán with our livestock that was still alive. The soldiers laughed at us.[66]

The children lived with an aunt for approximately six months before they were forced to flee once more after death threats against their aunt for taking them into her home.

Mariposa's aunt arranged for the children to live in San Lucas Tolimán. To get there, they first needed to pass an army checkpoint in the middle of the night near the town of Santa Cruz del Quiché, approximately fifty miles to the southwest. Mariposa recalled, "We were in a truck with people going to the coast to work and they carried us. When we got to Santa Cruz del Quiché we had to get out and the soldiers wanted to know who we were and where our parents were. One of the workers said our parents owned the truck and the driver was our father and they let us pass." They arrived in San Lucas Tolimán the following morning. Mariposa remembered that Schaffer received the children with food, clothing, and "a lot of love. It is a hard moment to describe because we finally felt free, and that nobody would be looking for us. That's how we arrived in San Lucas." Although the children were understandably traumatized by their journey, Mariposa recalled feeling that Schaffer, Father John Goggin, and San Lucas Tolimán's parishioners always protected them. When asked about her daily life in the parish at the time, she remembered that "we had everything we needed. My sister was cared for and had all she needed, all that I couldn't do for her. When I saw her starting to study in school, I cried tears of joy. [The parish] was very, very beautiful for us. . . . What I remember most about Padre is that when he would hug us, his beard always scratched us."[67]

Stories like Mariposa's were not uncommon, and several were published in the New Ulm Diocese's newsletter. In March 1978, Schaffer shared the story of Geronimo Ajpuac, a young boy who "probably [had] . . . polio as an infant, no one is sure, but from the knees down his legs and feet are best described as grotesque. They look like two sticks with a brown-paper bag of misplaced bones at the bottom." Schaffer then recalled a particularly difficult moment with Ajpuac after visiting a doctor: "Dr. Silva disbelievingly asked, 'How can that boy walk?' And then the verdict. Needed immediately, serious, long and terribly painful surgery on both feet. Can the guy handle it? I broke down then and cried. When I got together, we called him into the office and asked him what he thought. His first question was 'Padre, will they cut off my feet?' I choked but could answer, 'No.' Then, 'Will they cut off my toes?' Again, 'No.' 'O.K.,' he said, 'let's try.' Yesterday, we brought him home from the hospital after the first of his surgeries. It will take a long, long time."

Another newsletter issue from the period introduced readers to Dominga, another orphaned child living at Casa Felíz. According to mission priest Father David Roney, Dominga was "possibly the most mature twelve-year-old I have ever met. Maybe her maturity is due to the fact that a few months ago, in the middle of the night, she watched while her parents were dragged from their beds and shot. The killers were never identified." According to Roney, Dominga was one of eighty children living at Casa Felíz, which included "one little girl, about eight years old [who] still refuses to leave the parish grounds. It's the only place where she feels safe."[69] Roney asked readers to consider donating to complete construction on a new, larger orphanage.

Roney's report exemplifies a second common form of Catholic activism. News from and about Guatemala frequently appeared in Catholic newspapers across the United States during this period, as the US Catholic press reported on Guatemalans' reactions to Father Hermogenes López's murder in 1978; USAC's call for an end to "persecution" of religious, labor, and student leaders in 1979; and the CEG's pleas for peace after Father Walter Voordeckers' murder in Santa Lucía Cotzumagalpa in 1980.[70] In turn, *Catholic Worker* managing editor Peggy Scherer penned an introspective essay on a vigil for peace at the Pentagon in 1980. Reflecting on the experience, Scherer mused, "We carefully maintain the myths necessary to keep us from outrage—as in Guatemala, recently, when hungry peasants seeking redress against the stream of detentions and disappearances in their village went to the Spanish Embassy and were killed there. . . . We accept with little question the labeling of such peasants, thus discrediting them. Again and again, justice is not the issue—only 'order.'"[71]

More locally, diocesan newspaper carried the Catholic News Service's wire stories, offered local coverage, and published editorials from area priests or bishops on the crises that plagued Guatemala and, more broadly, Central America. In Davenport, Iowa, the *Catholic Messenger* reported on Father Thomas Buechele's return from Guatemala in late 1979. In remarks to Davenport-area Catholics, Buechele referred to Guatemala as a "hotbed" and said, "Church officials in Guatemala face persecution from the military government if they try to properly minister to their parishioners. However, if they tell the people that they must endure their poverty, they are not properly preaching the gospel."[72] Likewise, the April 3, 1980, edition of Dubuque, Iowa's *Witness* included an editorial on Central America's multiple political crises. Referring to the overthrows of Fulgencio Batista in Cuba, Somoza in Nicaragua, and Romero in El Salvador, the *Witness* editorial staff argued that the United States had supported each dictator until "it was obvious the revolutionaries would be victorious, but it was never soon enough to avoid being blamed for the repression of the regime. . . . This is the dilemma this nation is in presently with Nicaragua and El Salvador and will very probably soon face in Guatemala and Honduras."[73] Finally, in December 1980, Rochester, New York's *Courier-Journal* printed a syndicated Religious News Service report on the human rights challenges that President-Elect Ronald Reagan would face in Central America and noted that Catholics had become prime targets of government and right-wing violence.[74]

Diocesan newspapers also reported on local events and concerns related to Guatemala. The *Witness* reported in its February 22, 1979, edition that a group of 250 Dubuque residents would visit Guatemala City as part of a citizen exchange program. The program, known as the Friendship Force, offered classes and workshops to teach participants about their host country during a ten-day visit. The report also noted that a fund drive was currently underway to support the program and asked *Witness* readers for volunteers to host Guatemalans visiting Dubuque.[75] Elsewhere, the Corpus Christi, Texas, *South Texas Catholic* reported on Sister Siena Schmitt of Houston, Texas, who spoke about her experiences in Guatemala as part of the Leadership Conference of Women Religious, held in Castroville, Texas, in May. According to the report, the conference's theme was ways to "increase awareness of and to deal effectively with the social injustices existing in society and within religious congregations" and a follow-up meeting of the group's national assembly would be held in Castroville later in the summer.[76]

Catholic activists also played active roles in interfaith and secular grassroots organizations. One particularly notable example was the Guatemala News and Information Bureau (GNIB), a group formed in San Francisco, California, in 1977 that disseminated information about Guatemala and Central America across the United States. The GNIB worked with groups like the Oakland-based Network in Solidarity with the People of Guatemala, the Central American Non-Intervention Coalition, and the Bay Area Central American Peace Campaign and collected an impressive array of mailings, letters, and press clippings on Guatemala's violence and human rights abuses. Much of this material came from Catholic groups like the CEG, the United States Catholic Council, the Nicaragua-based Guatemalan Church in Exile, and the Saint Raymond's Church Social Justice Committee in Dublin, California. The group also collected information from individual sources, such as a priest's anonymous, month-by-month account of violence in the Ixil region from August 1979 to January 1980. The GNIB also circulated individual accounts of human rights abuses in their mailings: in a 1979 issue of the group's "Guatemala!" newsletter, the story of Miguel Archila's murder, Yolanda de la Luz Aguilar Urizar's rape, and letters to her uncle were printed on page two in both Spanish and English.

Guatemala's anti-Catholic repression increased as Catholic activists helped bring conditions in the country to greater public attention. On May 1, 1980, Father Conrado de la Cruz Concepción, a Filipino missionary serving in Tiquisate, Escunitla, and catechist Herlando Cifuentes were abducted in Guatemala City while watching a May Day demonstration. According to witnesses, "six heavily armed men" forced the two men into a gray Toyota jeep on the corner of Sixth Street and Eighth Avenue, just feet from the city's Metropolitan Cathedral. Their bodies were never found. On May 11, the archbishop of Escuintla, Monsignor

Mario Enrique Ríos Montt, brother of Lucas's successor, Brigadier General José Efraín Ríos Montt, protested the abductions during masses and public demonstrations in Escuintla and Santa Lucía Cotzumalguapa.

The next day, Father Walter Voordeckers, a Belgian priest and outspoken critic of the country's violence, was murdered in Santa Lucía Cotzumalguapa, where he had served the parish since 1966. According to Father Francesco Herren, a contemporary of the slain priest, Voordeckers received death threats while visiting family and friends in Belgium in 1979 but nevertheless returned to Santa Lucia Cotzumalguapa. Herren later recalled that Voordeckers' funeral mass drew an estimated ten thousand people from as far away as Santa Rosa and Petén and that Voordeckers had always "spoke from his heart" in homilies. Herren also noted that there was "a very big difference" between the murders of de la Cruz and Voordeckers, noting, "I was able to tell Walter's parents everything that happened and that we buried him, while with Conrado we never knew what they did with him."[77]

Less than a month later, Father José María Gran Cirera, known familiarly as "Padre Chemita," was fatally shot from behind on June 5 as he returned to Chajul after visiting some of the parish's more remote communities. Cirera's sacristan, Domingo del Barrio Batz, was also murdered in the attack. The men's deaths were exceedingly violent: del Barrio had been shot twice in both his stomach and chest and once through his eye, and Cirera had been shot at least five times and had had one arm severed. Additionally, the men's murderers left guerrilla "propaganda" with the corpses.[78] Cirera, a Spanish-born priest, had served in Quiché for five years prior to his murder, while del Barrio, a native of Ilom, Quiché, had been a longtime Catholic Action supporter and had frequently accompanied parish priests in remote areas to assist with celebrating communion and other sacraments. Their bodies were discovered almost a month later. On July 10, another Spanish-born priest, Father Faustino Villanueva Villanueva, was murdered in the parish rectory in Joyabaj, Quiché. Villanueva had served as a missionary in Quiché and Nandaime, Nicaragua, since 1959 and was the fourth of ten priests to be killed during the Lucas regime.

The regime's anti-Catholicism also took other forms. In January 1980, Guatemala's Jesuits published a statement in the newspaper *El Gráfico* that resoundingly condemned the country's inequality and violence. Among other examples, the Jesuits noted that while market prices for coffee, sugar, and cotton (Guatemala's primary exports) had risen substantially in recent months, workers' salaries had stagnated. At the same time, they argued, rising costs for necessities like food, electricity, and public transportation had similarly "crush[ed] the [urban] wage earners more every day in a comparable misery . . . to that of the agricultural sector." The letter also cited a *Diario Impacto* report that the country had endured 3,252 murders between January and October 1979 alone and grimly mused that "it is . . . a proverb that in Guatemala there are no political prisoners, only dead and disappeared."[79]

The following day, *El Grafico* published a rebuttal from Lucas's Public Relations Secretariat that accused the Jesuits of political subversion and of "trying to ridicule the Pope himself and the Catholic Latin American hierarchy," referencing the pontiff's admonitions about politically entangled clergy at Puebla the year prior. The Secretariat's letter also accused the Jesuits of "deliberately" ignoring "the criticisms of the Holy Father against 'priests' who have put aside their religious mission to dedicate themselves to political activism and . . . to nourish Marxist subversion as agents of a network of the enemies of Guatemala who operate from outside the country" in what the regime saw as "a case of clear intervention of foreigners in the internal affairs of Guatemala."[80] The statement concluded with a call for the order to recall "political Jesuit priests" serving in the country. Not to be outdone, the ESA issued its own statement a week later in which the organization threatened to kill every Guatemalan Jesuit in the country and expel all of the order's foreign-born members from the country. On January 29, the Washington, DC–based Jesuit Conference of the United States issued a press release that compared the threat with a similar one made by El Salvador's White Warrior Union death squad, noting that "a massive international protest against such inhumane threats [in El Salvador] was effective, at least in part, in preventing such threatened violence at the time."[81] Finally, the CEH later recorded multiple incidences of the army forcibly closing or occupying churches in Joyabaj, Zacualpa, San Pedro Jocopilas, Sacapulas, Nebaj, Chajul, San Juan Cotzal, Uspantán, Chiché, and Conillá, among other parishes, throughout 1980. In some cases, as in Chipaj, the army also forced Catholics to convert to evangelical Protestantism "under the threat of death."[82]

By any metric, the Lucas regime's first thirty months were exceptionally violent. According to Amnesty International, the Guatemalan army, police, and death squads killed more than six thousand people in 1979 and 1980 alone while the CEH recorded more than seven hundred documented human rights abuses, ranging from massacres and disappearances to deaths from violence-related illness and hunger committed between 1978 and 1980.[83] No sector of Guatemala, whether public or private, was immune to violence or terror.

Simultaneously, the lingering ambiguities after CELAM's Pubela conference allowed Liberationist and conservative Catholics alike to claim that the Pope had endorsed their particular social and political views. In Guatemala, this ambiguity was evident in the rift between Casariego and the CEG, as well as rank-and-file clergy, which was manifested in expected ways, like the CEG's letters, as well as the unexpected, which, at times, included the naming of neutered stray cats. While Catholic activists became more visible and vocal during the late 1970s, the Lucas regime viewed them as a growing, dangerous rival and sought violent reprisal in multiple ways. These developments had profound diplomatic consequences as Catholic activists brought pressure to bear on US policymakers to act on the Lucas regime's violence, urged Ortiz's recall as ambassador, and responded to the United States' own rightward shift following Reagan's election in 1980.

4

The Worst Possible Outcome

The Lucas regime's violence and lawlessness was apparent from its earliest days. Its response to the 1978 bus fare protests signaled that the country's repression and violence would continue under the new regime as death squads like the ESA, Ojo por Ojo, and Unidad pro Libertad Nacional contra la Agresión Comunista operated openly and with impunity. At the same time, massacres in Quiché, Alta Verapáz, and Huehuetenango grew more frequent as the war's violence shifted away from Guatemala City and into the country's western highlands following the Panzós massacre. Other types of human rights abuses, including rape, forcible displacement, malnutrition, and torture also increased under Lucas. Of the almost seven hundred known cases of human rights abuses that CEH recorded between 1978 and 1980, more than five hundred were attributed to the army and state-affiliated groups including the PN, civil patrols, military commissions, and *guardias de haciendas*, private security forces employed by wealthy *finqueros* like La Perla owner José Luis Arenas Barrera.

Lucas also seemed ready to continue Laugerud's refusal of US military assistance tied to Guatemala's human rights record. Like Laugerud, Lucas denounced the Carter administration's emphasis on human rights as a contemporary version of yanqui imperialism and criticized the United States' own human rights abuses, both at home and around the globe. Also like Laugerud, Lucas mitigated the absence of US weapons and munitions through multiple arms agreements with other countries and private contractors, which bolstered both dictators' blustery denunciations of US policy and brought the limits of the Carter administration's policies into sharper focus. The ensuing diplomatic trough impeded the administration's influence in Central America at the worst possible moment, as Nicaragua's Sandinista Revolution entered its final months and El Salvador plunged into civil war by decade's end. The administration's inconsistent and, at times, contradictory responses to these simultaneous crises led some policymakers and administration officials to acknowledge the United States' receding political influence in the region.

Guatemala's violence and human rights abuses also fomented division within the country's Roman Catholic Church and worsened its relationship with the Lucas regime. The CEG and Casariego publicly criticized each other, and the regime and the ESA openly threatened the country's Jesuits in the wake of the Spanish Embassy massacre in 1980. Similar conditions existed in El Salvador, where death squads like the White Warrior Union threatened to murder Jesuits, and posters and signs reading "Be a patriot! Kill a priest!" were a common sight. The Salvadoran army also murdered several priests, including Father Rutilio Grande and Óscar Romero, and, in 1980, raped and murdered US missionaries Sister Maura Clarke, Sister Ita Ford, Sister Dorothy Kazel, and lay missionary Jean Donovan. In Nicaragua, liberation theology intersected with national politics as the Marxist Frente Sandinista de Liberación Nacional government appointed Fathers Miguel d'Escoto Brockmann, Ernesto Cardenal, and Fernando Cardenal to key political positions after dictator Anastasio Somoza DeBayle's overthrow in 1979. All the while, the US Catholic press provided frequent and, often, in-depth coverage of each of these crises that brought Central America's turmoil and violence home for readers in parishes and dioceses across the United States.

This chapter explores some of the bureaucratic, ideological, and practical challenges that shaped US-Guatemalan relations during the late 1970s. It explores how disagreements over the Lucas regime's human rights record within the State Department during this period left its Bureau of Inter-American Affairs and Human Rights and Humanitarian Affairs Bureau at cross-purposes, especially on the topic of arms sales to the regime. Meanwhile, US policymakers like Davis Boster and Frank Ortiz, among others, caricatured Lucas as a plodding, inarticulate country bumpkin whose ascendancy had been the 1978 election's worst possible outcome. These challenges hamstrung any meaningful improvements in US-Guatemalan relations during the late 1970s, even as Catholic activists, the US Catholic press, and transnational human rights groups brought news of violence and unrest in Guatemala and Central America to greater public attention in the United States.

Human rights were a critical factor in US policymaking decisions on Guatemala during the late 1970s. In a cable dated July 18, 1978, Boster reported that the country's extreme left and right continued to assail the Carter administration's human rights and foreign policies. According to Boster, Guatemala's far left viewed the Carter administration's emphasis on human rights as "a sham—fine words belied by the alliance of US business interests, supported by the U[nited] S[tates] G[overnment] with the military and economic preservers of the status quo." On the far right, Lucas, like Laugerud, viewed the Carter administration's emphasis on human rights as an intervention in Guatemala's sovereign domestic affairs, and some Lucas regime leaders believed it was a pretext for supporting the United Kingdom in its ongoing dispute with Guatemala over territorial claims to Belize.[1]

Boster further noted that *Prensa Libre* had denounced US policy as hypocritical, given the United States' own human rights record at home and around the globe.

Boster also reported that although the Lucas regime viewed the Carter administration's emphasis on human rights as interventionism, it nevertheless pledged to improve Guatemala's human rights record. During Lucas's inaugural address, he had vowed to "establish a social peace based on the well-being of all Guatemalans" and that his regime would respect human rights as it pursued a "genuine democracy."[2] Lucas also pledged to create "new sources of employment" in the agricultural and manufacturing sectors to raise living standards across the country.[3] Likewise, at a meeting of the Organization of American States in Washington, Lucas's vice president, Francisco Villagrán Kramer, stated that the Carter administration's policies were becoming increasingly accepted across Latin America and that "we are moving in the direction of giving human rights an international dimension."[4] These statements led Boster to conclude that Lucas desired better relations with the United States and would be open to "quietly accepting" military assistance predicated on his regime's human rights record, a position that his successor, Ortiz, also took as ambassador.[5]

Not all State Department officials shared Boster's optimism. In a memorandum dated September 1, 1978, Richard Feinberg, a member of the State Department's Policy Planning Staff, enumerated several examples of Guatemala's ongoing human rights abuses that he observed on a recent visit to the country. In a passage that recalled the CIA's alarming report on Arana years earlier, Feinberg reported that Guatemala's interior minister, Donaldo Álvarez Ruiz, had not only praised death squad activity as a useful way to "clean" the country but also acknowledged that the squads operated with Lucas's approval and that Lucas had authorized police and military members' participation in death squad killings.[6] Feinberg also reported that ongoing violence in El Salvador and Nicaragua had left Lucas increasingly worried about maintaining order in Guatemala, a development that other administration and State Department officials would echo in the coming months.

While State Department officials dithered, members of the Lucas regime, including Lucas himself, cited human rights concerns as their motivation for purchasing US weapons. Lucas, Villagrán, and Foreign Minister Rafael Castillo Valdez had all separately inquired about purchasing five thousand rounds of tear gas from the United States on an urgent basis during 1978. Both Lucas and Villagrán framed their requests in the language of human rights: Villagrán told Boster that tear gas was a more humane means of quelling protest, while Lucas complained that "he would become a target of human rights criticism when policy finds it necessary to resort to clubs and ultimately firearms to disband unauthorized demonstrations and strike because tear gas had run out."[7]

Individual bureaus within the State Department disagreed on authorizing the request. The Bureau of Inter-American Affairs (ARA) endorsed the sale for multiple reasons, most notably that a refusal would be another impediment to improving US-Guatemalan relations under the new Lucas regime as violence and political unrest worsened in both Nicaragua and El Salvador. The bureau also argued that the United States had sold bullets to Guatemala for decades, and any time the regime shot and killed civilians, it "exposed [the United States] to criticism . . . for having sold Guatemala ammunition but not tear gas." In contrast, the Human Rights and Humanitarian Affairs Bureau (HA) discouraged the sale based on Guatemala's human rights record and cited the Harkin Amendments as a legal prohibition against the sale. The HA Bureau also observed that while Lucas claimed the need for tear gas was urgent, he had not sought it from other sources. The bureau found this notable because, as it argued, tear gas "could probably be obtained elsewhere," and it speculated that Lucas specifically wanted to use tear gas as a symbol of US support for his regime. There was some merit to this argument, since Lucas did indeed have multiple alternative sources for tear gas, guns, and bullets: between 1978 and 1980, the Lucas regime purchased weapons and supplies from a host of US allies, including Israel, Switzerland, and South Korea, among other countries. Additionally, both Israel and Argentina sent technical and tactical advisers to Guatemala during this period.[8] Similar conditions existed in Nicaragua and El Salvador, which also utilized multiple nations, particularly Israel, to purchase arms for those countries' dictatorships.[9]

The Lucas regime also acquired arms via private transactions with US-based companies. Under the Export Administration Act of 1979 and the Arms Export Control Act, private sales from companies to Guatemala were permissible if licensed by the State Department. License applications for Guatemala were reviewed by both the ARA and HA Bureaus, as well as the department's Political-Military Affairs Bureau. Under this arrangement, private companies sold almost one million dollars in weapons to the Lucas regime in 1979 alone, including more than eighteen hundred pistols and revolvers, eleven hundred rifles, ten submachine guns, and almost two and a half million cartridges of ammunition.[10] Additionally, an unnamed supplier sold five thousand rounds of tear gas to the regime in 1978.[11] This was not unique to the Lucas regime, as Laugerud had made multiple arms purchases from Smith & Wesson, International Armament Corporation, and Hamilton Associates while in power. Nor was this unique to Guatemala: as historian William Michael Schmidli has shown, arms manufacturers in the United States also privately sold weapons to Argentina during that country's Dirty War of the 1970s with State Department approval.[12]

While the ARA and HA Bureaus disagreed on the severity of the Lucas regime's human rights abuses, crises in Nicaragua and El Salvador plunged Central America into deeper disarray. The FSLN forces were in the midst of a final offensive by mid-1979, as large numbers of the group's armed forces streamed into the country via Costa Rica and engaged in what US Embassy officials described as "unusually heavy firefights" in the capital, Managua.[13] The FSLN toppled Somoza on July 19, ending the Somoza family dictatorship and, in the process, installed Latin America's third Marxist government after Cuba in 1959 and Grenada four months before the FSLN's victory.[14]

Meanwhile in El Salvador, campesinos, student and labor unions, and Catholic activists were among those Salvadorans that protested the country's crippling poverty and powerful oligarchy, culminating in General Carlos Humberto Romero Mena's overthrow in October 1979. A five-man junta, composed of three civilians and two army colonels, took power on October 15 and denounced the dictatorship's failure to rectify the country's "anarchic" conditions.[15] The junta announced its intention to form a cabinet composed of members from across the political spectrum and to implement a range of economic and social reforms that would redress the country's poverty and human rights abuses. Despite its goals, the junta crumbled as its civilian members resigned, opening the door for the military's return to total power and civil war by 1980.[16]

Central America's rapidly worsening crises prompted the Carter administration to order a second PRC review of US policy approaches to the region in 1979. Like the 1977 PRC, the 1979 committee comprised top-level officials from the State Department, White House, Joint Chiefs of Staff, and National Security Council, among other agencies, and met throughout that summer. Committee members viewed conditions in Nicaragua and El Salvador as more urgent than those in Guatemala: Deputy Secretary of State Warren Christopher characterized the Lucas regime as "a stable and conservative one," albeit one that "apparently sanctions official assassinations," while the assistant secretary of state for inter-American affairs, Viron Vaky, argued that although Lucas was unpopular and murderous, the United States had "more time" in Guatemala to take action than it had to address the Nicaraguan and Salvadoran crises. In contrast, the PRC continued to refer to Guatemala as "stable and stronger than its neighbors" and maintained that pressing Lucas for human rights and political reforms remained the top priority in bilateral affairs.[17]

As the PRC analyzed Central America's crises, Frank Ortiz assumed his post as ambassador to Guatemala on July 17. Ortiz had served the State Department in multiple capacities since 1951, including deputy executive secretary of state from 1975 to 1977 and as ambassador to Barbados and Grenada from 1977 to 1979. A

State Department press release praised Ortiz as a career diplomat whose "years of working in Latin America and his lifelong interest in the area" made him an ideal candidate for the posting to Guatemala.[18] The press release also alluded to Ortiz's reputation for candor and stated that Guatemala's strategic importance to the United States required an ambassador capable of forthright, open dialogue on key diplomatic issues.

Correspondence from Ortiz's first months as ambassador highlighted the State Department's contradictory policies toward Guatemala and the immediate challenges that Ortiz faced as ambassador. His cables and telegrams from this period included his assessment of Guatemala's increasingly unstable social conditions, as well as his contention that the Carter administration's human rights policies contributed to the Lucas government's sense of diplomatic and political isolation. This correspondence acknowledged internal disagreements on human rights and the Lucas regime's violence and demonstrated the State Department's inability to provide Ortiz with clear direction on how to engage Lucas on these issues. As a result, Ortiz had little diplomatic leverage in his negotiations with the Lucas regime on its human rights abuses as it continued to acquire weapons from alternative sources inside and outside the United States (Figure 4.1).

Figure 4.1. US Ambassador Frank V. Ortiz Jr. and Brigadier General Fernando Romeo Lucas Garcia, 1979. (Courtesy Palace of the Governors Photo Archives [NMHM/DCA], HP.2008.18.003.)

One of Ortiz's earliest telegrams from Guatemala City highlights many of these problems. On September 4, he presented a lengthy account of his first impressions of Guatemala, the country's human rights abuses, and the view of US-Guatemalan relations from Guatemala City. Writing about his initial impression of the country's citizens, Ortiz claimed, "Dominant Guatemalans see themselves as increasingly isolated and as the international target of a Marxist-inspired, hostile, coordinated campaign. . . . It helps create a siege mentality. It strengthens the hand of those in Guatemala who favor repressive responses even to constructive criticism and to legitimate pressures for change."[19]

Ortiz also reported that acceptance of the Carter administration's human rights policies had clear, explicit limits. According to Ortiz, while many Guatemalans believed those policies were central to good relations with the United States, they took on "strongly negative aspects when our public condemnations run counter to Guatemalan nationalism."[20] He also noted that the administration had emboldened Guatemala's far left by challenging the Lucas regime to improve its human rights record, albeit unsuccessfully. In his view, the best course of action for US-Guatemalan relations was to avoid overt criticism of the Lucas regime's human rights abuses while working quietly with Guatemalan leaders to find consensus on ways to halt the country's violence and defuse its siege mentality.

Miscommunication and misunderstandings on key diplomatic matters also complicated Ortiz's mission. In a letter to Ortiz dated October 13, 1979, Deputy Assistant Secretary of Defense John Bushnell acknowledged that all outgoing correspondence and direction to the US Embassy in Guatemala City was an amalgamation of policy recommendations from the ARA, as well as the State Department's Policy Planning Staff and the White House itself. The result was a contradictory policy that left Ortiz and embassy officials without clear direction on how to approach human rights and other diplomatic issues. As a result, Bushnell continued, "communications between Washington and the Embassy may not be as good as they should be on the key issue in Guatemala—human rights as a block to constructive US actions."[21]

Bushnell was particularly concerned with a misunderstanding over what State Department officials precisely meant in their directives on improving Guatemala's human rights practices. Bushnell wrote, "When you are instructed to ask Lucas to make a public commitment to respect human rights . . . what we are really saying is that we need concrete *actions* to demonstrate a real determination to stop the . . . killing. Broad public statements will not meet the bill because they are not credible."[22] Bushnell's instructions, however, remained essentially impossible to follow because Lucas was able to mitigate the loss of US military assistance by securing arms and munitions from other states and commercial merchants. As Ortiz noted,

Lucas had far less incentive to comply to US human rights standards if states like Israel and South Korea and companies like Smith & Wesson were willing and able to engage in arms sales to Guatemala.

Regional upheaval also raised US policymakers' concerns about Guatemala's violence. Romero had been overthrown in El Salvador just days before Bushnell's letter to Ortiz, leading Bushnell to comment that "with this week's events in El Salvador . . . I am afraid that some in Guatemala will react to events nearby by taking a tougher and more violent stand although I would hope the majority would move in the opposite direction." Bushnell emphasized Guatemala's increased importance to US interests following Romero's overthrow, stating, "I should stress again that real actions to protect human rights are needed by the [Lucas government] to change our current policy and develop a basis for cooperation."[23]

Finally, a third piece of correspondence from the autumn of 1979 highlights the State Department's internal disagreements over how to define human rights and execute human rights policies. In a letter dated October 19, the ARA's International Relations Officer, James Mack, provided Ortiz with an update on departmental discussions concerning Guatemala, which focused on human rights, arms sales, and embassy reporting from Guatemala City. On the topic of human rights, Mack reported that key State Department officials, including Vaky, former US ambassador to Guatemala and then assistant secretary of state for intelligence and research William Bowdler, and HA Bureau Secretary Patricia Derian, had recently met with members of the Guatemalan organization Amigos del País to discuss the country's human rights abuses. Mack reported, "We found ourselves talking about very different aspects of the problem. The Guatemalans outlined the steps that the [Guatemalan government] and the private sector have taken . . . to improve social security, labor legislation and medical care for the working class. Yet, as you know, the focus here is almost totally on the 'integrity of the human person' type of violations which are the fundamental cause of the difficulties in our relationship. The Guatemalans are going to have to respond to our concerns . . . to make the necessary converts in the Department and on the Hill."[24]

Mack also informed Ortiz that individual bureaus within the State Department still disagreed on Guatemala's status as a human rights violator and the extent of the Lucas regime's responsibility for halting human rights abuses. According to Mack, the ARA argued that the Lucas regime was required to take concrete steps to halt only those abuses directly attributed to the regime, such as those committed by the army or PN, before the State Department could remove Guatemala from its list of persistent human rights violator states but made no mention of violence committed by opposition groups like ORPA and the EGP. In contrast, the State Department's Office of the Legal Adviser believed that Section 116 of the

Foreign Assistance Act of 1974 required the Lucas regime to take steps to halt *all* human rights abuses in Guatemala, including those committed by the country's militant left, and argued that the regime's failure to do so kept it ineligible for military assistance.[25] Mack reported that this argument had persuaded Christopher and that this decision was instrumental in the refusal of a proposed Inter-American Development Bank loan to Guatemala aimed at bolstering the country's tourism industry earlier in the year.

Ortiz's personal feelings about Guatemalan leaders punctuated his correspondence with State Department officials. In addition to privately referring to him as the "killer president of Guatemala," Ortiz described Lucas as "handsome, tall, broad shouldered—sort of a John Barrymore type—but . . . a cold-blooded, vicious man [with] eyes like a cobra."[26] Ortiz also doubted Lucas's intellect, caricaturing him as a boorish simpleton ill-equipped to govern.[27] Ortiz was also distrustful of Villagrán, who he characterized as a scheming opportunist intent on replacing Lucas. Ortiz described Villagrán in a State Department telegram as being "possessed of a fertile and imaginative mind" but also having "a surprising lack of a sense of reality" when it came to his importance within Guatemalan politics. One notable example of this came during a lunch meeting between Ortiz and Villagrán on November 9, when Villagrán hinted at a potential coup and asked Ortiz if the Carter administration would recognize him as president if Lucas resigned or was overthrown. Ortiz deflected the question but reported that Villagrán wildly overestimated his popularity among the country's military and political leaders. According to Ortiz, "Villagrán's lack of a significant political base and the strong opposition to him on the part of many if not all the political parties would seem to make a Villagrán Kramer government one of the least likely scenarios for the future."[28] Ortiz also noted that Villagrán attempted to stoke fears of another direct US intervention by making public statements that the Carter administration sought to overthrow Lucas and install Villagrán as president.[29]

As policy debates on Guatemala swirled, Catholic activists continued calling attention to conditions in Central America, especially via the Catholic press. In the August 7 edition of the San Francisco Archdiocese's *Interchange*, for example, Monsignor James B. Flynn reported on the recent high-profile murders of Alberto Fuentes Mohr and Manuel Colom Argueta, as well as Guatemala's resurgent death squad activity and anti-labor violence, particularly against workers at Coca-Cola's bottling plant in Guatemala City. Flynn urged readers to write to Carter, congressional policymakers, the United Nations, Coca-Cola executives, and John Trotter, owner of the Guatemala City bottling plant, and noted that Trotter had "hired military officers as personnel, warehouse and security managers." Further, Flynn asserted, "union members have been threatened, [and] . . . if as alleged, he has attempted to destroy these rights and has cooperated with the Guatemalan government in the use of terrorist tactics, it is all the more repugnant because he is a United States citizen and acting in the name of a United States based company."[30]

Catholic activists were also prominent in human rights groups during this period. Maryknoll Father Edward Killackey worked with the Washington Office of Latin America, a Washington, DC–based human rights advocacy group, and Catholic leadership within the Inter-Church Committee on Human Rights in Latin America printed firsthand accounts of Guatemala's violence in the group's publications. Catholic activists also held leadership positions with groups like the Council on Hemispheric Affairs, the North American Congress on Latin America, and, later, supported Washington's Central American Historical Institute, whose newsletters kept readers informed about political and human rights crises across the region and excoriated US policy positions on Central America.

Bishops and clergy also called for economic boycotts of businesses that profited from human rights abuses. In a statement printed in the August 2, 1978, edition of the *Denver Catholic Register*, Archbishop James Casey announced that "faithful stewardship" of the archdiocese's finances precluded it from "investments in Companies who jeopardize World peace," including weapons and arms manufacturers, and companies whose products or services caused "undue social injury" or were contrary to "the moral teachings of the Church."[31] Casey also stated that the Denver Archdiocese was "ready to participate in corporate efforts with other Church-related groups in research and possible action for change through voting power in the area of Corporate Responsibility."[32] The following year, Monsignor Charles Owen Rice's weekly *Pittsburgh Catholic* column shared the story of Father Bernard Survil, a local priest who, Rice claimed, "was working with the poor in Nicaragua until the thugs banished him." According to Rice, Survil returned to Pittsburgh because the city was home to Guerrentz International Corporation, one of the United States' largest importers of Nicaraguan beef, an industry controlled by the Somoza family. Rice included Guerrentz International's local address and telephone number in his column and suggested that "a Mr. Joel Berg, who appears to be in charge, does not appear to have any quarrel with Somoza and should be reasoned with." Rice and Survil called on *Pittsburgh Catholic* readers to pressure Guerrentz International to end its relationship with Nicaragua's beef industry not only to deprive the Somoza family of financial resources but also to pressure the beef industry to return its considerable land holdings to poor farmers. Rice punctuated his thoughts by noting that "Somoza is a bad guy, but he is no worse than our men in Guatemala, El Salvador, or Honduras."[33]

Catholic activists also maintained a presence on Capitol Hill. On September 20, 1979, the United States Catholic Conference's adviser on Latin American and

Caribbean Affairs, Father Thomas E. Quigley, offered testimony on Guatemala at a House International Organizations Subcommittee hearing on disappearances and human rights abuses in which he compared Lucas to dictator General Jorge Rafael Videla, whose own repressive campaign was killing thousands of Argentinians at the time, and testified that Guatemala's violence was "far more pervasive" than either El Salvador's or Chile's. Also during that hearing, WOLA representative Heather Foote testified that "reports from Catholic and Protestant church services, the International Commission of Jurists and Amnesty International indicate that, despite the reliable optimistic interpretation of the State Department, repression continues [in Guatemala] today and that the government-directed and condoned disappearances are on the increase."[34] According to Foote, political murders and disappearances increased 35 percent during the Lucas regime's first six months; her testimony detailed seventy separate instances of state-sanctioned human rights abuses during that time.[35]

Finally, legislators introduced parish priests' reports from Guatemala into the record on the House floor. Ohio Representative Donald Pease read a statement from a priest in Quiché that contained a monthly account of violence in the department between August 1979 and January 1980, including dozens of previously unreported incidents that highlighted how military and civil patrols acted with impunity in the area. On October 19, for example, a group of soldiers entered a church in Nebaj during mass, kidnapped a teenaged boy, and "took the people out of the chapel, put the men against the wall and with threats of shooting them demanded to know who the guerrillas were."[36] The group then left in a jeep and robbed multiple local merchants of money and cases of beer on their way back to their garrison. In another incident, the priest reported that a woman was gang-raped by seven soldiers in Chajúl while other patrol members held her would-be rescuers at bay with machine guns. The woman had given birth just twenty days before her rape. Events like these prompted Ortiz to warn the State Department that Guatemala was "a blood-bath waiting to happen." He attributed this in large part to the ongoing crises in El Salvador and Nicaragua, which, he claimed, fueled Guatemalan rightists' siege mentality to a "paranoid state [where] they react violently, almost hysterically" to actual and perceived threats alike.[37] He also reported that the country's extreme right seemed capable of engaging in broad, indiscriminate atrocities at the slightest provocation that could endanger the country's eleven thousand US citizens, most of whom lived and worked in Guatemala City.

Conditions in Guatemala contributed to a diplomatic impasse with the United States. Ortiz understood that the Carter administration could not support a regime engaged in widespread human rights abuses. Neither could it fully abandon Lucas without contributing to his regime's siege mentality and paranoia or without appearing to support groups like ORPA and the EGP. For Ortiz, the Carter administration's only viable solution remained a "non-confrontational posture of unmistakable support for the essential political freedoms . . . and those factors essential to the functioning of a modern representational democracy." These included showing public support for the rule of law, respect of constitutional order and authority, and an impartial, independent, and uncorrupted judicial system. Ortiz wrote, "If this sounds to you as advocacy of such American staples as 'mom' and 'apple pie,' that is the point. This is what we understand; this is what we do best; this is what is expected of us and this is what would really get us on the right side of the power curve."[38] For Ortiz, then, this policy embodied the essence of American political values that the world expected from US diplomacy and contributed to the Carter administration's desired image as a facilitator of internal change, rather than as a foreign interventionist.

Ortiz's proposed strategy led some critics to charge that he was either incapable of or uninterested in confronting the Lucas regime over its human rights abuses. One such criticism came from the Council on Hemispheric Affairs, a Washington-based organization focused on economic, political, and human rights practices in the Americas. In a press release from its director, Larry Birns, the organization assailed Ortiz for being "unable to adequately recognize a situation where more people are being killed, in absolute terms, every day than in any other country in the hemisphere . . . regrettably, Ortiz has become an indefatigable apologist for one of the most miserable governments in the region."[39]

Ortiz also faced strong criticism from key congressional leaders. On June 10, Iowa congressman Tom Harkin sent a letter directly to Carter that sharply criticized Ortiz's record as ambassador compared with the United States' ambassadors to Nicaragua and El Salvador, Lawrence Pezzulo and Robert White, and accused Ortiz of having too close of a relationship with Lucas to be an effective diplomat. Harkin wrote, "All of my contacts in Nicaragua involved in the human rights efforts claim that Ambassador Ortiz is 'well known' to be on the side of the repressive right-wing element of Guatemala. I contrast this with my friends in El Salvador and Nicaragua who do not say these things about Larry Pezzulo or Bob White." Harkin concluded his letter by lobbying Carter to recall Ortiz from his post, stating that the administration's ambassador to Guatemala "should certainly be making more in-roads and contacts with the popular and democratic forces in that country."[40] Mack forwarded a copy of Harkin's letter to Ortiz, who directly responded to Harkin in a sharply worded letter on June 26. Ortiz alluded to the obstacles he encountered in his posting, stating, "You apparently have preferences as to Governments. While you do, the Ambassador does not. He has to operate in the situation in which he finds himself and seek to exert maximum influence always in the advancement of American interests." He called Harkin's allegations "malevolently wrong" and stated that Harkin would issue a complete retraction of his claims if Harkin was an "honorable man."[41]

News of Ortiz's potential recall from Guatemala had begun to circulate in both the US and Guatemalan press by late June. On June 28, the *New York Times* reported that Ortiz was to be replaced as ambassador "shortly" following what the story described as "a bitter internal debate over United States policy" toward Guatemala. The front-page story cited an anonymous "high-ranking" State Department official, who stated that "it had long been obvious that Mr. Ortiz's analysis of the Guatemalan situation was not shared by other administration specialists."[42] The US embassy in Guatemala City confirmed Ortiz's recall in a July 2 press briefing and characterized his departure as part of "many changes" to the regional diplomatic corps.[43] On July 3, Guatemala City's *La Tarde* newspaper ran a pair of stories on Ortiz's recall and noted Guatemalan political leaders' anger at the news. Julio Alegría Ceniz, a Guatemalan congressman and Social Democratic party member, expressed surprise at the brevity of Ortiz's posting, and MLN head Leonel Sisniega Otero expressed his hope that "the new ambassador does not become a scourge on Guatemala, like Bowdler or Pessulo [*sic*]."[44] *Prensa Libre* condemned Ortiz's recall in its July 4 edition and blamed his removal on what it described as an "interventionist" and "messianic" US foreign policy that had failed to gain traction in Guatemala, El Salvador, and Nicaragua.[45] Finally, the *Washington Post* reported on July 20 that Ortiz's recall was part of a broader diplomatic reorganization that included ambassadorial changes in Argentina, Colombia, Honduras, Paraguay, and Uruguay throughout the summer.[46] Ortiz was officially recalled on August 6, ending what he later described as the worst appointment of his career, and was temporarily assigned to the United States Southern Command in Panama as chief political advisor before being named US ambassador to Peru in 1981.[47]

The Carter administration's challenges in Central America fueled conservatives' foreign policy criticisms ahead of the 1980 presidential election. Foreign policy hawks like Carter's National Security Adviser Zbigniew Brzezinski, New York congressman John Murphy, and pundits like Jeane Kirkpatrick vigorously rejected the administration's human rights policies as Soviet and Cuban appeasement that had done little more than alienate erstwhile regional allies like Laugerud, Lucas, and Somoza. They viewed Central America and the Caribbean as the Cold War's battlefield for the 1980s, with some neoconservatives going as far as to call US-Soviet contestations in the region "the third phase of World War III," and pointed to the "loss" of Nicaragua and the Panama Canal Treaty as evidence of the Carter administration's failed policies and the end of the hemisphere's Pax Americana.[48] Only an unwavering policy of engagement and intervention, they argued, could restore the United States' regional hegemony and global strength. Multiple Republican Party and neoconservative-funded think tanks created broad policy statements during 1979 and 1980 predicated on these ideals, which formed the bedrock of the Reagan administration's policies toward Central America.

The Committee of Santa Fe was among the most influential of these groups. The committee was a five-man ad hoc group of policy critics with foreign policy-making, military, and academic backgrounds.[49] One committee member, Roger Fontaine, would later serve as the National Security Council's Latin American specialist during the Reagan administration, from 1981 to 1983. The committee's final report, *A New Inter-American Policy for the Eighties*, was a jeremiad against what it viewed as Carter's accommodationist tendencies and urged a bellicose policy predicated on increased military presence in Latin America, greater coordination with regional states to eradicate internal Marxist subversion, and sharp de-emphasis of human rights as the Carter administration had defined them. On human rights, the committee argued that the Carter administration needed to abandon its existing policies in favor of what it described as a "non-interventionist policy of political and ethical realism." The committee assailed what it viewed as human rights activists' relativist understanding of human rights and claimed, without any supporting evidence, that Latin Americans "find it repugnant that the United States, which legally sanctions the liquidation of more than one million unborn children each year [and] exhibits moral outrage at the killing of a terrorist who bombs and machine guns innocent civilians. What, they ask, about the human rights of the victims of left wing terrorism?" The committee also claimed that the most imminent threat to human rights in Guatemala and El Salvador was not regimes like Lucas's but rather "domestic revolutionary groups assisted by the Soviet-Cuban axis" that jeopardized US security.[50] For the committee, a foreign policy model that actively prevented Marxist influence in Latin states would naturally promote respect for concrete civil liberties and human rights throughout the region without the need for arms restrictions, as had been the case in Guatemala.

Committee members took a similar position against Catholic activists, who they believed fomented unrest by fighting for human rights and criticizing the United States' historical encounters with Latin America. They recognized Catholicism's historically close ties to the region's politics and argued that US foreign policy needed to counter liberation theology and liberal clergy, which the committee accused of "manipulat[ing] the information media through church-affiliated groups and other so-called human rights lobbies."[51] The committee report claimed that unidentified "Marxist-Leninist forces" had infiltrated the Latin American church and had utilized it as a "political weapon" to gin up political upheaval across the region during the 1970s. This portion of the committee's report would prove influential in the Reagan administration's engagement with Catholic activists in Guatemala and the United States during the early 1980s.

The late 1970s, then, was a pivotal moment for the US foreign policy in Central America. In Nicaragua, the Sandinista Revolution had installed the second Marxist government in Latin America by 1979, and the first in Central America since Árbenz's presidency a generation earlier. Relatedly, Somoza's ouster also meant the loss of the United States' oldest and most reliable regional ally, leading administration officials like Christopher and Vaky to worry that conditions in El Salvador could lead to yet another potentially successful Marxist revolution there. Instead, Romero's overthrow and the junta's subsequent collapse helped spark a civil war that would claim one hundred thousand Salvadoran lives by 1990. The Carter administration's inability to forestall either of these crises fueled administration critics' assertions that the United States' long-standing hegemony in the region had drastically faded, a conclusion bolstered by the Carter administration's decision to revert control of the Panama Canal back to the Panamanian government in 1979.

Additional diplomatic challenges in Guatemala bolstered these assertions. Laugerud and Lucas exposed a critical flaw in the Carter administration's envisioned policy for Central America after they refused US military assistance. Both were able to purchase weapons from a variety of sources and demonstrated that aid restrictions and embargoes can only be effective if the sanctioned country has no alternatives to procure restricted or embargoed goods and supplies. Further, from a historical perspective, Guatemala's ability to buck the Carter administration should not be underemphasized. Indeed, just twenty-five years earlier, the Eisenhower administration had approved an invasion of Guatemala and deposed its democratically elected president in a matter of days, provoked in large part by corporate insistence. Clearly, US-Guatemalan relations had changed by the end of the 1970s.

The end of the 1970s also marked the beginning of a rightward shift in US politics that would have significant foreign policy consequences. The Reagan administration's approach to Central America would prove far more bellicose than Carter's, calling for increased military assistance to the region and causing some to fear a commitment of US military forces to El Salvador. While those fears never materialized, Reagan administration officials nevertheless mulled assassinating Fidel Castro and sending troops to El Salvador, used Honduras as a staging ground for covert operations in the region, and funded a proxy war in Nicaragua by supporting the country's right-wing Contras via illegal arms sales to Iran during the 1980s. Nevertheless, human rights concerns remained part of the Reagan administration's foreign policy calculus during the early 1980s: administration officials and policymakers' decisions on Guatemala did consider, to a degree, how human rights activists, the public, and Catholic activists would react to these decisions. At the same time, some administration officials would argue for seeking closer, more cordial relations with Catholic activists to gain a critical ally on Central American matters and, as some maintained, to prevent similar political unrest from taking root in the United States. These events would have consequences for the Reagan administration's approach to Guatemala during the early 1980s, just as the war's violence rose to even more astonishing levels under Lucas and his successor.

5

"We Need the Closest Possible Cooperation with the Church"

On January 16, 1981, the *Spokane Daily Chronicle* published a story on Bishop Lawrence Welsh's recent visit to the Diocese of Spokane's sponsored mission in Sololá, Guatemala. Speaking at a press conference upon his return, Welsh stated that he told the mission's three priests and nine nuns that they were free to leave the country if they desired, in order to escape what he described as "extreme physical danger and possible martyrdom" in Sololá. According to Welsh, he and Monsignor William Van Ommerman decided to visit the mission to show support for its staff and gave his personal assurance that "if and when [they] decide it to be necessary . . . to withdraw from Guatemala, we . . . will support you fully in this decision and will do all in our power to facilitate and guarantee your safe and immediate return."[1]

A second account of Welsh's press conference from the National Catholic News Service reported that he had also recalled the "evidence of extreme human suffering" that he had witnessed in Sololá. According to Welsh, corpses discovered in the area during his visit bore clear evidence of torture that included missing fingers, pierced eardrums, burned mouths, castrations, and other horrific degradations. Welsh also acknowledged the connection between Guatemala's poverty and violence, noting that "this brutal suffering is afflicting a people who are already suffering the crushing burden of poverty. Children who live on the floor, in smoke-filled houses, without even enough corn to eat, are suddenly faced with the loss of their father, the one who was providing the little they had." Welsh added that both the US government and the US Roman Catholic Church had a "vested interest" in Guatemala: according to the bishop, "individually and collectively we share the responsibility of demanding of our Church and our country that those interested be based on the Gospel value of human dignity and not on what is politically expedient."[2]

Four days after Welsh's press conference, the *Minneapolis Tribune* printed an open letter from the Guatemala Solidarity Committee of Minnesota to Ronald Reagan, who had been inaugurated as the fortieth president of the United States that same day. The group reminded Reagan that the Eisenhower administration and CIA had been responsible for Jacobo Árbenz Guzmán's overthrow in 1954 and that in the aftermath "millions of American tax dollars have been used for military and economic aid to support the government there. The wealthy, the high-ranking officers, and foreign investors have profited from this arrangement, while most of Guatemala's 7 million people have become poorer and more alienated from the political process."[3] The group's letter also noted that two-thirds of Guatemalans worked in the agricultural industry without owning any of the land they worked and that more than 80 percent of Guatemalan children suffered from malnourishment.

The letter also lamented that "when [Guatemalans] organize to improve their standard of living and secure their basic human rights, their leaders—church people, workers, peasants, professors, and students—are called Communists and are subject to the most brutal repression. That means kidnapping, torture, and murder, not arrest and imprisonment."[4] The group also warned that anti-Catholic violence in Guatemala was on the rise and urged Reagan to make human rights a cornerstone of his new administration's foreign policy and ban all cash arms sales and military aid to Guatemala. Nearly four hundred people and groups signed the letter, including local and state political leaders, other grassroots organizations, local labor unions, and multiple clergy and faith-based groups, including many Catholics and Catholic organizations.

Coverage of Welsh's press conference and the Guatemala Solidarity Committee's letter to Reagan are two examples of how Catholic activists attempted to influence US policy decisions on Guatemala during the Reagan administration. First, both the letter and the coverage of Welsh's remarks were forms of human rights reportage through their inclusion of statistical information and firsthand accounts of Guatemala's human rights abuses and called on the new administration to take concrete steps to help improve conditions in the country. Second, although the Guatemala Solidarity Committee was not a faith-based organization, dozens of priests, nuns, and groups like Catholic Charities of the Archdiocese of Minneapolis-Saint Paul, the Minneapolis Saint Joseph House, and the Maryknoll Fathers endorsed the letter alongside many academics, area Lutheran and Mennonite churches, and groups including the US-Grenada Friendship Committee, American Indian Movement, and both the El Salvador and Nicaragua Solidarity Committees of Minnesota.

These examples also underscore that Central America and Catholic activism were two crucial and, at times, entangled concerns for the Reagan administration in its earliest months. Administration officials and conservative pundits viewed Central America as beset by a series of crises born from the Carter administration's human rights–based foreign policy. In addition to the Carter administration's "loss" of Nicaragua and decision to cede control of the Panama Canal to Panama in 1979, many hawkish policymakers believed that increased Cuban, Soviet, and Nicaraguan support for Marxist compatriots in El Salvador and Guatemala, as well as Grenada in the Caribbean, seemingly portended a new red tide washing over the hemisphere.

For some within the Reagan administration, the church seemed a crucial partner in Central America. These administration officials, as well as other conservative pundits and policymakers, believed that Pope John Paul II's strident anticommunism was an ideal complement to their own bellicose positions toward Cuba and the Soviet Union and that the Pope was a potentially invaluable ally in Eastern European and Latin American diplomatic affairs. The pontiff had successfully mediated a peaceful settlement between the Argentine and Chilean governments over territorial claims to the Beagle Channel in 1978 and offered to do likewise in a similar conflict between Guatemala, Britain, and Honduras over claims to Belize that same year. For some Reagan administration officials, securing the church's assistance in resolving Central America's myriad conflicts was important enough that multiple administration officials and federal agencies attempted to make overtures throughout 1981 to not only the Pope but also Catholics in both Central America and the United States, to gain support for the administration's preferred policy approaches to the region. In June 1981, Reagan's assistant for national security affairs, Richard Allen, informed William Wilson, Reagan's personal representative to the Holy See, that "we need the closest possible cooperation with the Church in securing democracy, stability, and social justice in the region. You may wish to convey . . . that the President places the highest priority on achieving a working relationship with the Church in securing our mutually shared goals for Central America."[5]

Although administration officials like Allen and Wilson clearly desired a close working relationship with Catholic leaders and laity on Central American matters, others demonized Catholic activists as Marxist sympathizers and dangerous radicals. After members of El Salvador's army murdered Sisters Maura Clarke, Ita Ford, Dorothy Kazel, and lay missionary Jean Donovan in December 1980, both Jeane Kirkpatrick, who Reagan had nominated to serve as the US ambassador to the United Nations, and Secretary of State Alexander Haig outraged Catholics around the globe with their characterizations of the women and the circumstances surrounding their murders. Additionally, the CIA speculated that some of Guatemala's priests had begun actively assisting ORPA and the EGP, while some State

Department officials believed that US missionaries serving in Central America could foment anti-US sentiment in their home parishes upon their return. These conflicting assessments coincided with increased violence and anti-Catholic repression in Guatemala, making a close relationship unlikely.

Finally, Catholic leaders like Welsh, United States Catholic Conference (USCC) president Archbishop John Roach, and Father Bryan Hehir, among many others, criticized the new administration's desire to restore arms sales to the region in the face of persistent anti-Catholic violence: in Guatemala alone, the Lucas regime murdered six priests between February and August 1981, kidnapped a seventh, and openly threatened others. The Guatemalan army also killed hundreds of civilians affiliated with Catholic parishes and Christian base communities across the country's western departments. Many US Catholic newspapers, organizations and affiliated grassroots groups, and individual Catholic activists criticized the Reagan administration's Central American policies as truculent and devastating for the region's poor, leading some policymakers and administration officials to believe that Catholic activists threatened the Reagan administration's diplomatic and strategic goals for the region.

Clashes like these precluded the Reagan administration from achieving the close working relationship that it desired with Catholic leaders and groups and led some policymakers and administration officials to reassess the Reagan administration's positions on Central America. In some cases, they also worried that Catholic activists returning from Guatemala and other places in Central America could foment anti-Reagan or anti-American sentiment in their home parishes, especially those with large Latino populations. Ultimately, by 1982, US policymakers had begun to re-examine the administration's relationship with Catholic activists and, more specifically, whether it could redress activists' criticisms without simultaneously alienating congressional conservatives, anti-communist allies in Guatemala, or conservative Catholics in the United States. While administration officials attempted to navigate this narrow diplomatic strait, Guatemala's anti-Catholic violence continued to worsen as the Lucas regime's grip on political power began to slip, culminating in its overthrow in March 1982.

This chapter explores some of the many ways that Catholic activists attempted to safeguard Guatemalans' human rights and influence the Reagan administration's policies toward the country during the early 1980s. It offers several examples of individual and collective Catholic activism, including the rescue of orphaned children from massacre sites, reports of Guatemala's human rights abuses from priests and the Catholic press, congressional testimony from the USCC, and the facilitation of local action. It also recounts the Lucas regime's staggering human rights abuses during this period and the Reagan administration's tepid response to the country's violence. Finally, it examines how Catholic activism complicated the administration's relationship with the church on diplomatic and political matters, ultimately placing the two sides largely at odds with each other on Guatemala and Central America by Lucas's overthrow.

The Reagan administration faced multiple escalating crises in Central America during its earliest months, including civil wars in Guatemala and El Salvador, a Sandinista-led Nicaragua, arms trafficking to both countries via Honduras, and both international and intraregional refugee crises in which thousands of Central Americans fled their countries' violence for refuge in Honduras, Mexico, the United States, and Canada, among other places.[6] The new administration blamed these crises in part on Cuban and Soviet intervention in the region, particularly in El Salvador, where Cuban support for the country's guerrillas raised alarm among key administration figures eager to escalate the Cold War. Haig, for example, wrote in February 1981 that a Marxist El Salvador would be "a major reversal" in the balance of regional power that would profoundly erode US credibility in the region.[7] Haig also alarmed cabinet members when, during a National Security Council meeting the following month, he proposed an attack on Cuba and told Reagan, "You just give me the word, and I'll turn that fucking island into a parking lot."[8] Likewise, Reagan's director of central intelligence, William Casey, had previously described El Salvador as "symbolically, the most important place in the world" for the US defense and foreign policies and argued that covert action in the region was the best strategy for advancing the administration's regional goals.[9] Finally, Kirkpatrick, who *Pittsburgh Catholic* columnist Monsignor Charles Owen Rice once described as "that dreadful woman," agreed that El Salvador was the administration's most pressing regional concern and suggested employing proxy forces to battle the region's guerrilla groups.[10]

After Haig's ludicrous proposal to turn Cuba into a parking lot was rebuffed by other administration officials, he turned his attention to El Salvador. Haig urged deploying troops to the country as a show of force to Cuban and Soviet leaders. He also believed that any conflict in El Salvador would be quick and decisive and told Reagan that "this is one you can win"—an important consideration in the wake of the United States' defeat in the Vietnam War.[11] For other administration officials, however, El Salvador raised the specter of Vietnam and called for increased military aid to the country instead. According to LeoGrande, an "inner circle" of Reagan advisers that included Attorney General Edwin Meese, White House Chief of Staff James Baker, and Deputy Chief of Staff Michael Deaver all opposed intervention in El Salvador and urged Reagan to focus on his domestic agenda instead.[12] Lacking consensus, the administration did not finalize an official policy on El Salvador until late February, when it requested more US military advisers and an additional twenty-five million dollars in military aid be sent to the country and Reagan authorized the CIA to conduct covert operations there.[13]

Bishops and dioceses across the United States condemned the new policy. In Minneapolis-Saint Paul, Roach lamented that "the restoration of military assistance . . . enhances the possibility of more violence from the security forces and associates the United States with acts of oppression which can only alienate the majority of people in El Salvador." James Hickey, the archbishop of Washington, DC, also criticized the administration's decision as a "great disappointment" and declared it was "most unfortunate that our government has chosen to give military assistance to strengthen [Junta Revolucionario Gobierno leader Jose Napoleón] Duarte despite the lack of solid proof that he can control the very military forces we shall be aiding."[14] Elsewhere, the Archdiocese of Portland, Oregon, criticized the administration for abetting what it called "the flagrant denial of human rights, continued violence and thousands of assassinations" in El Salvador and demanded a halt to all military aid to the country.[15]

The USCC also condemned the administration's policies. Father Bryan Hehir represented the group at a House Foreign Operations Subcommittee hearing on February 25, 1981, and testified that "the USCC believes that the long-term interest of the United States in Central America will hardly be served if the majority of the people there believe we have chosen to subordinate their quest for justice . . . at the price of rendering an entire population simply an instrument in a larger strategy." Hehir reiterated Salvadoran archbishop Arturo Rivera y Damas's call for a global moratorium on weapons sales to Central America and warned that those weapons would continue to be used to kill Catholics, including US missionaries serving in the region. Hehir also testified that "if we simply lift this whole conflict out of context and make it an East-West faceoff, we lose sight of the essence of the problem," which, he argued, was Central America's historical, institutionalized economic and social inequality.[16]

Three weeks after Hehir's testimony, Haig drew widespread condemnation for his tactless and baseless speculation about the murders of Clarke, Ford, Kazel, and Donovan during his own congressional testimony. Haig, whose brother, Frank, was a Jesuit priest, implied the nuns were partially to blame for their own murders during a House Foreign Affairs Committee hearing on March 18. Haig told the committee, "I would like to suggest to you that some of these investigations would lead one to believe that perhaps the vehicle the nuns were riding in may have run a roadblock or may have been perceived to be doing that, and that there was an exchange of fire in which perhaps those who caused the casualties sought to cover it up."[17] Newspapers across the country printed Haig's comments, which were roundly criticized for their attempt to blame the women for their own murders.[18] Members of the women's families, as well as some members of Congress, also denounced Haig's comments and the Reagan administration's desire to intervene in El Salvador's civil war. "Our sisters died down there," William Ford, Ita Ford's brother, told reporters. "Thousands of others have died. To say that it is a communist plot is just an excuse to turn El Salvador into a national cemetery."[19] Likewise, New York congressman Richard Ottinger, whose district included the Maryknoll Mission House, described Haig's remarks as "shocking and thoughtless speculation" that endangered other Americans in the region. Salvadoran officials dismissed Haig's comments out of hand, as one Foreign Ministry official remarked that the Secretary of State had an "incredible imagination."[20] Haig attempted to soften his remarks the following day during a Senate Foreign Relations Committee hearing, where he stated that "anyone who suggests that what I said yesterday was in that direction has got to be mischievous or not very bright," but he maintained that his baseless conjecture was "one of the most prominent theories" surrounding the murders.[21]

Although policymakers and Reagan administration officials had clearly prioritized El Salvador in their regional calculus, they also believed Guatemala remained the most valuable prize in Central America for Cuba, the Soviet Union, and their allies because it had the region's largest population, strongest economy, ports on both the Caribbean Sea and Pacific Ocean, oil and mineral deposits in the northern Petén department, and the Northern Transversal Strip's natural resources. Lucas attempted to use the Reagan administration's positions on Guatemala to his advantage and met with US ambassador to Guatemala Melvin Sinn on March 9 to discuss multiple issues, including restoring arms sales. Lucas acknowledged that El Salvador's violence had caused the international press to vilify Duarte and that US efforts to assist the Salvadoran government had created "a good deal of conflict domestically and internationally."[22]

Lucas also assured Sinn that the Guatemalan government "wanted at all costs to avoid compromising the U.S. or create [similar] problems" in US-Guatemalan relations. He told Sinn that his regime was entrenched in a war for the country's survival against a guerrilla force that had received supplies and training from Cuba and that the military was in danger of being overpowered. Furthermore, although Lucas had managed to mitigate the loss of US military aid to a degree, he told Sinn that his regime's human rights record precluded the Reagan administration from selling him arms to help win the war. For these reasons, Lucas claimed, he had refused "repeated recommendations" from his cabinet to publicly request the opportunity to purchase arms from the United States. Instead, he asked Sinn to help arrange an off-the-record meeting with Reagan administration officials, or Reagan himself, in which Lucas would privately request that arms sales resume.

Sinn reported that "with some emotion [Lucas] declared that the only thing he asked . . . was that we not block efforts to purchase the items they needed to defend themselves. He was not asking for gifts or charity; he would somehow find the cash to pay for what was needed. [Lucas] indicated . . . he could promise the utmost secrecy and discretion in any discussions on this question."[23] Lucas also complained that "all the international press could see [in Guatemala] was a repressive military regime [and] insisted that he would like to see some objectivity" in coverage of the country's violence.

The international press characterized Guatemala as suffering under a repressive military regime because Guatemala was, in fact, suffering under a repressive military regime. Statistically, the war had reached its most violent period to date: the CEH recorded more than eleven hundred cases of human rights abuses nationwide during 1981, more than doubling the approximately five hundred abuses committed the previous year. Of these, more than seven hundred took place in the department of Quiché, an area the same size as the city of Juneau, Alaska. The abuses were also profound. In La Democracia, Escuintla, soldiers abducted a FAR member from his home and tortured him before killing him. His widow later testified to the CEH that "there were about twelve [soldiers] . . . they took my husband out of bed. . . . Right there on the patio, with his own machete, they [castrated] my husband. . . . On January 26 . . . some workers saw that a person was burning who was not yet dead and tried to extinguish him with branches but others said not to do it because the authorities had burned him . . . it was [my husband], I only knew him by his big toe, which was very short, because he was completely burned . . . his body had signs of torture, burned completely, wrapped in wire."[24]

Massacres were also frequent during 1981 and overwhelmingly committed by the regime. Of approximately two hundred known massacres during the year, the army, PN, death squads, and other state forces were responsible for more than 190.[25] On multiple occasions, the army used helicopters to kill their victims: in Cobán, Alta Verapáz, for example, soldiers in a helicopter murdered seven people hiding in the Nimblajacoc mountains, including Teodoro Cucul, a newborn.[26] The *New York Times* published four stories on Guatemala's violence in six days in February 1981 alone, and the *Chicago Tribune, Los Angeles Times*, and *Washington Post* also reported on Guatemala's violence and human rights abuses throughout the year.[27]

Unsurprisingly, the US Catholic press also continued to report on conditions in Guatemala. Wire service reports from the Catholic News Agency were frequently reprinted in diocesan newspapers across the country. Additionally, national newspapers like the *National Catholic Reporter* continued to offer readers frequent, in-depth reporting on Guatemala and Central America. In 1981, for example, the *National Catholic Reporter* offered extensive coverage of Rother's murder and anti-Catholic violence across the region, alongside measured insights in essays by the newspaper's Latin American and Vatican correspondents, Penny Lernoux and Peter Hebblethwaite, respectively, and former congressman Father Robert Drinan, a Jesuit priest.[28]

Diocesan newspapers also continued to accentuate local connections in ways that their national counterparts simply could not match and helped individual Catholics across the United States forge their own personal ties to Guatemala. In Davenport, Iowa, the *Catholic Messenger* reported on Davenport native Sister Betty Campbell's national speaking tour, which focused on Central America's violence, and on local priest Father George Dorsey's blunt contention that Guatemala was suffering "a bloodbath" and "a genocide of the Indian population."[29] Likewise, the *Denver Catholic Register* featured a lengthy interview with an anonymous Jesuit priest on a variety of topics related to Guatemala.[30] Similar local-themed stories appeared in the *Catholic Sentinel*, the *Dubuque Witness*, and the *Pittsburgh Catholic*, among others.[31]

Diocesan newspapers also reported on area children's connections to Guatemala and their understanding of the country's violence. In one notable example, the *Catholic Messenger* reported on an Iowa City Catholic Grade School class assignment in which every student wrote a letter to a family in Guatemala or El Salvador. According to Sister Agnes Giblin, younger children "just drew pictures and sent a little message—Hi, how are you today? We're thinking about you, that kind of thing," while older students "introduce[d] themselves . . . [and told] the family that we were thinking about them and praying for them." She also told the *Messenger* that the assignment had left the children "very conscious of the news. . . . They'll come to me and say, 'did you hear in the news about . . . ?' or 'do you think we should pray for . . . ?' I guess the thing I wanted to get across to the children was that, even though they didn't know these people, as Christians we were touching someone else's life, and that's what we're all about."[32]

Administration officials from multiple agencies believed that a better relationship with Catholic activists and the church would increase public support for its policies toward Guatemala. In a lengthy report to Haig in February 1981, for example, Sinn offered his thoughts on the state of US-Guatemalan relations and called for sustained dialogue with legislators, private groups, and religious leaders so that they would better "understand what we are doing, why we are doing it, and what we desire in response."[33] The National Security Council's Latin American directorate, Roger Fontaine, suggested a similar approach to Nicaragua and advised administration officials to "encourage such major and credible figures as the

Archbishop [Miguel] Obando y Bravo of Nicaragua to convince the skeptical, particularly in Western Europe, of the nature of the Sandinista revolution."[34]

Sinn reiterated his concerns about anti-Catholic violence and the church in a report to Haig dated June 18, 1981. In it, Sinn noted that "over the last ten months relations between the Catholic Church on the one hand and the G[overnment] O[f] G[uatemala] and extreme right on the other have reached a point of high tension."[35] Among multiple examples, Sinn cited the Lucas regime's expulsion of the Jesuit Society from the country in 1980, the Quiché Diocese's closure due to the area's profound violence, and the Lucas regime's refusal to readmit the diocese's bishop, Juan Gerardi Conedera, into the country upon his return from an audience with the Pope. What alarmed Sinn most, however, was that six priests had been murdered in the country in the previous twelve months.[36] He also reported that Escuintla bishop Mario Enrique Ríos Montt, Father Cesar Jerez, and two American-born priests, Rother and Father Ronald Burke, had all recently appeared on death lists and that in Quiché, "a car belonging to a group of Canadian nuns was riddled with submachine gun bullets. One of the nuns reportedly saw a person, presumed to have been a soldier, throw a grenade into the parish house."[37] In all, the Lucas regime murdered six priests during 1981 and abducted Father Luis Pellecer in June and held the priest captive for three months before releasing him. For Sinn, these acts seemed to affirm an ominous promise that Lucas had made in 1980 when he warned, "If the priests and clerics do not attend to the business of saving souls, we will carry them out" of Guatemala.[38]

Sinn also reported that violence also brought the Guatemalan church's internal divisions closer to the surface. In his analysis, Guatemala's church had split into three principal factions in recent years. The first was composed of the country's rank-and-file priests, many of whom served parishes in Guatemala's rural areas. Sinn noted that 496 of the country's 556 priests were foreign-born and that most native-born priests were members of orders like the Jesuits or Salesians, which did not have seminaries within the country. Similarly, only 271 of the country's 989 nuns were Guatemalan, and most, like the country's priests, had been educated elsewhere. As a result, Sinn argued, "with many having come from countries where political systems were at least more democratic than authoritarian, these liberal clergymen and women found it difficult to accept the perceived injustices perpetuated by the military regime and the silence of their own Church leaders." One consequence of this was that "the religious community has become more aggressive and critical. In recent months there have been a number of visits to the embassy by both Guatemalan and American priests and nuns who have been less reluctant than in the past to share their accounts of massacres, murders and abductions of members of their congregations by elements of the GOG or far right."[39] This also contributed to Lucas's ongoing siege mentality, which former ambassador Frank Ortiz had warned the State Department about as early as 1979.

Sinn's analysis of Guatemala's clerical population included two important insights. First, he argued that although many of what he described as the country's "rural clergy" were politically liberal, they were not Marxist. To the contrary, Sinn reported that "at most" less than five priests actively supported the country's guerrilla groups, and no more than 5 percent were sympathetic to the far left at all. Second, he estimated that as many as 90 percent of the rural clergy was "opposed to the GOG's harsh methods of dealing with the left and potential Indian collaborators." Despite these distinctions, however, the Lucas regime was wary of both foreign-born and rural clergy, who were murdered far more frequently than their native-born counterparts: of the nine priests ultimately murdered in Guatemala between 1980 and the end of 1981, only one, Father Carlos Gálvez Galindo, was Guatemalan (Table 5.1).

Table 5.1 Catholic priests murdered or abducted in Guatemala, 1981	
Name (Place of death or kidnapping)	**Date of death or kidnapping**
Father Conrado de la Cruz Concepción (Guatemala City)	May 1, 1980
Father Walter Voordeckers (Santa Lucía Cotzumalguapa)	May 12, 1980
Father José María Gran Cirera (Xe Ixoq Vitz)	June 4, 1980
Father Faustino Villanueva Villanueva (Joyabaj)	July 10, 1980
Father Juan Alonso Fernández (Uspantán)	February 13, 1981
Father Carlos Gálvez Galindo (Tecpán)	May 14, 1981
Father Pedro Aguilar Santos (Quiché)	May 21, 1981
Father Luis Pellecer (Guatemala City)	Kidnapped June 8, 1981, released September 30, 1981
Father Marco Tulio Maruzzo (Izabal)	July 1, 1981
Father Stanley Rother (Santiago Atitlán)	July 28, 1981
Father Carlos Pérez Alonso (Guatemala City)	August 2, 1981

The CEG represented the second faction. Sinn characterized the bishops as a more politically diverse group than the country's rank-and-file clergy, composed of four liberals, three conservatives, and seven moderates. While the CEG had historically taken a moderate path, Sinn reported that a change seemed to be underway, citing a pastoral letter issued in April in which the CEG "declared that they would continue their denunciation of the injustices suffered by the poor and to call for respect for human rights."[40]

While the two factions differed politically, they shared an antipathy for the third faction, Cardinal Mario Casariego. Casariego's staunch conservativism left him profoundly unpopular with the country's rural clergy: one mission's priests had named a neutered cat after the cardinal, while the CEG had clashed with Casariego in the press and an unnamed priest denounced him as "a scandal, something out of the Middle Ages, ill-prepared to represent or lead the Church in these times."[41] Likewise, Sinn argued that the CEG's more aggressive language in its April pastoral letter was evidence of the ongoing "gradual estrangement" between the conference and Casariego. Sinn warned that these internal tensions, coupled with the country's anti-Catholic violence and persecution, could potentially push individual priests, nuns, or bishops to the extreme left and support groups like the FAR, ORPA, and EGP.

One month after Sinn's report, Father Stanley Rother was murdered inside the rectory of his church in Santiago Atitlán, Sololá, on July 28 (Figure 5.1). Rother was the first US-born priest to be murdered in Guatemala since Father Bill Woods in November 1976, and his murder generated significant press coverage in the United States due in large part to US news outlets' increased attention to Guatemala's violence. Rother's murder also strained US-Guatemalan relations even further as Catholic activists, as well as some members of the US church's hierarchy, pressed Congress and Reagan administration officials for a full, transparent investigation and prosecution of Rother's killers. Although these efforts were ultimately unsuccessful, Catholics' activism in this case did help foil the Lucas regime's attempt to imprison three innocent men for the crime.

In some ways, Rother was ideally suited for mission work in Santiago Atitlán. Rother was the only mission priest in Santiago Atitlán with farming experience, and his affinity for repair work and other forms of manual labor addressed a critical need in Santiago Atitlán, as agricultural production was one of the mission's four principal initiatives. After Rother's murder, Oklahoma City Diocese archbishop Charles Salatka recalled that Rother had been "very, very aware of the condition of [the] people," a sentiment shared by many who knew him in Santiago Atitlán.[42] Diego Ixbalan Tacaxoy, who worked as a watchman and wood-carver with the mission, described Rother as "a very good person . . . like an elder of the whole community." In an interview with Father Dave Monahan, he recalled when

Figure 5.1.
Father Stanley
Rother. (Used
with permission,
Archdiocese of
Oklahoma City.)

his wife, Andrea, contracted tuberculosis, Rother purchased the necessary medication and routinely visited their home and often shared meals with the couple.[43] Likewise, local priest Father Adan García's most vivid memory of Rother was the rescue and relief efforts he personally led in Patzún, Chimaltenango, following the country's catastrophic 1976 earthquake. In an interview with Monahan, García said that Rother "was the only one strong enough and brave enough to go into the ravines where the poor people lived. . . . He filled [his] pickup with all kinds of equipment from the hospital here . . . he brought injured people on his own shoulders up the slopes."[44] Finally, Sololá bishop Angelico Melotto noted that Rother had told him "I want to stay here all my life" and that the Oklahoma native showed "love for the poor. . . . He always had a poor beggar eating lunch with him. That impressed me. Sometimes we think of the Americans as too elegant."[45] Rother's actions, as well as his effort to learn Tz'utujil, endeared him to parishioners, who referred to him as *A'Plas*, a translation of his middle name, Francis.

Santiago Atitlán was relatively insulated from the war's violence until 1980, when ORPA members visited the town to recruit new members. Rother alluded to the visit in a letter dated July 9 of that year, reporting, "A leftist group came in to here while I was gone, and the people seem to have accepted them. . . . About ten days ago a quasi-leftist group threw out bulletins and reprimanded the government about some things that have been going on in the department." Rother also expressed mixed feelings about the groups' cordiality toward the area's clergy and religious. Rother wrote, "They consider us on their side. Actually they are meeting upstairs right now. It kind of compromises me, but almost all of them in the group are catechists."[46]

Rother's personal letters from late 1980 and early 1981 also chronicled the army's repression in the area. In a letter dated November 20, 1980, Rother informed his friend Sam Leven that the army had moved into the area on October 21 and encamped outside town. Two days later, Gaspar Culán, the director of the mission's radio station, Voz de Atitlán, was abducted and had not been found in the ensuing weeks. The station's offices were also ransacked in the days after his disappearance.[47] Three more people disappeared following Culán's abduction, leading Rother to acknowledge that a perceptible climate of fear had descended on the town. Rother told Leven that "the people were terrorized. Hundreds stayed in the Church at night for mutual defense, even some stayed here in the rectory to protect us. After dark you just wouldn't find anyone on the streets."[48] He was even more direct in another letter from this period, when he admitted to Salatka that "the reality is that we are in danger."[49]

Rother then arranged for several local mission workers to leave the area for their own safety. In a letter to friend and frequent mission volunteer Sister Bertha Sánchez, Rother wrote that "the radio people, some catechists, co-op leaders etc. are all out of town . . . the young teachers are all gone."[50] He also acknowledged that both he and his assistant priest, Father Pedro Bocel, had experienced "various stages of panic and fright" in recent weeks. Despite this, Rother still maintained an outwardly calm, almost resigned outlook on the situation. In another letter to longtime friend and frequent mission volunteer Frankie Williams, Rother acknowledged that "when things like [disappearances] go on, no one . . . feels secure either. Fr. Pedro and I have been afraid like anyone else, but we are fine. Most of our classes and other meetings are cancelled. Sometimes we even have to change the places where we sleep just in case they look for us. . . . It is a shame that this has to happen, but it is part of a process going on in these parts of the world. I guess we will get used to it little by little."[51] As the violence worsened in Santiago Atitlán, the threat to Rother's life grew larger: by early November, Rother informed Salatka that conditions at the mission had deteriorated, recounting the disappearances and use of the church as a refuge. Rother was worried enough about the threats to his safety that he included a copy of his will and other legal documents with the letter in the event of his murder.[52]

Rother also had a contentious meeting with a local army captain three days after his letter to Salatka. He offered a vivid account of this meeting in his letter to Leven, reporting that the captain had

> walked into the mayor's office and immediately pointed me out
> and asked me to translate for him. He acted like he knew who

I was, how long I had been here, etc. I begged off and had Pedro do it. After he finished his p.r. speech and all that bullshit, he asked for questions. My hand shot up like a jack-in-a-box and among other things I told him that it would be hard for them to get the confidence of the people because all of this started 2 days after they arrived and when certain ones were taken out of their houses, the whole area was surrounded by [the army]. Well, he wasn't exactly happy about my comments. He asked if I wanted to make more formal charges, and I said that I was just repeating what I had heard on the street. He finally cooled down and we shook hands when the meeting was over. The cofrades later said they were glad that I said it and they didn't have to. The prot[estant] ministers only praised him for their presence there and they even gave him a bible as a gift.[53]

The meeting placed Rother and the army farther apart and contributed to a spike in violence specifically targeted at the mission and its workers in 1981. On January 12, Rother alerted US Embassy officials in Guatemala City that a detachment of soldiers assigned to the area had killed a man as he was shooting ducks at the Chacaya coffee finca outside of Santiago Atitlán five days earlier. The victim, who the detachment had seen hunting in the area on multiple occasions, was the father of Rother's cook at the Iglesia Parroquia Santiago Apostól church. Rother and other parishioners speculated that the detachment mistakenly believed the man to be a guerrilla, which in turn precipitated an army massacre that morning. Rother reported a total of seventeen victims.[54] He also told embassy officials that he had witnessed an army truck moving the bodies out of town and that the bodies were discovered several days later "some distance from Santiago" (Atitlán) in Cocales and San Andres Senetabaj.[55] The corpses were returned to Santiago Atitlán, where family members identified the victims. Rother also reported seeing an army helicopter flying overhead during the massacre, which, he speculated, may have helped transport bodies out of the area.[56]

Rother also reported multiple recent acts of harassment and intimidation in the parish. In one instance, four men kidnapped Diego Quic Ajuchian, a parish catechist, in front of the rectory. In a letter to friends in the United States dated January 5, Rother offered an account of Quic's abduction:

He had been eating and sleeping here, and usually visiting his wife and two kids in the late afternoon. . . . Saturday night about 7:45, he was intercepted by a group of four kidnappers. . . . He got to within 15 feet of the door and was holding on to the bannister [sic] and yelling for help . . . by the time I realized what was happening they were putting him in a waiting car. I realized that I had just witnessed a kidnapping of someone that we had gotten to know and love and [was] unable to do anything about it. I can still hear his muffled screams for help . . . this friend was being taken off to be tortured for a day or two and then brutally murdered for wanting a better life and more justice for his *pueblo*. He had told me before, "I have never stolen, have never hurt anyone, have never eaten someone else's food, why do they want to hurt me and kill me?"[57]

A short time after his abduction, passengers "on a bus coming into town saw the same car preceded and followed by army jeeps. People in the bus, including multiple parishioners from Santiago Atitlán, reported hearing screaming from the car."[58] Diego Quic, thirty years of age, was never seen alive again. He was survived by his wife and two sons, aged one and three (Figure 5.2).

Figure 5.2. Quic family photo, undated. (Used with permission, Archdiocese of Oklahoma City.)

Rother also reported that he had been added to a list of people to be killed in Santiago Atitlán. Army jeeps had followed Rother's car on multiple occasions, and embassy officials reported that in one such incident "he was in such fear that he hit 80 miles an hour and outran the jeep."[59] In another, an army patrol stopped Schaffer's car while searching for Rother. The patrol checked his license plate against their list at a checkpoint on the road to Santiago Atitlán, where Schaffer heard one soldier say "*no es Rother*," before letting him pass.[60] Despite incidents like these, Rother did not initially request assistance from the US Embassy because, as he told Sinn, "he was an American, which still might mean something."[61] He did, however, ask embassy officials for assistance in evacuating Bocel to Oklahoma City because, Rother believed, Bocel was in certain danger as a Mayan Catholic priest.

Soldiers tried to murder Bocel on January 16, two days after Rother's visit to the embassy in Guatemala City. That day, Bocel had agreed to perform Mass for one of the massacre's victims but had reconsidered after being warned that he would be killed. According to a State Department telegram, "nuns reported that soldiers surrounded the church at the appointed hour and remained there for some time afterwards . . . to pick [Bocel] up or worse."[62] This incident, along with warnings from Schaffer and fellow priest Father Patrick Green that an army operation to murder Rother and Bocel was underway, prompted both men to leave Santiago Atitlán for Guatemala City. Schaffer drove Bocel to the capital, smuggling him out of the parish hidden under blankets in his car.[63] Rother and Bocel remained hidden in Guatemala City safe houses for twelve days before departing the country for Oklahoma City on January 28.

Rother was unhappy in Oklahoma, expressing his desire to return to Santiago Atitlán in multiple letters to friends during early 1981. He also refrained from discussing conditions in Guatemala with the press. In March, Rother turned down an offer to participate in a national speaking tour about Central America's unrest. He did, however, speak about Guatemala while celebrating Mass at Saint John the Baptist Church in Edmond that month, excoriating the country's violence and the US policies that, he believed, perpetuated it. Rother's comments had tragic consequences, as one attendee, Don White, wrote a letter to Salatka expressing his "disappointment" in Rother's remarks and what he described as Rother's apparent "support for communism."[64] He also praised the Reagan administration for its hard-line foreign policy and called on Salatka to clarify the church's position on communism and Central America's crises.

White then sent another, unsigned letter addressed to both the CIA and the Guatemalan Embassy's military attaché in Washington and stated, "I was able to witness [at the Mass] a political action speech by a Catholic priest advocating the overthrow of your present administration in Guatemala. . . . As a Catholic I was revolted to [the] point of disgust, in listening to this Father Roost [sic] advocate Central American Revolution in Guatemala, El Salvador, and Costa Rica, while offering support for the current leftist and Marxist elements in Cuba and Central America."[65] White closed the one-page letter with his wishes that "God Protect Your Country From These Invaders." Rother and Bocel remained in Oklahoma until April, when Rother learned that neither he nor Bocel remained on death lists circulating in Sololá. They returned to Santiago Atitlán that month, unaware that their names had been placed back on the list, most likely after the Edmond mass.

Early that month, as Rother and Bocel returned to Santiago Atitlán, the CEG issued a pastoral letter titled "Man, His Dignity and Rights: The Mission of the Church and its Members in the Present Moment" that forcefully denounced Guatemala's inequality, violence, and dictatorial regime. The letter included information from a recently completed Central American Episcopal Council (CEDAC) study that found that 2 percent of Guatemala's population owned more than 70 percent of the country's land, one in five Guatemalans were unemployed, and more than half the population was underemployed. Among employed Guatemalans, 80 percent earned just seventy-seven centavos per day on average. CEDAC's study also found that more than 60 percent of Guatemalans over the age of seven were illiterate, and the average life expectancy was fifty-six years in the country's urban areas and just forty-one in the countryside.

The CEG attributed these abysmal facts to the state's historical failure to protect the common good. Moreover, the bishops charged that the state would never be able to do so until it took seriously the concept of economic and social rights as the basis of a just and prosperous society for all people. "It is anti-Christian," the bishops wrote, "the attitude of those who remain insensitive or indifferent to the poverty of the great majority . . . [or] to tenaciously oppose the good of the community and . . . hinder projects of positive collective benefit. And it is truly scandalous to want to legitimize this essentially anti-evangelical attitude to instrumentalize the Church or the religious values of simple people." The letter then praised organizations and people that worked to improve living conditions in places like Guatemala and reiterated that it was the duty of all Christians to "organize Guatemala on the basis of justice and unrestricted respect for human rights" and mourned the priests, religious, and catechists murdered across Central America by state forces.[66]

Rother continued to protest Guatemala's inequality and violence in his homilies during the spring and early summer, until July 28, when three masked men entered the Santiago Atitlán church rectory and forced Bocel's brother, Francisco, at gunpoint to lead them to Rother. Bocel later wrote,

> It was one in the morning, when I heard a knock at my door, I
> thought it was Padre Francisco and I said "What!" I opened the
> door and I was surprised by three hooded men, with a stature like
> Padre and a Spanish accent when he spoke.... It did not seem to
> me that they were indigenous, they carried knives and guns. Un-
> der threat of death, they forced me to bring them to Padre's room.
>
> With great fear I said "Padre, they are looking for you!" Padre
> opened the door.... I only heard Padre say "kill me here!" then I
> heard fighting... with great fear I [hid] in my room.... After five
> minutes, I decided to go out to find out what happened and... I
> found a cardboard box. I opened it and saw a pistol with ammu-
> nition. I left it... [and saw] Padre lying on the floor dead. I saw
> blood and broken objects everywhere.[67]

Word of Rother's murder quickly spread. In an interview with Monahan, Schaffer recalled that he learned the news later that morning from two nuns who had traveled to San Lucas Tolimán. He sent the nuns and fellow San Lucas Tolimán priest Father John Goggin to Panajachel to alert Salatka and the US Embassy. Schaffer and Sister Ana María González then traveled to Santiago Atitlán and viewed the dressing of Rother's body. Schaffer credited González for organizing the gathered crowd for an impromptu Mass. According to Schaffer, "her doing that kept violence from erupting. I'm convinced that kept people from an insurrection." Describing the scene, Schaffer remembered that "a little old Indian woman... kneeling on the end of a pew [was] crying her heart out... she kept repeating, 'they have killed our priest. He was my priest, our priest.... He spoke our language.'"[68] Rother's body was repatriated to Oklahoma except for his heart, which was removed and placed inside the church in Santiago Atitlán.

Guatemalan officials initially denied that Rother's murderers had acted at the government's behest and that Rother had ever been targeted for death. United States intelligence agents at the CIA's Guatemala City station accepted this information at face value and noted in a heavily excised report, "It is highly improbable that the Guatemalan high command would have authorized the assassination of a United States priest at this time. There is still no conclusive evidence concerning the identity of the attackers." Instead, Guatemalan and US officials attributed Rother's murder to a botched robbery attempt by local bandits and suggested that Francisco Bocel had acted as an inside man that had helped plan the robbery.[69]

Physical evidence and eyewitness reports from the crime scene, however, challenged this explanation. First, Sister Linda Wanner, present at the murder scene, found a nine-millimeter caliber shell casing on Rother's bookshelf; the casing matched the ammunition used by Guatemala's military and police forces. Second, Bocel stated that Rother's murderers spoke to him in accented Spanish that was different from the local dialect. However, as in many parts of rural Guatemala, Spanish is often a locality's second language. This was the case in Santiago Atitlán, where Tz'utujil was the local lingua franca. Had Rother's killers truly been local bandits, they would have addressed Bocel—a Mayan man—in Tz'utujil instead of Spanish.[70] Finally, nothing was reported missing from the alleged robbery. Despite these inconsistencies, PN officers arrested three local men, Miguel Angel Mendoza Tucún, Esteban Cocheleanda, and Juan Quijo Cuj, for Rother's murder in August 1981.[71]

Religious leaders and groups in the United States rejected the idea that Mendoza, Cocheleanda, and Quijo were the killers. In Oklahoma City, Salatka deemed the men's arrests a "miscarriage of justice" and lobbied Reagan administration officials, including Reagan himself, to press the Lucas regime to release the men and reopen their investigation.[72] Further, the Religious Task Force on Central America, in conjunction with NISGUA, asked its members and supporters to honor Rother with "services involv[ing] a general perspective of non-intervention and self-determination for all the people of Central America, emphasizing that those were the principles which Stan stood for."[73] The NISGUA called for multiple forms of protest that included funeral masses "for reflection on Stan's life, the meaning of his martyrdom, the persecution of the Church, the situation of Guatemala and U.S. policy in Central America," letter-writing campaigns, and public demonstrations demanding no US military aid to Guatemala or anywhere else in Central America. The task force urged protesters to mention Rother in these letters. It made similar exhortations in a second letter on the one-year anniversary of Rother's murder and asked its members to "lift up the life of Father Rother as an example of the Church's preferential option for the poor . . . and we ask that whatever you do be brought to the attention of the media so that other people in the U.S. hear these voices. FATHER STAN ROTHER IS ALIVE IN CHRIST AND IN THE PEOPLE OF GUATEMALA!"[74]

United States political leaders also voiced their skepticism of the investigation. In a letter to Haig on September 3, 1981, Minnesota congressman James L. Oberstar demanded "a full and fair investigation" into Rother's murder because he did not believe the Lucas regime's explanation of a botched robbery and added, "The Guatemalan government should realize that public opinion in America regarding repressive rightwing governments has been changed dramatically following the murder of American citizens by rightwing elements." These murders included Rother and Clarke, Ford, Kazel, and Donovan in El Salvador the previous year.[75] Oklahoma senator David L. Boren in his own letter to Haig also demanded that the Reagan administration "spare no effort" in identifying the killers.[76] Finally, Texas congressman Ron Paul wrote a letter to Guatemala's ambassador to the United States, Doroteo Monterroso, on November 6, 1981, to express his anger that "the most likely suspects" in Rother's murder remained free and that "if this matter is not dealt with in a satisfactory and expedited manner, I will actively support special measures to halt all aid to your government."[77] Monterroso's response, dated December 3, exhibited annoyance with Paul's use of the phrase "the most likely suspects" and gave curt assurances that US Embassy officials in Guatemala City had full access to all pertinent facts in the case. Monterroso forwarded a copy of the letter to PN officials and requested the most updated information on the case, citing pressure from officials like Paul and Oberstar, as well as US press coverage of the murder.[78]

Rother's murderers were never positively identified. Despite Oberstar's bluster and Paul's threats, no sanctions were placed on the Lucas regime to reopen the investigation. Nor was there a congressional investigation into the crime. Likewise, the question of who alerted local authorities in Sololá about the accusations in White's letter has never been answered. Finally, neither the Reagan administration nor the US Embassy in Guatemala City sent a representative to a mass commemorating the one-year anniversary of Rother's death. Like Bill Woods's murderers in 1976, Rother's killers eluded justice for their crime. Reflecting on Rother's murder years later, Schaffer asked, "What could we as Americans do to pursue it? There are people . . . who know. Would they come forth? Probably not. Will somebody leave it in memoirs someplace? Maybe. Even with all of those horrible situations . . . there [were] some very good people around who felt embarrassed about all this. . . . I'd love to see something come out."[79]

The USCC issued a comprehensive statement on Central America on November 19, 1981. It recognized that the region had become "a focal point of concern and attention in the United States" in recent years and that the region's turmoil was especially resonant for Catholics around the globe because "the Church . . . is so intimately identified with the people of those countries in their pilgrimage of faith and pursuit of justice."[80] The statement then lauded CELAM's advocacy for the poor and, as Oberstar had, decried the state-sanctioned murders of Catholic clergy and missionaries across the region. The statement also provided country-specific synopses of ongoing violence and Catholic persecution in El Salvador, Guatemala, and Nicaragua. Its description of Guatemala was particularly grim, citing the State Department's estimate of one hundred political murders per month during the year and the CEG's declaration that "the acts of violence among us have taken on unimaginable forms: there are murders, kidnappings, torture and even vicious desecrations of the victims' bodies."[81] It also echoed the CEG's contention that the year's clerical murders suggested that the Lucas regime had declared war on Catholicism in both word and deed.

The statement also demanded changes in US-Guatemalan relations and declared that "U.S. diplomacy should be directed toward enhancing the protection of human rights and assisting the meeting of basic human needs, especially the need for food and capital investment for food production." It also assailed the Reagan administration's interest in reinstating military assistance to Guatemala and demanded that US policymakers instead heed the pope's exhortation to "seek out the structural reasons which foster or cause the different forms of poverty in the world . . . so you can apply the proper remedies." The statement concluded with an expression of the USCC's solidarity with their Central American brethren and the hope that "our continuing prayer for the Church and the people of that region may be contemplated by our public support in this country of their human rights and needs."[82]

Individual parishes in the United States also became contact zones in which clergy, missionaries, and catechists shared their experiences in Guatemala with US parishioners to raise awareness of the country's crises and strengthen both countries' bonds of solidarity. One example was Schaffer's effort to raise funds in the United States for mission projects in San Lucas Tolimán, most notably a health clinic for Luqueños. Schaffer believed that Guatemalans' voices were more important than his own and asked a mission employee to accompany him to speak to parish audiences on fundraising trips to Minnesota.[83] She later recalled in an interview why the clinic was needed at the time:

> One day a woman with a very sick child came to see Padre Gregorio. He couldn't help with medicine because we didn't have doctors or anything. The Mayan people just treated themselves with medicinal herbs, they didn't know of western medicine because they didn't have doctors or pharmacists or anything here, or any money to pay for medicine. So, the woman came to ask Padre to give a blessing on her child, maybe with this it would cure her child, and when she gave the child to Padre, it died in his arms. This was very hard for Padre, and he said the next day "to see this woman crying for her child and I couldn't do anything, we need to look for help and money from the U.S. I'm going to help you go through the embassy to get a visa and passport and you can go with me to the U.S. to help." So, I went with him to help look for money.[84]

She also told audiences about the toll that Guatemala's violence had taken on the country's children, recalling trips into Quiché to rescue children like Mariposa and Pastor, who had been orphaned by the violence:

When I took this one group from Quiché it was very hard. There was a family of five and another family of six . . . the army had killed their parents and the children had seen it happen, so they went to seek refuge in the church in Quiché. Because Padre already had *Casa Feliz* [a mission orphanage] here, the father from Quiché wanted the children to be able to come here [to San Lucas Tolimán] but it was so dangerous in those years because the military was everywhere. . . . I told Padre I would go get them, but I was very afraid of the army. We left, but when we were coming back the army stopped us and the children began to shake because they had seen how their parents had died, so I told them to not cry and if the army asks, tell them I am your mother and we came to visit Quiché and we are going home to San Lucas. . . . They let us pass, but at another checkpoint a soldier asked, "Why are you carrying so many children?" I got out of the car and asked him what the problem was with going home, we weren't carrying anything but my children and the food we brought. They let us go, but I was very afraid . . . thanks to God we got home.[85]

Testimonies like these not only offer an intimate account of local conditions in Guatemala but also show how individual Catholics engaged and directly intervened to save lives and forestall additional human rights abuses. Further, the mission employee's testimony offered US parishioners a Guatemalan perspective that was often absent from press accounts and congressional hearings. For her, however, it was an obligation: "The lives of people mattered to me because I knew how harsh it was, because every mother who stayed with their children, how can you not think of trying to help?"[86]

By any measure, 1981 had been an incredibly violent year in Guatemala. Little seemed to have changed by early 1982, as massacres attributed to both the army and the EGP occurred in the Ixcán and Sacuchum Dolores, San Marcos, among other places, in January, and San Juan Cotzal, Quiché and Chisec, Alta Verapáz the following month. Explicitly anti-Catholic violence also persisted, most notably the murder of La Salle Brother James Miller in Huehuetenango on February 13. Like Rother, Miller had been a longtime missionary, having served as the head of a La Salle school in Bluefields, Nicaragua, for a decade before volunteering for mission work in Guatemala in 1981, where he served as the director of three such schools in Huehuetenango.

Although the Brothers had actively encouraged greater educational and vocational opportunities for poor Mayan boys in the Huehuetenango area, they were largely ignored by the army and police. Relations soured in February 1982, after soldiers forcibly conscripted multiple La Salle students by abducting them from the city's marketplace. One of Miller's fellow Brothers, Paul Joslin, negotiated the boys' release by furnishing copies of their school registration, which exempted them from service. Joslin made three such visits to an area army base in early February. After Joslin's third visit on February 10, the Brothers learned they were in imminent danger. In an interview, Joslin recalled that "the youngest member of the [La Salle] community said to us, 'Señor Ortiz wants to speak to a Brother in his home as soon as possible' and he said 'I'm free this afternoon, I can go.... That evening, we said to him at dinner, 'what happened when you went to Señor Ortiz's house?' Ortiz was no ordinary person—he was someone who had just retired from the Guardia de la Hacienda [and] his son was a La Salle Christian Brother, so he had our best intention at heart, he really did. His information was that the G-2—as soon as he said it, everybody just shuddered, [because] that was the death squad—was looking for the 'subdirector de La Salle.'"[87]

According to Joslin, the news was met with "confusion" because the La Salle community had three such subdirectors: Joslin, Miller, and a local Guatemalan Brother. The three Brothers met on the evening of February 10 to decide whether to remain in Huehuetenango or to flee. Joslin believed that the G-2 was looking for him because of his repeated appearances at the local army base, noting that "that was probably a nuisance to the military authorities." Joslin noted that after collectively agreeing to remain in Huehuetenango for as long as possible, "Señor Ortiz told us to remain inside, but if we had to go out to be accompanied by someone else.... At the end of the meeting, James came up to me and said 'what are you going to do about it?' and I said 'I know what I'm *not* going to do, I'm not going back to that base.'"[88] Instead, Joslin met with Lee Powell, a visiting representative from the charity Christian Children's Fund, which sponsored multiple La Salle students in Huehuetenango, including one of the conscripted boys. Powell agreed to speak to base officers about halting the forced conscriptions.

Miller was shot to death on February 13 as he attempted to patch the exterior wall of Casa Indigena, one of the Brothers' three area schools. According to witnesses and police, the shooters had opened fire with machine guns from a passing car.[89] Joslin and fellow Brothers Martin Spellman and Gregory Cavalier met with US Embassy officials in Guatemala City that evening and reported that the recent conscriptions had raised tensions with local army commanders. Joslin and

Cavalier added that the Colegio La Salle, one of the Brothers' schools, had been included on a recently circulated list of targets for attack by local guerrillas, who were suspicious of Miller's years working in Nicaragua and his cordial relationship with deposed dictator Anastasio Somoza Debayle. In his report to the State Department, US ambassador to Guatemala Frederic Chapin remarked that "it was clear that [Joslin and Cavalier's] first instinct was to attribute [Miller's] death to GOG security forces. . . . They are aware of the deaths of several Catholic priests which have been generally attributed to GOG security forces. . . . They appear also to be aware of the possibility that guerrillas might have been responsible for [Miller's] death, given the reported guerrilla threat against the Colegio La Salle, Miller's work in Nicaragua and the guerrillas' certain knowledge that if the murder could be made to look like a government hit, it would surely complicate further U.S. cooperation with Guatemala."[90] Citing these uncertainties, Chapin reported, "In short, the questions surrounding this crime make it impossible to draw any conclusions so far regarding who did it and why." The La Salle Brothers closed the Huehuetenango mission after Miller's death. Like Rother and Woods, no one was prosecuted for his murder.

In addition to complicating US-Guatemalan relations, Guatemala's continuous violence also impeded the Reagan administration's desired relationship with Catholic activists. While some administration officials did indeed seek "the closest possible cooperation with the Church" on crises like Guatemala, conditions in the country made that cooperation an impossibility. As a result, some State Department officials began to take a more critical approach to Catholics and, more generally, the church itself. In early 1982, Richard Brown, a career State Department Foreign Service Officer with an extensive diplomatic background in Latin American affairs, wrote a comprehensive analysis for the National War College that detailed Catholicism's changes since CELAM's 1968 Medellín Conference and their implications for US foreign policy.[91] Brown's study, titled "The Challenge to the U.S. of Liberation Theology in Latin America," framed the philosophy and the changes it wrought as a clerical effort "to take advantage of the long-standing anti-American sentiment in the Hemisphere to attract the public (especially the youth and the intellectuals) back into the fold and to serve as an added justification for totally restructuring the political and economic systems, and countering the tyranny as they saw it of the 'national security state doctrine.'"[92] In Brown's estimation, Latin America's Marxists, particularly Fidel Castro, capitalized on liberation theology's spread and had further radicalized liberationists' desire for revolution by providing Cuban financial and material support.

Brown also argued that while foreign-born priests outnumbered native-born priests in virtually every country in Latin America, national churches with larger numbers of foreign priests were more amenable to Marxism because foreign priests had typically received advanced education in Europe or the United States, where they had been introduced to Marxist philosophy during their studies. This, he claimed, led "most foreign religious personnel (who are in large part either American or European) . . . to view their surroundings through liberationist lenses [and] feel less constrained by the secular power structure of their host countries and certainly possess loyalties to convictions that extend beyond national borders."[93] Brown used the Guatemalan church as an extreme example of this relationship, citing the same demographic totals that Sinn had reported to Haig a year earlier. He also cited US Embassy reports from Tegucigalpa, Honduras, that French, Spanish, and US Jesuits were allegedly funneling food and money to guerrillas in neighboring El Salvador, where Archbishop Arturo Rivera y Damas claimed that approximately a dozen priests had taken up arms in the countryside and that "at least twenty" priests occupied "key positions" in Nicaragua's government, including Foreign Minister Miguel d'Escoto Brockmann, a Los Angeles, California, native.[94]

Brown also argued that "an increasingly vocal and effective Church lobby in the U.S." sought a similar disruption and "internal revolution" in the United States. He argued that Catholic activists, most notably Jesuit and Maryknoll-affiliated clergy and missionaries, sought to block US military assistance to Central America not out of Christian concerns for human rights but rather to facilitate Marxism's spread throughout the region. According to Brown, Catholic activists' participation with grassroots groups like NISGUA, sponsorship of seminars on Central American politics in US in parishes, and public criticism of US policy goals all worked toward this goal. He was also concerned about Catholics' lobbying efforts that included letter-writing campaigns to Congress like those described in the *Catholic Messenger*: according to Brown, "during 1979–81, the Office of Central American Affairs in the Department of State received thousands of letters from American nuns and priests as well as from adult parishioners and Catholic parochial schoolchildren. These letters . . . sought . . . to condemn and castigate. The schoolchildren's letters in particular were apparently written as class assignments."[95] Brown warned that Catholic activists' efforts had begun to influence evangelical groups like the National Council of Churches, which had adopted resolutions that condemned the Reagan administration's support for military regimes in El Salvador and Guatemala at their national conference in 1981, and that Catholic activists were especially eager to mobilize the Latino population in California and Texas, which, he noted, had sizable Central American and refugee populations.

Brown concluded that this seemingly resurgent Catholic activism "complicate[d] the ability of the U.S. to conduct business in the Western Hemisphere" and, if left unchecked, posed a security threat within the United States. To meet this challenge, Brown advised a strategy centered on dialogue with Catholic activists in the United States and Central America to find common ideological ground that would, he wrote, "expose the fallacies and false hopes of liberation theology" and the changes it had brought to the church and beyond.[96] Specific to Catholic activists in the United States, Brown advised that Reagan administration officials and policymakers "be especially persistent" in emphasizing what he termed the "inherent errors and bankruptcy" in liberation theology and Marxism in open, cordial discussions with Catholic activists and leadership. He argued that this approach would be diplomatically beneficial because it prevented the Reagan administration's foreign policy critics in Central America from claiming that the administration had dismissed their criticisms out of hand. Finally, he urged administration officials to let Vatican and US Catholic leadership take the lead in engaging Catholic activists on political matters. He believed that treating the matter as a primarily religious one would "permit other, more qualified advocates to carry on the long-range effort to free the Church of an alien force" and avoid potential conflicts with the Holy See over US interference in what Brown urged US policymakers to see as an internal Catholic issue.

Brown's study was well received among senior administration officials. National Security Adviser William Clark was impressed with its content and perspective and directed Deputy Assistant to the President for National Security Affairs Robert McFarlane to forward a copy to Cardinal Pio Laghi, the apostolic nuncio to the United States. He also requested that a copy be sent to William Wilson, Reagan's personal representative to the Holy See, to "engender a dialogue" with church officials in Rome, including the pope, on how to best engage with Catholic activists on the topic of Central America. The Ríos Montt regime's violence, however, doomed these efforts.

Catholic activism was as multifaceted and visible as ever during the early 1980s. In some cases, priests like Schaffer and Rother engaged in direct intervention to advocate for their parishioners' human dignity through fundraising appeals, offering employment and shelter for the poor, and celebrating Mass in Tz'utujil or K'iche. In others, individual parishioners like the mission employee practiced an even more direct intervention by rescuing children from Quiché, risking her own life in the process. Rother's murder underscored the risks of direct intervention and, at the same time, brought greater public attention to Guatemala's ongoing violence.

Human rights reportage was also central to Catholic activism during this period. Like direct intervention, reporting took multiple forms, ranging from Rother's meeting with Sinn to discuss local conditions in Santiago Atitlán to Welsh's firsthand account of his experiences in Guatemala during his visit. Additionally, the Catholic press offered extensive coverage on all Central America's crises, including Guatemala's, during the early 1980s. Diocesan newspapers played an especially critical role in this process, as they were able to offer their readers locally focused stories and editorials that nationally circulated newspapers like the *National Catholic Reporter* or wire services like the CNA or RNS could not.

Catholic activists likewise remained prominent among critics of the US policies toward Central America. The USCC articulated many activists' concerns about the region's violence and human rights abuses and directly appealed to the Reagan administration to halt all military aid to the region and commit to finding peaceful, equitable solutions to the region's economic, political, and social disparities. In other cases, priests like Hehir offered congressional testimony on the region's crises, and bishops like Salatka and groups like the Religious Task Force on Central America and NISGUA exerted sustained pressure on the US government and the Reagan administration for a full investigation into Rother's murder and rejected the Lucas regime's initial claims that his death was the result of a simple strong-arm robbery. Congressmen like Oberstar, Borer, and Paul responded to these demands by lobbying Guatemalan officials in Washington and Guatemala City alike to reopen the investigation and free Mendoza, Cocheleanda, and Quiju from police custody. Although Rother's true killers were never identified, Catholics' activism did help free three innocent men from prison for a crime that they did not commit.

Acts like these contributed to the Reagan administration's complicated relationship with the church during the early 1980s. Some administration officials, like Brown and Sinn, recognized that Catholic activists' organization, international movement, and willingness to engage Guatemalan and US political leaders made them a key partner, along with the pope, in diplomatic and political matters across the region. However, that alliance could not be secured without broad changes in the administration's policy approaches to Central American politics and human rights that, if adopted, would bring both sides ideologically closer. Brown's policy suggestions also acknowledged that neither foreign nor domestic policies developed in separate vacuums. Instead, they were two mutually reinforcing halves of the same apparatus: direct intervention, reporting on the country's human rights abuses, congressional testimony, reports and editorials in the Catholic press, and calls to reopen the investigation into Rother's and Miller's murders could—and did—shape many US Catholics' views of Guatemala and US foreign policy. These events compelled policymakers like Brown to take greater notice of Catholic activism and its potential diplomatic and domestic consequences. These consequences would become even more urgent following Lucas's overthrow in

March 1982 as his successor, Brigadier General José Efraín Ríos Montt, committed genocide in the country's Ixil region and other rampant human rights abuses during his brief dictatorship. Catholic activists' responses to the Ríos Montt regime, however, exacerbated tensions with the Reagan administration, precisely as Guatemala's civil war reached its bloody apex.

6

"In More Than One Office a Picture of Che Guevara"

Guatemala's war had reached a strategic stalemate by early 1982. Although the army, police, and death squads had committed thousands of human rights abuses since Lucas assumed power in 1978, they failed to defeat either ORPA or the EGP in the ensuing four years. Instead, US and Guatemalan policymakers alike reported that both groups had received supplies and training from the Cuban government and, in February 1982, ORPA and the EGP, along with the FAR and PGT, established the Unidad Revolucionaria Nacional Guatemalteca (URNG), a coalition that would represent the country's far-left political groups for the war's duration. In response, the Lucas regime increased its repression even more during what would be its final months in power. These abuses took numerous forms, including murder, massacres, rape, and abduction, and were especially prevalent in Huehuetenango and Quiché's Ixil Triangle region.[1] These atrocities were part of the Victoria 82 campaign, a scorched-earth plan designed to eradicate the country's militant left, their sympathizers, and civilian collaborators. By year's end, this violence would account for more than twenty-five hundred known human rights abuses in 1982, an average of nearly seven per day. More than eleven hundred of these occurred in Quiché, where the military committed acts of genocide on the order of Lucas's successor, Brigadier General José Efraín Ríos Montt.

At the same time, Catholic activists remained a prominent voice within US policymaking decisions about Guatemala. Catholic newspapers across the country continued to report on the country's violence throughout the year and continued to accentuate local ties to Guatemala in reporting on local refugee resettlement, fundraising drives, the formation of local-level activist groups, and any number of talks, films, and public demonstrations to bring greater public attention to Guatemala's crises. Further, both the CEG and USCC denounced the country's ongoing violence and the Ríos Montt regime's repression more directly and unequivocally than ever before, and individual priests and missionaries continued to practice multiple forms of activism. As had been the case during the Lucas regime, Catholic activists in Guatemala and the United States directly intervened to halt the Ríos Montt regime's human rights abuses while also offering expert testimony during US congressional hearings on Central America, lobbying elected officials and policymakers, and working with other grassroots organizations devoted to finding peace and justice for the beleaguered region. Finally, the pope himself denounced the violence plaguing Central America during his visit to the region in 1983, which included a contentious stop in Guatemala that precipitated a crisis for the Ríos Montt regime just weeks before its collapse.

Their continued advocacy came at a cost, however, as Catholic activists' relationship with the Reagan administration demonstrably soured while Ríos Montt ruled Guatemala. Administration officials like William Clark and Robert McFarlane had lauded Richard Brown's strategy for securing Catholic support of its intended Central American policy in February 1982, just prior to Ríos Montt's ascension to power. By September 1983, however, the Reagan administration's approach to Catholic activists had changed enough that Morton Blackwell, the White House's coordinator for its Central America Working Group and Special Assistant to the President, advised Faith Ryan Whittlesey, the director of the State Department's Office of Public Liaison, that she should exclude the USCC from weekly Working Group meetings. According to Blackwell, "The USCC staff is militantly anti-Reagan, militantly antidefense preparedness and, according to one report, sports in more than one office a picture of Che Guevarra [sic]."[2]

Brown's study and Blackwell's memorandum are useful historical markers for understanding the Reagan administration's approach to the Ríos Montt regime. Brown's report circulated in the weeks preceding the coup that installed Ríos Montt, while Blackwell's memo was dated September 3, 1983, just weeks after the dictator's overthrow on August 8 of that year. They also reflect how the administration's clashes with Catholic activists during the Ríos Montt regime facilitated a shift from policymakers seeking "the closest possible cooperation with the Church" to Blackwell's depiction of the USCC office as a nest of Marxist subversion lovingly festooned with Marxist iconography.

This chapter examines the numerous ways that Catholic activists and the Reagan administration clashed over the Ríos Montt regime's violence. It recounts Lucas's final months in power during 1982 and the events surrounding the coup that brought Ríos Montt to power, as well as the CEG's initial response. It also explains how the Ríos Montt regime's atrocities strained its relationship with the Reagan administration. These included acts of explicitly anti-Catholic violence that included using churches as sites of mass killings and torture, forced religious conversion, and the army's continued persecution of missionaries, priests, and nuns serving in the country. It also offers multiple examples of Catholic responses to these outrages on local, national, and global levels that show how Catholic activists remained a prominent voice within US policymaking decisions toward Guatemala as the country's violence surged and its relationship with the United States grew more complicated.

Two questions framed Guatemala's 1982 elections. The first was a question of legitimacy. United States policymakers had long criticized the country's lack of true democratic structure, especially after the 1974 and 1978 contests had been flagrantly rigged. They also viewed open and honest elections in 1982 as a cornerstone of human rights: as early as 1980, US ambassador to Guatemala Frank Ortiz had viewed a clean election with civilian candidates as an important measure of Guatemala's progress on human rights issues that would facilitate improved bilateral relations.[3]

The second was a question of precisely *who* would run for president. As anthropologist Jennifer Schirmer has noted, years of unchecked military rule had created a bloated, kleptocratic structure that saw the dictatorship in control of more than forty state-run enterprises, including public utilities, cement production, and tourism agencies, among others; had created deep pockets of corruption and graft that enriched high-ranking officers; and had simultaneously failed to defeat the country's guerrilla forces. Instead, the Lucas regime's repression had seemingly galvanized the far left, and its human rights abuses had alienated Guatemala diplomatically and contributed to capital flight as violence surged under Lucas. Finally, Lucas's advisers believed that Guatemalans would be more likely to vote— and accept the election's results—if the military did not field any candidates.[4]

Finding a willing civilian candidate, however, proved difficult. Seeking to prolong his influence, Lucas initially offered his support to longtime friend Alfonso Ponce Archila, an ophthalmologist from Alta Verapáz, who declined the offer. Lucas then turned to his finance minister, Hugo Tulio Búcaro, who also declined.[5] Faced with no willing civilian candidate, Lucas's advisers suggested endorsing his defense minister, General Aníbal Angel Guevara Rodríguez, as a last resort. The CIA took a dim view of Guevara and warned that while Guevara was "less rigidly right wing than President Lucas," a Guevara regime would almost assuredly continue repressing the country's left and "unaccommodating" moderate factions.[6] With Lucas's endorsement, Guevara campaigned against conservative Gustavo Anzueto Vielman, the Christian Democrat–endorsed Alejandro Maldonado Aguirre, and far-right stalwart Mario Sandoval Alarcón.

Contrary to the CIA's predictions, Guevara campaigned on a platform of "resolv[ing] promptly and firmly the grave problems from which the people of [Guatemala] have suffered for so long."[7] According to Guevara, the country's bloodshed could not end until the government enacted meaningful economic and social reforms that addressed poverty and class discrimination. To this end, he proposed a land reform program that would create a reserve of federal land allocated to landless campesinos to own and farm their own plots in what he described as a form of "collective agricultural patrimony."[8] Guevara argued that this policy would increase food production and reduce Guatemala's dependence on food aid and imports. He also called for new infrastructure projects that would modernize the countryside, stimulate Guatemala's construction and heavy industrial sectors, provide greater access to water and electricity, and grow the country's skilled labor force and middle class. Guevara's social policies also included provisions to "vigorously" support education programs for Mayans, a nationwide vocational training program, expanded federal health and welfare schemes, and greater efforts to provide employment opportunities for women. Guevara argued that the net effect of this platform would "make all Guatemalans believe that they are human beings who can fully identify with our country."[9]

The US embassy officials in Guatemala City monitored the campaign closely and sought insight from political insiders. On January 12, former Guatemalan president and Central Auténtica Nacionalista (CAN) party founder Carlos Arana Osorio met with Chapin to discuss several election issues including political violence, Guevara's prospects for victory, and, presciently, his ability to remain in power if elected. Arana called Guatemala's violence an "intractable problem" exacerbated by a lack of foreign investment and tourism in recent years and told Chapin that although all four candidates declared ending the country's violence their top priority if elected, none—including his own candidate Anzueto—had presented a viable solution for doing so. He also acknowledged that Anzueto had no chance of winning and agreed with recent polls that had projected Guevara as the victor. Arana also told Chapin that while he considered Guevara a friend and a good soldier, he was "rather limited intellectually and had narrow experience for a successful president." Chapin later noted that this comment had surprised him and understood it as an insinuation that Guevara would be little more than an acquiescent stooge for the MLN and far-right generals. Arana explicitly rejected the possibility of a coup, however, because "times [had] changed" and the officer corps was more ordered and disciplined than ever.[10] Arana instead told Chapin that he believed a multiparty, coalition government would work within a Guevara cabinet and that the CAN was prepared to work with Guevara if asked.

The URNG had a different perspective. The organization's initial public announcement on February 8 declared that it sought to build a "revolutionary, patriotic, popular and democratic government commit[ted] . . . to the Guatemalan people" via a five-point plan that guaranteed "the supreme human rights of life and peace" to all citizens and would eliminate the country's oligarchic rule, provide legal avenues for racial equality, offer all political parties recognition in the democratic process, and promise nonalignment with either superpower in foreign affairs. They also charged that all four candidates represented the country's military and business sectors, and the people of Guatemala had not had a candidate of their own since Árbenz in 1950. Relatedly, they claimed that, irrespective of whoever won, "no one [in Guatemala] believes in the grand deceit of elections" and that none of the four candidates represented the country's poor.[11]

The campaign had also failed to produce a clear front-runner. The polls that Arana cited in his meeting with Chapin had shown Guevara holding a consistent, albeit minor lead since November 1981 (Table 6.1). However, a late surge from Maldonado in February made the race a statistical dead heat, and US officials worried that Guevara's sudden razor-thin edge in the polls would prompt the military to manipulate vote totals to ensure his victory and delegitimize his presidency before it even began. CIA officials were particularly concerned about this possibility, as Sandoval had stronger support among army officers than Guevara thanks to Sandoval's campaign pledge of higher salaries and new equipment for the army if elected. On March 5, two days before the election, the CIA's Guatemala City station warned that "at home and abroad, a victory by Guevara will be widely assumed to have been achieved through fraud" and that Sandoval was likely to claim fraud and provoke his supporters to protest violently if he lost.[12]

Table 6.1. Guatemalan electoral polling data, November 1981 to February 1982 (percent totals)			
	November 1981	December 1981	February 1982
Anzueto (CAN)	9.76	14.12	12.85
Guevara (PR-PID-FUN)	21.83	22.99	23.21
Maldonado (PNR-DC)	16.08	15.46	22.26
Sandoval (MLN)	11.73	13.30	16.66
Undecided/other/null	40.60	34.13	25.02

Almost one million people voted on March 8, a 30 percent increase over the 1974 and 1978 elections. When the results were announced the following day, Guevara, who had held a 1 percent lead over Maldonado in the final preelection poll in February, enjoyed a 10 percent margin of victory over Maldonado and beat third-place finisher Sandoval by sixteen points. As Arana had predicted in January, Anzueto finished a distant fourth. Guevara's margin of victory prompted immediate accusations of fraud: Maldonado accused the regime of delaying results from departmental capitals to manipulate vote totals, and Sandoval, as had been expected, urged his supporters to protest the result. On March 10, Sandoval, Maldonado, and Anzueto supporters protested the election together and demanded a new election within sixty days.[13] The Lucas regime ordered the army and police to break up the protest by force and jailed all three losing candidates until the demonstration subsided. United States officials in Guatemala City concluded that fraud had indeed occurred and expressed their concerns to Guatemalan military and political officials. During a meeting with Lucas's chief of staff Colonel Hector Israel Montalván on March 11, Chapin said the United States "would find it impossible" to work closely with a Guevara-led government due to the questionable circumstances surrounding his victory and that "the popular consensus in Guatemala and abroad was that significant fraud had taken place."[14] Further, a CIA report on March 22 speculated that "with Guevara at the helm, the government will be hard pressed to remedy the problems" that his presidency would face after officially taking power on July 1.[15]

Guevara never had the opportunity to assume power. The day after the CIA issued its report, Lucas was overthrown and replaced by a three-man junta composed of retired Brigadier General José Efraín Ríos Montt, Colonel Hector Luis Gordillo Martínez, and General Horacio Egberto Maldonado Schaad. According to a State Department report issued after the coup, Guevara had been unpopular among senior officers who felt he would be an ineffective leader and resented Lucas for not consulting them on Guevara's nomination.[16] An initial coup attempt had been planned for March 21 by a group of officers from the Guatemalan Air Force and the army's Honor Guard but was delayed until March 23, when junior officers ordered tanks and troops to surround the Palacio Nacional and demand Lucas's resignation, new elections without military candidates within sixty days, and a peaceful transition of power to whoever won the election.[17]

Initial cables from Defense Department officials on March 23 reported that the coup had been nonviolent, that Guatemala City remained "absolutely calm," and that several unpopular regime members like PN director Brigadier General Hernán Chupina Barahona and his secretary general, Randolfo Catalan Pazos, as well as Lucas's advisers Jorge and Raúl Garcia Granados, had been arrested. United States officials held little regard for any of the four men. Chupina had authorized the police's violent responses to the bus fare and PMA protests in 1978 and was purportedly linked to the ESA death squad, while the Defense Department viewed Catalan as "a thug and killer" in his own right and described the Granados brothers as "a crook [and] an even bigger crook."[18] Additionally, the Defense Intelligence Agency (DIA) also reported that while the coup had been successful, the officer corps remained fractured over the dueling coup plots, and warned that further upheaval was possible.

For Ríos Montt, the journey to the presidency had been a long one. A Huehuetenango native, he enlisted in the army in 1943 and had been promoted to corporal by July of that year. After attending the army's officer training academy, the Escuela Politécnica, from 1946 to 1950, Ríos Montt received additional training at the School of the Americas in the Panama Canal Zone and at the US Army's Special Warfare School in Fort Bragg, North Carolina. By June 1972, Ríos Montt had risen to the rank of brigadier general and was appointed chief of staff of the Guatemalan Army the following year. A US Army report described Ríos Montt as both "a sincere, intelligent, hard-driving officer who may be counted on to do a job in an excellent manner" and a "lone wolf" and unwittingly foreshadowed his regime's astounding violence and genocide, noting that the general displayed "a fervent approach to mission accomplishment."[19]

The year 1974 was notable for the Ríos Montt family. That year, the general's brother Mario Enrique was ordained as a Catholic bishop while the general campaigned for the country's presidency. Ríos Montt received the Christian Democratic Party's endorsement and ran against Laugerud, who had been Arana's defense minister and preferred successor. Arana's endorsement of Laugerud was not a purely political decision, as Ríos Montt's polarizing personality repelled as many people as it attracted. According to historian Carlos Sabino, Ríos Montt's foes saw the general as "a psychopath" and an "unstable, 'deranged' man . . . manipulative and unpredictable," while his allies lauded his "unquestionable leadership abilities, his democratic and anti-communist convictions . . . and austere life."[20] United States Embassy officials had been long aware of Ríos Montt's apparent unpopularity: US ambassador to Guatemala William C. Bowdler reported that Ríos Montt, along with another newly promoted general, Ricardo Peralta Méndez, were "widely regarded as the Army's most politically Left senior officers" and that other officers had blatantly ignored the two at a party honoring their promotions during the summer of 1972.[21] Unsurprisingly, Laugerud won a flagrantly fraudulent election in March 1974 and Ríos Montt was dispatched to Spain, where he served as a defense attaché until his retirement and return to Guatemala in 1977.

Soon after his return, Ríos Montt experienced a profound personal transformation and became a born-again Christian. As historian Lauren Turek has noted, multiple US-based evangelical associations, like the Southern Baptist Foreign Mission and the National Association of Evangelicals, coordinated large-scale relief efforts for Guatemala after the country's catastrophic 1976 earthquake left more than one hundred thousand people dead or injured and over a million more homeless.[22] In addition to aid and supplies, evangelical groups like California's Gospel Outreach Church also sent missionaries to Guatemala, where they led Bible study groups, proselytized, and established churches like the neo-Pentecostal

Verbo Ministries, which Ríos Montt subsequently joined in 1977. Ríos Montt remained bitter about his loss and, according to Turek, was drawn to Verbo's "promise of individual salvation, energetic worship, and tight-knit community" and committed himself deeply to the church.[23] By decade's end, Ríos Montt had shared his personal testimony with Gospel Outreach leadership in California and taught at Verbo's primary school in Guatemala City. Ríos Montt's affiliation with Verbo defined his regime from its very beginning: as Virginia Garrard-Burnett has noted, Verbo's official account of the coup claimed that Ríos Montt was at the school on the afternoon of March 23 when he was summoned to the Palacio Nacional, unaware that he had been selected to lead the junta.[24]

The URNG immediately rejected the new junta. On March 24, the organization declared that "Ríos Montt, Maldonado Schaad, Gordillo and the rest are equally stained by the blood of the people as were Lucas García and the generals who were displaced by their pals." Its leaders also claimed that while the coup had exposed factionalism within the army's high command, "no one should have illusions about rapid victory. . . . Now we must prepare to . . . achiev[e] new and more important victories in the just and necessary path of the Popular Revolutionary War of all the Guatemalan People."[25]

In contrast, the CEG initially reacted with cautious optimism. After the coup, CEG members met with the new junta and presented it with a communique that expressed the bishops' "profound interest" in the junta's plan to improve Guatemala's human rights record. According to US Embassy reports of the meeting, Mario Enrique Ríos Montt asked his brother to open the meeting by leading the group in prayer.[26] After the meeting, Bishop Ríos Montt told the press, "my brother, the general, reacted positively to our petition and we are hopeful that things will indeed improve for the Church, and Guatemala as a whole."[27] A week later, the bishops published an open letter to the junta that offered the Guatemalan church's "selfless cooperation" with the junta and its perspective on social issues in exchange for the junta's guarantee that it would not interfere with the church's evangelical or humanitarian activities.[28] CEG president Monsignor Próspero Penados del Barrio also called on the country's priests and Christian community leaders to lead their parishes in a day of prayer for peace in Central America on Maundy Thursday, observed that year on April 8. Penados reminded Catholics of Maundy Thursday's significance to Christians, specifically Jesus's command to his disciples to love and serve one another during the Last Supper. In this spirit, Penados asked all parishes to participate in a nationwide offering of money, clothing, blankets, and basic goods to be redistributed by the Guatemalan church and affiliated organizations like Caritas and Oxfam to Central Americans who had lost their homes and possessions during their countries' wars. Penados asked Guatemalans "to share the little that we have with our brothers who have been left with nothing" and reminded them of "the fraternal solidarity" that religious and secular groups around the globe had shown Guatemalans after the 1976 earthquake and subsequent escalation of the war.[29]

US policymakers' reactions to the coup were more reserved. Although Ríos Montt's reputation for honesty and professionalism had been impeccable, reports from multiple agencies noted that many of the military's junior officers had become disgruntled with the junta almost immediately after it had assumed power. The officers resented the junta's decision to allow corrupt officials like Montalván and Central Bank director Luís Alfredo Castillo Corado positions in the new regime, as well as Ríos Montt's appointment of family members to cabinet positions and Verbo ministers as his personal advisers. The officer corps also objected to the junta's decision not to arrest or deport either Lucas or his brother Benedicto, who served as the army's chief of staff during his brother's regime.[30] US Embassy officials also worried that pressuring the junta to hold immediate elections would lead to Sandoval's election, placing the country's most right-wing party, the MLN, in power, and, in Chapin's words, bring with it "all that would mean in terms of highly authoritarian policies."[31] Chapin discussed these matters with Ríos Montt during a meeting on April 8 and assured the dictator that US leaders "were not trying to rush him but that the time table for a return to constitutional norms was an issue which foreign governments and world public opinion were interested in." According to Chapin, Ríos Montt told him that while God had destined him to be president, he had little desire to remain in power and instead wanted to resume his life as a retired officer and Sunday school teacher. However, he needed to first attend to "the complicated business of cleaning up corruption" before stepping down.[32] The DIA also predicted that Ríos Montt would likely resign following new elections and characterized him as the junta's true leader.[33]

New elections never came, Ríos Montt never resigned, and human rights abuses persisted under his rule as army patrols killed thirty-seven people in Xalbal and Kaibil in the Ixcán region of Quiché during the regime's first weeks.[34] On April 3, soldiers raped dozens of women and girls in Chel, a village north of the town of Chajul, before murdering ninety people, including children and pregnant women, with machetes before burning the village.[35] Soldiers returned to Chel three weeks later and shot forty-five more people. That same month, the Ríos Montt regime organized the first of the country's Patrullas de Autodefensa Civil (PACs) in Quiché. As Schirmer has noted, the PACs served as the army's "eyes and ears" throughout the country's western highlands and comprised local campesino conscripts.[36] For campesinos, the patrols were in no way voluntary: one former *patrulla* testified, "They told us 'if you don't join the patrol, we will [kill] you as we did these guerillas.'"[37] According to Schirmer, approximately three hundred thousand Guatemalans had been forced to serve in PACs in 850 villages across the country by the end of 1982.[38]

While PAC conscripts were not officially soldiers, they were forced to provide multiple services to the army, including patrolling villages, reporting suspected guerrillas and sympathizers, providing supplies and labor for the army, and participating in raids and massacres, at times in their own villages. In testimony to the CEH after the war, a former PAC conscript from Huehuetenango recalled his role in a massacre in the town of Santa Crúz Barillas: "After having shot everyone . . . it seemed that not all of them were dead, so some soldiers had to put their weapons in the chests of the three who were still living and sho[o]t them . . . [A lieutenant] said 'now we are going to make mincemeat of [them] but you have to do it, because I'm tired.' . . . That's how the lieutenant spoke to encourage all of us present, to give us the courage to participate in the slaughter . . . then soldiers, patrol officers and military commissioners began to machete corpses until only pieces were left."[39]

In another massacre in April 1982, approximately 140 soldiers and PAC members entered Acul Quiché, a small community of 250 families, and executed twenty-five men before forcing survivors to join PACs.[40] These atrocities marked the beginning of a bloody five-month period that claimed the lives of approximately ten thousand Guatemalans and, notably, destroyed more than four hundred Mayan villages throughout 1982 as part of the Ríos Montt's regime's genocidal violence.[41]

Atrocities like these were common during the junta's earliest days. However, some policymakers in Washington viewed it as an improvement over the Lucas regime and asked Congress to authorize resuming arms sales to Guatemala as a goodwill gesture and an incentive to improve the country's human rights record. Deputy Assistant Secretary for Inter-American Affairs Stephen W. Bosworth lauded Lucas's overthrow in remarks before the Senate Foreign Relations Committee in April and praised the coup as an event that "may have ended the political paralysis which has gripped the country."[42] According to Bosworth, the Ríos Montt–led junta had taken concrete but unnamed steps to eliminate the country's corruption, and he viewed the coup as part of a broader wave of democratization in Central America, alongside recent elections in El Salvador and Honduras. Bosworth hoped the junta would "continue to make progress . . . and that we in turn will be able to establish a closer, more collaborative relationship with this key country." He asked the committee to authorize an immediate 250,000 dollars in military training for Guatemala's armed forces, with four million dollars' worth of helicopter parts in to follow 1983 "in the expectation that conditions there may improve sufficiently."[43]

Some communities suffered protracted waves of violence. On May 18, 1982, soldiers entered the community of San Antonio Sinaché, Quiché, and killed forty-five people, wounded four, and tortured two. One survivor testified, "I watched the people in front of me fall as if they had stumbled, but they fell because they were hit by bullets or because grenades were [exploding] nearby, and people would fly up and fall like dolls when this happened . . . we did not even turn to look back, we all ran like crazy from one place to another."[44] Another survivor recalled being forced to leave an elderly family member behind, recalling, "We couldn't take [him] because he could not run like younger people, so we thought to leave him hidden in our house. . . . He agreed to stay behind and we ran away so they wouldn't kill us. But when the soldiers came to the house, they found him and slit his throat."[45] In all, the army killed fifty-one villagers on May 18 and killed an additional forty using machetes on May 30. The two massacres were part of a protracted wave of violence in San Antonio Sinaché: soldiers had previously murdered 108 men, women, and children in the village in March of that year. Atrocities like these prompted the CEG to issue a pastoral letter on May 27 that assailed the junta's actions and stated in part that "the consequences of this irrational violence cannot be more dismal" and that "never in our national history have such serious extremes been reached. These murders are already in the realm of genocide. We must recognize these acts are in major contradiction to the divine commandment, 'thou shalt not kill.'"[46] The bishops also expressed concern for Guatemalans that had fled to Mexico, which the *New York Times* estimated to exceed one hundred thousand later in the year.[47]

Ríos Montt also attempted to dismantle Guatemala's political structure in favor of autocratic rule during the summer of 1982. On June 9, he disbanded the junta, dissolved the National Assembly, and declared himself commander of the country's armed forces. Ríos Montt also removed all the country's mayors and replaced them with his own appointees before declaring a one-month nationwide state of siege under Decree Law 45–82 on June 30. The state of siege permitted the country's police and military to conduct warrantless searches and arrests, repealed citizens' rights to carry arms, banned gatherings of more than four people without prior authorization, enacted civic curfews, and suspended all constitutionally guaranteed civil liberties. Alongside the state of siege, an additional decree, 46–82, authorized secret kangaroo courts in which "individuals caught in the act of subversive activities [would] be tried on the spot" and either imprisoned or executed if convicted.[48] Ríos Montt justified bankrupting Guatemalan democracy by claiming that "those who have brought chaos to Guatemala [are] those who offer the red paradise of slavery [and] . . . have unleashed a chain of death" and that "it is time to begin to manage this situation as it should be managed, as God orders, as we all want it to be managed." That management included Ríos Montt's Frijoles y Fusiles (Beans and Rifles) program, which offered food aid to citizens who pledged allegiance to the state. One high-ranking officer described the plan more succinctly: "If you are with us, we'll feed you; if you are not, we'll kill you."[49]

In addition to revoking all civil liberties, the regime also launched Victoria 82, a comprehensive strategic plan to destroy the guerrillas and win Guatemalans' hearts and minds during the summer of 1982. The plan called for the regime to announce a three-week amnesty for the country's guerrillas to surrender to the army beginning June 1. The regime also launched a concerted advertising campaign touting the amnesty decree in Mayan dialects, including Kak'chiquel, Kiché, Kekchí, and Ixil. The plan also called for a partial mobilization of the army on June 13 "as a show of force" before declaring a state of emergency in areas with continued guerrilla activity.[50] After the amnesty lapsed, field commanders were given carte blanche to "annihilate" guerrillas and, according to a DIA cable, "each commander [had] as much freedom as possible" to do so. The cable also underscored Ríos Montt's own culpability in his regime's genocide, noting that Ríos Montt told senior officers that he "expected results" and "wanted each commander to take special care that innocent individuals would not be killed; however, if such unfortunate acts did take place he did not want to read about them in the newspapers."[51]

Victoria 82 also sought to improve military-civilian relations and foster greater order within the ranks. Some senior officers believed Lucas's indiscriminate violence had eroded the military's credibility and public image. This was especially true in the country's western highlands, where, according to Victoria 82's architects, "the great masses of indigenous people of the Altiplano . . . have found an echo in the proclamations of subversives because [of] the scarcity of land, immense poverty and due to the many years of *concientización* they have received, [and] they see the army as an invading [force]. . . . Adding to this a good amount of mistakes made by the troops such as vandalism, rapes, robberies, and destruction of crops, have been skillfully exploited by national and international subversion."[52]

Notably, Victoria 82 required troop detachments to hold pro-regime rallies across the country that included themes like the amnesty program, guerrillas' purported massacres of campesinos, and the horrors that had followed Marxist victories in Cuba and Nicaragua. It further stipulated that "concentrations of the civilian population for the army and repudiation of subversion will be encouraged, taking special care that these [events] appear to be an initiative of the population."[53] The regime believed that creating this type of Potemkin Guatemala would justify the army's violence not only to the country's citizens but also to Reagan administration officials who remained concerned about the potential backlash against closer US-Guatemalan relations.

Parallel to this, a program designed "to maintain the combative spirit of our troops" was scheduled to begin on June 21. Officers were directed to explain to their troops what "the country [was] going through and the need to exterminate the enemy."[54] This included briefings on a wide range of topics including the soldier's duty to society, atrocities purportedly committed by guerrillas, and methods of subversion, among others. Additionally, officers were ordered to keep soldiers apprised of successful battles, purported guerrilla atrocities, and demonstrations of public support for the army and regime. Finally, it authorized "recreation areas" for soldiers to take leave that would include facilities for laundry and bathing, a store, and "contact" with women. In addition to boosting troop morale, these provisions were also meant to forestall another junior officer coup such as the one that had overthrown Lucas just months before. Ríos Montt's expectation for the guerrillas' annihilation and disingenuous concern for civilian deaths led to multiple atrocities during the summer of 1982 that included torture at the Playa Grande military base in Ixcán, as well as in Quiché and in Guatemala City. Additionally, soldiers committed massacres in San Mateo Ixtatán and San Miguel Acatán, Huehuetenango; participated in disappearances in Zunil, Quetzaltenango; and murdered children in Quiché.[55] In the San Miguel Acatán massacre, the victims were forced to dig their own graves before being murdered.

Explicitly anti-Catholic acts were also common under the Ríos Montt regime. In some cases, churches themselves were sites of abuses. In Chajul, soldiers and PAC members massacred ninety-six workers at the Estrella Polar finca and, according to eyewitnesses, executed the workers inside a Catholic church before forcing other workers to remove and bury the bodies.[56] Soldiers also occupied churches in San Juan Cotzal, San Pedro Jocopilas, and a Marist boarding school in Chupal, among other places in Quiché. According to CEH testimonies, soldiers used belfries as observation posts and the churches for torture and executions.[57] In other cases, instances of abuses had a sectarian dimension: in Panzós, a witness recounted in testimony to the CEH that "two Mayan priests were kidnapped from their house by soldiers. [They had been] denounced by [an] evangelical pastor who said that they practiced magic rites. The evangelical pastor was also a military commissioner." In other cases, Catholics were forced to become members of evangelical churches. One forced convert recalled, "[We] had to become evangelicals because that is what the Army said. We had to forget about our organizations that we had in our community before the violence."[58] Another noted, "In 1982 and 1983 [the army] was crazy, [they] wanted everyone to become evangelicals and for a while we are evangelicals, and we are going to pray that they don't kill us, then we leave [evangelicalism]."[59]

The regime's abuses primarily targeted Mayan Catholics, but Mayan Protestants suffered horrific violence as well. In August 1982, soldiers kidnapped and tortured a Q'eqchi' Protestant pastor over the course of six days. According to the pastor, "One day I was going to do a bit of work when the soldiers took me. They beat me and gave me no food for six days. . . . When the soldiers were beating me they tied me up and hung me by my hands . . . they never stopped abusing me. They stuck wires in my throat." He convinced his captors to loosen the ropes binding his hands and escaped as the soldiers slept. He fled to the mountains and survived on wild fruits for "many days" before arriving at the home of relatives: "They were terrified when they saw me. They thought I had gone crazy. I was badly hurt and naked. I wept and they had compassion on me. They gave me clothes and a pair of shoes. . . . A fellow believer gave me some money for boat fare. Weeping and praying I went along the road. Many brothers asked me, 'are you all right?' I answered, 'I am very well, thank you. . . . ' I travelled in the mountains for 6 days. On the eighth day I arrived near my house with much fear. Because I was afraid, I didn't go to my house, but to the house of one of the members of my congregation."[60]

The pastor's testimony also recalled how his community responded to his return and ordeal. According to the pastor, "The whole community, especially one of my Catholic brothers, was very sorry about what had happened to me. My Catholic brother wept with me for we were good companions. We loved each other as God loved us. . . . At night my wife arrived and treated my wounds." The pastor also left no doubt as to who had been responsible for the country's violence, noting, "The soldiers and the secret police do the killing. . . . They told me so when I was their prisoner. They said the order comes from Gen. Ríos Montt that they are free to kill whoever they want. . . . We are afraid of these new laws of Ríos Montt. . . . There are many dead in the roads, in the army camps, everyplace."[61]

The USCC denounced Guatemala's violence and regime in a letter to CEG president Bishop Próspero Penados del Barrio on July 28. In it, Minneapolis-Saint Paul archbishop John Roach lamented "the sorrowful situation which confronts much of the church in Central America and, in a special way, the church in Guatemala . . . the seemingly unrestrained violence visited upon the most defenseless and long-suffering of your people, the indigenous *campesinos* and villagers." Roach stated that Guatemala's violence and atrocities were visceral reminders of ties between both countries' Catholics and, like the CEG had, described the repression as a genocide. Roach assured Penados that the USCC would "do all we can to help alleviate the suffering of so many [and] urge the authorities of our country to do nothing to increase the irrational violence but to offer only such assistance as will enable the Guatemalan people themselves to resolve the conflict and heal the wounds of civil strife."[62]

Despite atrocities in the countryside and Ríos Montt's suspension of all civil liberties, embassy officials in Guatemala City reported that human rights conditions in the country were improving. In a lengthy cable on August 2, the embassy reported on a wide range of diplomatic concerns and speculated that "the [Guatemalan] government might not be able to survive beyond five years without external assistance." Embassy officials also attempted to explain how Guatemala's human rights conditions had improved when Ríos Montt had effectively nullified all vestiges of democracy. According to embassy officials, "Ríos Montt's stated intention for declaring a state of siege has been to bring order and legality to the country" and "states of exception exist in a number of countries without leading to bloodbaths, including Colombia, where there has been one for many years owing to insurgent activities." Further, they reasoned that "in a country such as Guatemala, one must first obtain some control of the situation and establish a base upon which a state of law and respect for human rights can be built. We believe that the Ríos Montt government has begun this process, a process that may help avoid the possibility of a bloodbath."[63] A State Department Bureau of Intelligence and Research analysis issued later in the month offered similar conclusions, reporting that the army's human rights abuses had decreased under Ríos Montt, who the bureau credited for the "improvement."[64]

How—and why—could embassy officials provide Congress and the State Department with demonstrably false claims about the Ríos Montt regime? First, embassy reports of massacres and violence during 1982 consistently blamed ORPA and the EGP with no mention of the army. This was a significant departure from similar Carter-era reports that offered relatively more balanced information. During the Reagan administration, however, Bureau reports avoided implicating the army at all costs. In many cases, cables detailing civilian massacres used ambiguous language like "alleged massacre" and "allegations of government violence."[65] In others, embassy officials claimed that guerrilla units had "been dressed in army uniforms" during an April massacre in the Petén and in Huehuetenango in July.[66] Finally, embassy reports classified massacres in places like Petanac and Finca San Francisco in Huehuetenango, Nebaj and San Juan Cotzal in Quiché, and Quimal in Chimaltenango as either "unverifiable" or entirely fabricated.[67] In one case, Chapin reported that a massacre in Choatalun, San Martín Jilotepeque, "did not happen; the story is considered to have been a deliberate fabrication and one that should not be permitted to serve the Marxist cause."[68]

Why embassy officials took this approach is less clear. No presidential directive or administrative correspondence explicitly ordered Chapin or other US embassy officials to deny that these massacres occurred or to absolve the military from its culpability. However, a broader perspective on US policy approaches to Central America in 1982 offers one explanation. Although US policymakers still regarded El Salvador as the bellwether of regional stability at the time, Guatemala was Central America's most populous country, had the region's highest per capita income, ports on both the Atlantic and Pacific coasts, and the Northern Transversal Strip's resource wealth. Administration officials also pointed to the URNG's formation as evidence of Cuban-Soviet support for a Marxist insurgency in Guatemala that justified reinstating military aid to the Ríos Montt regime.

Finally, Guatemala was one of the only remaining legal avenues for the Reagan administration to influence Central American politics. Congressional legislation like 1982's Boland Amendment prohibited military assistance to El Salvador, and newly elected Costa Rican president Luis Alberto Monge pledged that he would not intervene, or support any other state's intervention, in Nicaragua.[69] Further, Honduran president Roberto Suazo Córdova turned down the Reagan administration's request to train Salvadoran military forces in Honduras because of the two countries' ongoing territorial disputes over the Gulf of Fonseca.[70] Implicating Ríos Montt's forces in massacres and repression would severely constrict that avenue and validate concerns of congressional human rights advocates like House Appropriations Subcommittee chairman Clarence D. Long, who told the Council on Hemispheric Affairs that the Ríos Montt regime "would never get another penny" of US aid.[71]

Catholic newspapers across the United States condemned the Ríos Montt regime's violence when the Reagan administration would not. In Portland, Oregon's *Catholic Sentinel*, sociologist Frank Fromherz recounted his visit to a refugee camp in Chiapas, Mexico, where more than nine thousand Guatemalans had fled in just two weeks during the summer of 1982. Fromherz also noted that the Guatemalan army had begun a cross-border operation in which soldiers entered the camps disguised as refugees to gain information on indigenous communities and leaders. The military's incursion into Mexican territory would later include kidnapping refugees and forcibly returning them to Guatemala and, in some cases, murdering them in Mexico. Fromherz excoriated the State Department's refusal to implicate the Ríos Montt regime and asked readers, "Do you believe these stories? Have I been sold a bill of goods by the Cuban-Soviet conspirators? We must ask ourselves whether we in clear conscience can permit the United States government to allow the Guatemalan government to take whatever steps it wants to counter aggression, particularly if it involves support of such brutal regimes."[72] Elsewhere, Albany, New York, *Evangelist* columnist Daniel Halloran criticized the Reagan administration's decision to resume military aid to Guatemala, and fellow *Evangelist* columnist Sister Cecilia Holbrook lamented that "little is heard of the Indian people in Guatemala, of their struggle, their suffering and their cruel deaths because our nation prefers to present a picture of a changing government both there and in El Salvador."[73] Similar essays and letters appeared in the Dubuque *Witness, Denver Catholic Register,* and *Pittsburgh Catholic,* among others.[74]

Catholic newspapers also continued to report on local activists' efforts in dioceses across the United States. In December 1982, the Association of Pittsburgh Priests issued a statement in support of the burgeoning Sanctuary Movement, in which churches across the country harbored refugees from Guatemala and El Salvador. The group's press release stated that "sanctuary emphasizes God's compassion and justice even above civil law and in the case of refugees from Central America offers protection from . . . imprisonment, torture, and death from their own government . . . and offers them support in the face of the harassment of the U.S. government."[75] Other diocesan newspapers also highlighted local connections to Guatemalan refugees. In Dubuque, the *Witness* printed a story on Fay Hauer, a local woman who had recently adopted a young, orphaned Guatemalan girl while serving as a Maryknoll missionary in Guatemala City, and *Denver Catholic Register* reporter James Fiedler shared with readers the horrific conditions that Guatemalans faced in refugee camps along the country's border with Mexico.[76] Fiedler's reporting included photographs taken by Steve Stephen, a member of Englewood, Colorado's Saint Thomas More's Parish and, according to Fiedler, "Stephen's experiences in the refugee camps . . . are good reasons for parish groups and other organizations to invite him in as a speaker." Elsewhere, several Rochester, New York, diocesan leaders established a campaign for peace in Central America, and Portland, Oregon's Mount Angel Seminary hosted Fromherz for a talk on Guatemala as part of the seminary's lecture series on justice and peace issues.[77] Finally, the *Catholic Voice* offered readers news on multiple Guatemala-related events in the Omaha diocese, including meetings of the local Amnesty International devoted to the country's human rights abuses, as well as fundraising efforts by students at Roncalli High School, who raised money to support Christian Brothers education programs in Guatemala.[78]

Catholic newspapers also contributed to secular coverage of Guatemala. The *Des Moines Register* published excerpts of Maryknoll Father Ron Hennessey's letters to his sister and fellow Maryknoll missionary, Sister Dorothy Marie Hennessey, of Dubuque, Iowa. After the *Register* printed the excerpts on the front page of their September 12 edition, they were subsequently disseminated across the United States by the National Catholic News Service, a wire service for diocesan newspapers. In his letters, Hennessey recounted some of the army's atrocities in and near San Mateo Ixtatan, Huehuetenango, during July of that year. Hennessey's reporting included news that soldiers had decapitated ten people, forced one group of indigenous citizens to kill another, and murdered children. "The guerrillas are not the answer," he wrote to his sister, "[but] I know of no case where

"In More Than One Office a Picture of Che Guevara" / 133

they have indiscriminately killed. This is not to say they have *not* killed innocent people, but nothing like all the people of a village." On politics, Hennessey wondered whether "the United States knows what is going on here. I cannot tell if Ríos Montt is . . . really a genocidist in the guise of a Christian prophet." He concluded his letter with a plea that his sister "please use this and anything else I sent to try to get others to help stop this madness."[79]

The USCC continued to make its voice heard as well. After its letter to the CEG in July, the organization issued a press release on November 5 that questioned the Reagan administration and State Department's claims about Ríos Montt's human rights record. Roach wrote, "From a wide variety of independent sources, but especially from Church sources within Guatemala . . . we draw the inescapable conclusion that respect for human rights in Guatemala is at its nadir." The release also noted that while foreign policymaking was not in the USCC's purview, "the extensive data available to us suggests that the previous pattern of violations [was] . . . only becoming worse" and demanded that the administration make no determination on authorizing military assistance until more "substantial and verifiable proof" of human rights improvements was presented to US policymakers.[80]

Finally, John Paul II also expressed his outrage over human rights conditions in Central America, including Guatemala. During his homily at San Salvador, El Salvador's Metropolitan Cathedral on November 28, Bishop Gregorio Rosa Chávez announced that the pope would make an apostolic journey to Central America and Haiti in early 1983.[81] The announcement came after the pontiff's remarks about Central America during a homily earlier in the year when he expressed his sorrow over the "fratricidal struggle which stifles rightful, legitimate aspirations for a civilized, peaceful way of living together and an orderly progress."[82]

The Ríos Montt regime's predilection for violence also contributed to the Reagan administration's decision to snub the dictator on two occasions in 1982. The first occurred in October when, prior to attending a three-day retreat in Hot Springs, Virginia (home of Robertson's Christian Broadcasting Network, which had hosted telethons for Ríos Montt and Nicaragua's Contras), Ríos Montt requested a meeting with Reagan at the White House as part of an official state visit. National Security Council officials warned that "it would be a mistake for President Reagan to receive Ríos Montt at this time [because] . . . the President's prestige could be damaged. However low profile a meeting, it will receive publicity— probably adverse."[83] Administration officials subsequently advised that Reagan also avoid visiting Guatemala on his December trip to Latin America for the same reason and instead offered to hold a "working meeting" with Ríos Montt in San Pedro Sula, Honduras's airport. Both decisions infuriated the dictator: Chapin reported that during a cabinet meeting Ríos Montt "said that there was no reason for him to go to Honduras [and] that he would not bow down to President Reagan and that Guatemala could not live under the U.S. boot."[84] Ríos Montt was further incensed after his cabinet ministers voted that he should accept Reagan's invitation to meet in Honduras and told them that "now that you have voted, I will abide by your decision, but I will not accept any conditions and I will not bow down to the U.S. I shall go with total independence and as an honorable Guatemalan who will give nothing away."[85] According to Chapin, eight of Ríos Montt's ministers voted in favor of the meeting, with four against.[86]

Reagan met with Ríos Montt in a brief, intense encounter in San Pedro Sula's La Mesa Airport on December 4. A memorandum of the meeting noted that Ríos Montt "launched into a half hour monologue" about Guatemala's history and ethnic composition and the country's need for weapons, ammunition, and prefabricated buildings and told Reagan that "there were no refugees in Mexico but [only] persons affiliated with the guerrillas." He concluded by denouncing human rights groups' reports about the country's repression and violence and asked Reagan "for an unspecified amount of money to counter false communist propaganda" about his regime.[87]

Ríos Montt's tirade seemed to overwhelm Reagan, who told the dictator that he had given him "a lot to think about" and would take Ríos Montt's remarks under advisement. Reagan praised the half-hour meeting as "a useful exchange of ideas" to reporters. In a question and answer session with the press aboard Air Force One that evening, Reagan said that Guatemala had "some very real problems" and that, in his opinion, Ríos Montt had "been getting a bum rap" in the international media.[88] Despite Reagan's comments, Ríos Montt continued to criticize the administration even when it tried to placate the dictator. After the State Department announced that the US government had approved the sale of spare helicopter parts on a cash-and-carry basis on January 6, 1983, Ríos Montt announced that his regime could not afford to purchase the parts and instead demanded that the parts be given as "gifts" from surplus US stocks.[89] Ríos Montt's announcement caused Chapin to remark that both countries were "talking past each other" on diplomatic issues.[90]

Just one day after Ríos Montt's meeting with Reagan, members of the Guatemalan army's special forces unit, the Kaibiles, were dispatched to the village of Dos Erres in the Petén to search for guerrillas and, according to the CEH, "to kill the villagers."[91] According to witnesses, "around two in the afternoon on December 6, the massacre began when a boy of three or four months was thrown alive into a well" while other children were beaten with a hammer before also being thrown into the well. According to one witness, "when the well was almost full

Figure 6.1. President Ronald Reagan and General José Efraín Ríos Montt, San Pedro Sula, Honduras, December 1982. (Courtesy Ronald Reagan Library.)

some people were still alive and they tried to get out."[92] Kaibiles also committed multiple rapes, beat pregnant women until they miscarried, and systematically murdered the village's children, women, and men. In all, as many as 350 civilians were murdered between December 6 and 10 in one of the war's worst atrocities. One survivor testified that during the massacre, "[one] night the Kaibiles celebrated having killed everyone and the rapes they had committed and . . . that there was no one left."[93]

The Dos Erres massacre amplified human rights activists' condemnations of Ríos Montt and Reagan's meeting with the dictator in Honduras. In a press release, the Council on Hemispheric Affairs called Reagan's decision to meet with Ríos Montt "shameful" and noted that Guatemala's armed forces had killed thousands of citizens since the March coup. The Council also rejected Bosworth's congressional testimony for "justify[ing] savage Guatemalan government policies in antiseptic language and . . . [for] blam[ing] the victims" of massacres for their own torture, disappearance, or murder; it further noted "hundreds" of reports from the international press, foreign states, human rights NGOs, and the church that detailed the Ríos Montt regime's bloody repression.[94] Elsewhere, Monsignor Charles Owen Rice remarked in his *Pittsburgh Catholic* column that "one wonders that even an obtuse and heartless man such as President Reagan can talk as he did about . . . Ríos Montt as having a bum rap. . . . His isolation from reality was not disturbed by his recent swing through parts of Latin America in which he talked only to oppressors." Rice punctuated his comments with a recollection of a Mass he had attended at a Franciscan church in the colonial capital of Antigua Guatemala in 1974, and the "truckload after truckload of Indians and peasants" in attendance that day. "Have they been caught up in the slaughter?" he asked. "They may well have been because, for a Catholic priest, nun, or lay person to organize the people for anything means risk of life."[95]

United States Catholic leaders continued to condemn the Ríos Montt regime's human rights record and the Reagan administration's policy approach to Guatemala in 1983. In a letter to Secretary of State George Shultz on January 27, Oklahoma City archbishop Charles Salatka sharply criticized the administration for its lack of progress on identifying and trying Stanley Rother's murderers and ignoring Catholic clergy's reports of the Guatemalan army's crimes to facilitate resuming military aid to the country. Salatka wrote, "As an American citizen I protest this unwise decision. As an American Catholic Archbishop of an archdiocese which sponsors a mission in Guatemala and which has mourned the loss of one of our own Oklahoma priests murdered in Guatemala, I am saddened by this decision. As a member of the Roman Catholic hierarchy I am angered that the picture of the situation in Guatemala as spelled out in consensus by American and Guatemalan bishops apparently is given little or no credence by this administration."[96]

Salatka also criticized the Ríos Montt regime's failure to understand that Guatemala's chief problem was not Marxist insurgency but rather "a corrupt social system which does not give equitable treatment to the indigenous peasant peoples" and, he argued, produced the conditions for insurgency.[97] He concluded his letter by concurring with both the CEG's and USCC's description of Guatemala's crisis as an ongoing genocide and asked Shultz to reconsider the administration's decision to offer military aid to Ríos Montt.

Shortly after Salatka wrote his letter to Shultz, the Ríos Montt regime provoked a confrontation with the Holy See that threatened the pope's upcoming visit to Guatemala. On February 16, the Holy See's apostolic nuncio to Guatemala, Monsignor Oriano Quilici, presented Guatemalan foreign minister Eduardo Castillo Arriola with an official message from the pope that "expressed his profound sadness and preoccupation" over the fate of six men who had been condemned to death under Decree 46–82 and asked the regime for clemency. The intercession failed, and all six men were shot on March 3, just three days before the pope's scheduled arrival in Guatemala City. Quilici denounced the executions as a calculated affront to the pope and said that "the Vatican finds this deplorable act incredible because of its possible national and worldwide repercussions."[98] He also declined to answer whether the pope would cancel his visit to Guatemala. Regime officials exacerbated the situation by announcing that another fifteen executions were scheduled for the three days of the pope's Guatemalan visit. On March 5, a Council on Hemispheric Affairs press release stated that Ríos Montt ordered the executions to proceed after his advisers convinced him that clemency would be perceived as an act of capitulation and that "this argument helped to provide a rational buttress to Ríos Montt's predilection to treat the Pope's visit with contempt because of his distaste for Catholicism, born from his evangelistic fervor."[99]

The pope visited Guatemala as scheduled and made multiple references to the executions and Guatemala's human rights crises. When he arrived in Guatemala City on March 6, the pontiff remarked that "this nation has been several times, even in recent times, the scene of calamities that have sown death and destruction . . . and today continues to suffer the scourge or the struggle between brothers that causes so much pain."[100] The following day, he celebrated Mass for an estimated one million people and criticized the executions as the most grievous of sins and said that "when man's right to life is violated, a crime and a very grave offense to God is committed."[101] Later that day, he celebrated a second Mass for another estimated one million people in Quetzaltenango, where he challenged the regime to enact legislation that offered stronger human rights protection for the country's Mayan majority and instructed those in attendance to "organize associations for the defense of your rights."[102] The pope then returned to Guatemala City and left the country for Honduras the following day.

Politics and religion were central themes throughout the pope's visit to Central America. In Costa Rica, he addressed the Inter-American Court of Human Rights in San José and told the assembled judges that he endorsed the court's legal mission, that he encouraged people and states within the court's jurisdiction to seek its remedy in human rights disputes, and that states and transnational bodies needed "effective instruments . . . and, where necessary, appropriate sanctions" to enforce human rights laws and covenants.[103] The pope experienced a hostile reaction the following day in Nicaragua as Sandinista government supporters interrupted his homily in Managua and attempted to cut his microphone, prompting him to admonish the crowd and call for silence on multiple occasions. His remarks in Managua centered on his opposition to Catholic priests holding positions of political power in the Sandinista government and warned against "a charismatic, new, or popular church separate from the episcopal authority."[104] Finally, the pope recalled the Sermon on the Mount during his homily in San Salvador on March 6, referring to its adage "blessed are the peacemakers, for they shall be called children of God" and stated, "I see in this crowd and all of Central

America . . . immense desire for reconciliation and peace. You are rightfully thirsting for peace. A clamor raises from your chests and throats: we want peace!"[105]

The pope's visit to Guatemala took place amid a remarkable religious shift in the country. As historian Virginia Garrard-Burnett has noted, approximately 30 percent of Guatemalan Christians had converted to some form of evangelical Protestantism by the early 1980s, making Guatemala "the most Protestant country in all of Spanish-speaking Latin America."[106] Moreover, the millenarian aesthetic of Ríos Montt's particular *type* of evangelicalism, alongside the paternalistic bombast he had cultivated as a Pentecostal Sunday school teacher, were on full display during Ríos Montt's *discursos*, a series of televised sermons he delivered every Sunday evening. He often referred to the audience as family members and blamed the country's problems on a larger moral failing that could only be solved through a renewed national relationship with God. One example of this came in his discurso "los protagonistas del futuro," in which he stated, "If you and I know who God is, the world will realize the miracle of Guatemala and there will be no more war . . . there will be peace, security, and prosperity; that God hears us and that our testimony is the fruit of our compromise!"[107]

National identity was another frequent discurso topic. For Ríos Montt, a true, authentic sense of national identity, Guatemalidad, could not exist until the nation was born again as "una nueva Guatemala" that rejected foreign influences like yanquísmo and Marxism, which, he argued, had shaped what it meant to be Guatemalan. In his jeremiad "no hemos aprendido a ser Guatemala" he proclaimed, "Some wanted Guatemala to integrate communism, others [wished] that we were capitalists, some that we were nationalists, others fascists, in short, a collection of mentalities imported from all the latitudes, all the philosophies, all the political doctrines that rule the universe." The result, he claimed, was that "we are marginalized, but we marginalized ourselves. We have given ourselves to the imitation of other cultures without building on our own."[108] For Ríos Montt and other evangelists, wholesale massacres and attacks on Catholics were not just combat strategies but also spiritually necessary acts that would hasten Nueva Guatemala's creation by destroying the old.

However, the pope's ability to draw more than two million people in two cities on the same day was a clear indication that Catholicism remained alive and vibrant in Guatemala. Like their evangelical counterparts, many of Guatemala's Catholics also yearned for a new Guatemala but rejected the millenarian type of rebirth that Ríos Montt seemed eager to hasten. Instead, the pope reiterated what the CEG and individual missionaries like Woods, Schaffer, and Rother had advocated for years: a reformed Guatemala with solidarity and justice as its political and social anchors. That desire for reformation was central to the way that the

CEG and Catholic activists understood their mission in places like Guatemala. Furthermore, the pope's condemnation of the Ríos Montt regime's human rights abuses and repression during his homily in Quetzaltenango echoed other proclamations he made in El Salvador and Nicaragua and reinforced the human rights advocacy he had exhibited during his visit to Mexico in 1979.

The pope's visit also energized the CEG, which issued a series of messages after his departure. The first, published on March 9, congratulated Guatemalan Catholics and declared, "We have shown, perhaps as never in our history, that we are a noble, peace-loving people of deep Catholic roots." They also called on their parishioners to reify their faith to "free us from the . . . hatred, resentment, and injustice that are the principal cause of so much of the pain, sadness, death, and tears that our people have suffered."[109] A subsequent message issued in April asked all Guatemalans to use the pope's visit as "a reason for penance, forgiveness, and deep reflection" if they desired peace. Finally, a pastoral letter issued on June 5 condemned Guatemala's "progressive militarization," specifically the country's PACs that "almost exclusively" consisted of Mayan campesinos forced into service. The bishops' letter also took the unusual step of criticizing evangelical Protestant sects for their aggressive proselytization and warned that "Protestant aggressiveness could easily lead to a war of incalculable consequences."[110]

The regime also faced criticism from an unlikely source. On June 5, Brigadier General José Guillermo Echeverría Vielman took Ríos Montt to task in an open letter read on Guatemala's top-rated news program *Aquí el Mundo* that asked why the dictator had not yet set a firm date for national elections, demanded civilian presidential candidates and a return to constitutional democracy, criticized Ríos Montt's use of the presidency as a "pulpit" for his faith, and called for the military to withdraw from national politics.[111] United States Defense Department officials called the letter a "bombshell" because it was the first time that a senior military officer had broken ranks against the regime and "publicly articulated as his own those same complaints being made against Ríos by politicians of practically every hue. In effect, Echeverría has opened the way for other critics of Ríos to feel free to weigh in."[112] The Defense Department's prediction proved accurate: two days after Echeverría's appearance on *Aqui el Mundo*, Roberto Castañeda Felice, a prominent Guatemalan agricultural leader, called on US Embassy chargé d'affaires Paul Taylor to discuss Echeverría's letter and voiced his own concerns about the regime. Castañeda told Taylor that Victoria 82's offensives had destroyed the national economy and created political and social conditions that strengthened the URNG and that he, like Echeverría, believed that "the army had been running the country for too long and should return to its barracks for its own good."[113] Castañeda reported that "Echeverría spoke for a large group of Guatemalan army officers" who resented Ríos Montt's fervent evangelicalism and wanted a civilian government so that the military could devote its resources and energy to defeating the URNG. According to Castañeda, "several" officers had already met to organize a coup, specifically naming five officers that had already committed to ousting Ríos Montt.[114] Longtime MLN chairman Leonel Sisniega Otero added his voice to the military's criticisms later in the month and demanded an immediate return to civilian rule.

Ríos Montt faced another formidable challenge on June 28, when former junta member Colonel Francisco Gordillo denounced the regime on *Aquí el Mundo*, saying, "Ríos Montt thinks it was God who made him President, but in reality it was we who appointed him." Sisniega also appeared on the program and openly demanded a coup, calling Ríos Montt a "traitor" and "religious fanatic."[115] The following day, Ríos Montt's public relations director Gonzalo Asturías addressed the nation and announced, among other things, that the country's Supreme Election Tribunal would be convened on June 30 as the first step toward national elections the following year.[116] Asturías's address was the regime's last-ditch effort to remain in power: US Embassy officials estimated that 70 percent of the military's officer corps supported a coup and that by early July "only the guard of honor . . . part of the Mariscal Zavala Battalion [and] part of the Air Force, and [Interior Minister] Ruíz [are] willing to be counted as loyal" to Ríos Montt.[117] Military officials and cabinet members also believed that two members of Ríos Montt's church, Francisco Bianchi and Álvaro Contreras, exerted undue influence on policymaking decisions through their positions as presidential advisors.[118] Bianchi and Contreras later stated that Ríos Montt's standing with Guatemalan civilians had also fallen sharply because "public employees . . . had been threatened and annoyed by Ríos Montt's continuous exhortations to more honest services" and that "his blunt accusations of immorality or lack of patriotism" had alienated large segments of the population.[119] These challenges were too much for Ríos Montt to surmount, and senior military officials forced him to resign the presidency on August 8. His defense minister, General Óscar Humberto Mejía Victores, assumed power the following day.

José Efraín Ríos Montt left an indelible, bloody stain on Guatemala. The CEH recorded more than twenty-five hundred known massacres, disappearances, and instances of torture and forced displacement, among other types of human rights abuses, during 1982 alone, and approximately half of the abuses recorded by the CEH occurred during Ríos Montt's seventeen-month regime. Quiché and Huehuetenango continued to suffer the worst of the war's violence under Ríos Montt, with approximately 1,600 of 1982's known human rights abuses occurring in those two departments: in all, more than half of Guatemala's twenty-two departments experienced an increase in human rights abuses during the Ríos Montt regime. The regime also committed approximately two dozen human rights violations in Mexico as soldiers and death squads kidnapped and murdered Guatemalan refugees.

The regime's violence also complicated its relationship with the Reagan administration. Although many administration officials and policymakers viewed Guatemala as an important regional ally, they also understood the political backlash that such a relationship would incur. As a result, Chapin and other US Embassy officials took great care to obfuscate—and in some cases outright lie about—who had been responsible for massacres, torture, and other human rights abuses in Guatemala. This approach gave the administration the diplomatic cover necessary to portray Ríos Montt as a devoted anti-communist leader who, in Reagan's words, had suffered "a bum rap" from his critics, even as the dictator committed genocide in the Ixil region and authorized horrific massacres in places like Dos Erres, Santa Crúz Barillas, and Chajul, among many others. This approach, however, was largely a failure: Congress did not remove prohibitions on direct military aid to Guatemala until 1985, and Ríos Montt viewed the administration's refusal to grant him a state visit, as well as having to meet Reagan in Honduras, as personal and national insults. The administration's policy failures in Guatemala were emblematic of its broader regional challenges, particularly in Nicaragua and El Salvador, as US influence in Central America seemed to wane.

Finally, Catholics in both countries continued to bring Guatemala's human rights abuses to greater public attention during the Ríos Montt regime. Both the CEG and USCC issued sharply worded condemnations of the regime's violence during 1982 and, for the first time, publicly characterized the violence as a genocide. Likewise, Catholic leaders like Roach, Salatka, Penados, and Quilici—and the pope himself—all condemned the Ríos Montt regime's human rights abuses in letters and direct appeals to political officials in Guatemala and the United States. Although they were unable to bring Guatemala's violence to heel in 1982, Catholic activists and leaders alike were nevertheless a highly visible, influential voice in US policy debates that Reagan administration officials could not dismiss out of hand. Meanwhile, in Guatemala, seismic changes within the country's Catholic hierarchy during the Mejía regime gave the CEG its strongest voice in decades, just as the country attempted to return to civilian rule.

7

Burning the Devil

General Óscar Humberto Mejía Victores's rise to power was, in some ways, unsurprising. Like his predecessors, Mejía attended the Escuela Politécnica and took command of an infantry battalion in Jutiapa upon graduating as a second lieutenant in 1953. By 1963, Mejía, by then a major, led the army's Honor Guard and had returned to the academy as an instructor. He subsequently held command at the Felipe Cruz army base in Escuintla as a colonel during the 1960s before his promotion to brigadier general in June 1980. Mejía then served as Ríos Montt's minister of defense, a position that Laugerud, Lucas, and Guevara had all previously held and that was a de facto final step on the way to the country's presidency. Mejía, however, seemingly sought to distance himself from his predecessors in both word and deed. After assuming power on August 8, Mejía acknowledged that the country's evangelicals had enjoyed disproportionate political and social influence under Ríos Montt by virtue of his relationship with Francisco Bianchi and Álvaro Contreras and that under his rule neither the army nor the state would function as "the defender, custodian, or protector of the interests of a particular group, be they religious, economic, or political" in nature. He also struck a conciliatory tone in his remarks and emphasized his commitment to the "complex task" of bringing peace to the beleaguered country, claiming that "with faith in God and . . . my comrades in arms and with the assistance of the different social, economic, and political sectors, we will resume the path to peace . . . [as] neither winners nor losers, [but as] Guatemalans in a common and united effort of sacrifice, dedication and service."[1]

Mejía also rescinded some of the Ríos Montt regime's most stringent legal decrees. Decree 91–83, for example, mandated that citizens could no longer be arrested or detained without cause or a signed warrant, restored the writ of habeas corpus for citizens in custody, and reinstated the right of personal legal defense in court proceedings. Additionally, Decree 93–83, issued on August 11, abolished the extrajudicial special tribunals that the Ríos Montt regime had established and transferred to the country's Supreme Court. The decree also abolished the death penalty and ordered that anyone awaiting execution would have their sentence commuted.[2]

The new regime's ascendancy also coincided with major changes within the country's church. Guatemala's longtime archbishop, Mario Casariego, died in June 1983 and was succeeded by Prospero Penados del Barrio, who had served as bishop of the San Marcos diocese since 1971. Penados, who was also president of the CEG, led the Guatemalan church in a more assertive direction that condemned the country's violence, criticized regime members by name, and, most importantly, encouraged Guatemalans to vote in the country's long-awaited elections in 1984 and 1985. In turn, the Mejía regime denounced Penados and the CEG for a perceived lack of patriotism and for interceding in politics, especially in the wake of Franciscan Superior Father Augusto Ramírez Monasterio's murder in November 1983. At the same time, the two sides showed some signs of understanding and conciliation. From the beginning of his episcopate, Penados encouraged dialogue between the Guatemalan church and regime, a development that US Embassy officials monitored closely. Additionally, the regime's deputy public relations secretary, Ramón Zelada Carrillo, and interior minister, Gustavo Adolfo López Sandoval, publicly apologized to the CEG for their earlier comments about the bishops, and Mejía appeared at masses and church events. Penados, in turn, blessed the newly elected National Assembly at the body's request in 1984.

This chapter examines the Mejía regime's relationship with the CEG as the country returned to civil government in December 1985. The CEG was more assertive than ever during this period, most notably by repeatedly encouraging Guatemalans to vote in the country's elections for a new National Assembly in July 1984 and for president in November 1985. It did so despite Penados's personal misgivings about the country's political climate and his resignation from a multiorganizational coalition that sought a negotiated end to the war. United States Embassy officials in Guatemala City frequently reported on the status of the CEG's relationship with the regime while the Catholic press and activist groups continued to press for an end to Guatemala's violence and greater respect for Guatemalans' human rights. Embassy officials also reported multiple coup attempts and rumors of Mejía's rivals' plots against him. Amid this tension and violence, Mejía ceded the presidency to Marco Vinicio Cerezo Arévalo in 1986 after a legitimate election ended the country's military dictatorship.

In the United States, initial reactions to the Mejía regime were largely skeptical. On the afternoon of the August 8 coup, Vice President George H. W. Bush brushed aside the notion of an imminent improvement in US-Guatemalan relations under Mejía without demonstrable reforms and a decrease in violence.[3] Similarly, a State Department official told the *Baltimore Sun*, "After all, the officers who threw [Ríos Montt] out are the same ones who put [Mejía] in," and speculated that the coup would further destabilize the region.[4] This position, however, was not unanimous: the *New York Times* reported on August 10 that US ambassador to Guatemala Frederic Chapin had met with Mejía the previous day and received the general's assurance that he intended to restore civilian democratic rule, which a State Department press release described emptily as a "positive step" for the new regime.[5] The *Times* also reported that anonymous Reagan administration officials expected that US-Guatemalan relations would improve in Ríos Montt's absence, contradicting Bush's initial skepticism.

Other agencies and policymakers also commented on the new regime. A DIA cable dated August 15 described the coup as led by a "minority faction" of officers intent on prolonging the army's grip on the presidency and predicted that a countercoup would depose Mejía within ninety days.[6] Additionally, Maryland congressman Clarence Long expressed little confidence in Guatemala's new head of state. Long went as far as comparing Mejía to Ríos Montt, stating, "Ríos Montt at least kept up a front of sanctimonious sermonizing. [Mejía] gave me the impression of total ruthlessness."[7] In an interview with the *New York Times* after the coup, Long recalled he had been "very disappointed" with Mejía following a meeting with the dictator earlier in the year and that, in his view, Mejía did not "care about human rights for Guatemalan Indians." Long also told the *Times* that "we ha[d] better uses for our money" than military aid to Guatemala and that he was skeptical Mejía would have any positive effect on the country.[8]

Finally, some US Catholic newspapers and leaders were also wary of Mejía. J. Richard Ham, then an auxiliary bishop with the Saint Paul-Minneapolis Archdiocese, visited Guatemala in August and upon his return told reporters that while the prospect of Mejía—a Catholic himself—leading Guatemala "sound[ed] good for the Church," the country's violence was far too indiscriminate to assume that Catholics in the country would be safe.[9] Ham, who had been a missionary in Guatemala from 1958 to 1979, reported that during the trip his delegation had learned of a July 29 massacre that allegedly claimed 210 lives and that the number of military bases in the country had tripled in just four years.[10] The Dubuque *Witness* reported on Ham's trip and noted that he had been accompanied by a handful of US bishops, including Archbishop Charles Salatka of Oklahoma City, whose parish had suffered Rother's murder, and Bishop Raymond Lucker of New Ulm, Minnesota, whose parish sponsored the San Lucas Tolimán mission. Elsewhere, *Pittsburgh Catholic* columnist Monsignor Charles Owen Rice continued to excoriate Guatemala's dictators and the Reagan administration in equal measure by characterizing the former as "murderous generals" and part of a "rotten" government and warning the latter could, and presumably would, commit military forces to the region and create "another Vietnam" in Central America.[11] More succinctly, *Our Sunday Visitor* noted that "whether or not . . . Mejía Victores will be an improvement remains to be seen. Probably not," while an editorial in Portland's *Catholic Sentinel* warned that any US support for Mejía would be a "big mistake."[12]

Misgivings about the Mejía regime were well founded. In addition to the US Embassy's lengthy report on Guatemala's ongoing political violence, the Inter-American Commission on Human Rights recorded 635 disappearances in the country between August 8, 1983 and April 30, 1984, an average of more than two per day.[13] Additionally, army and PAC forces committed numerous atrocities during this period, including massacres, disappearances, and torture in Alta Verapáz, Chimaltenango, Quetzaltenango, Quiché, San Marcos, and Totonicapán, among other departments.[14] In October 1983, soldiers and PAC members tortured, raped, and murdered forty-eight people in Maricaj, Salac, and Setzapec, villages near Cahabón, Alta Verapáz. According to the CEH's report, the victims were killed in "groups of three or four. One of the victims managed to survive by jumping into the [Oxec] river before being shot."[15]

In other cases, families fleeing the violence were captured and murdered as suspected guerrillas. In San Juan Ixcán, Quiché, a one-week-old baby, María Chávez Matom, died from hunger as her family fled from the army and PACs.[16] Elsewhere, soldiers arrested and tortured Fernando Jom, a CUC member and community leader from Natilaguaj, Alta Verapáz, after he attempted to surrender to the army during the Mejía regime's amnesty for guerrillas. According the CEH, Jom was detained and tortured in Cobán while the rest of Natilaguaj's population was sent to what the CEH termed a "reeducation camp" in Sacol, Peten, before being sent to Acamal in northern Alta Verapáz. The CEH also recorded accounts of the army's role in child trafficking: in a passage that recalled the Rafel Videla dictatorship in Argentina, the CEH reported that "the soldiers selected twenty-five orphaned children under the age of ten and took them to an unknown destination. . . . In 1995, one of the children . . . returned to Natilaguaj as an adult and said that several of the children were given to other families abroad."[17]

Anti-Catholic violence also persisted under the new regime. On September 8, plainclothes police abducted Guadalupé Pérez Siguán, Domingo López Popol, and Román Reyes in Santa Lucia Cotzumalguapa, Escuintla. All three were catechists and had ties to Father Walter Voordeckers, who the army murdered in Santa Lucia Cotzumagalpa three years earlier.[18] Fourteen more people, including a ten-year-old child, were abducted on October 2. None of the victims were seen again. Two weeks later, an armed patrol opened fire on a group of Catholics in Escuintla and abducted Father José Alfredo García, tortured him, and abandoned him on the side of a road.[19] The PAC members also murdered seminarian Prudencio Mendoza García in Aguacatán, Huehuetenango, on December 15 and in Santa Cruz del Quiché murdered Carmen Manuel Xiquin Tzoc on Christmas Day and Paulino López on December 27. Both men had been members of Catholic Action; Xiquin was also a member of CUC.[20]

Mejía also clashed with Pope John Paul II. In early November, all fourteen CEG members traveled to Rome on an *Ad Limina Apostolorum* visit, where the pontiff met with the CEG and privately with each individual bishop.[21] During the larger meeting, Penados lamented Guatemala's endless violence as "a society torn apart" and reassured the pope that although the CEG had criticized Guatemala's politics, "all we are trying to do is proclaim Christ the Lord's Gospel in order to build a new Guatemala 'with new skies and new land where justice and love reign.'" The pope acknowledged "the long list of priests and members of religious families who, in their testimony of faith and service to their people, have shed their blood or been kidnapped." He then repeated the admonition he had made of the Ríos Montt regime during his homily in Quetzaltenango: "No one should ever again confuse genuine evangelization with subversion, and ministers must be able to carry their mission in safety and without hindrance."[22]

Mejía responded to the pontiff's remarks during a press conference on November 6 in which he reminded the pope that "soldiers have also died" in Guatemala and that "two months ago the Mexican missionary Antonio Pérez Luna and two Nicaraguans were arrested with extremist propaganda and were deported to Mexico, and we have proof that some religious have been siding with the left for a long time."[23] The following day, Franciscan Superior Father Augusto Ramírez Monasterio was abducted and murdered while on his way to Antigua Guatemala's Catedral de San José (Figure 7.1). Before his murder, Monasterio had been arrested and tortured by an army patrol in Chimaltenango, where he was negotiating the release of a suspected guerrilla from military custody.[24]

Monasterio's murder coincided with a series of changes within the CEG that shaped the organization's relationship with the Mejía regime. Casariego suffered a fatal heart attack on June 15, 1983, that newspapers reported was brought on by exhaustion coordinating Pope John Paul II's visit to the country earlier in the year.[25] His episcopate, which began in 1964, spanned nearly the entirety of the war to that point and had been shaped by both his staunch conservatism and refusal to condemn the dictatorship for its flagrant human rights abuses as he blessed army tanks with holy water and told reporters, "If I had not been a priest, I would have been a soldier."[26] Casariego also made the struthionine decision to deny that there had been *any* priests murdered in Guatemala, telling *Time* magazine that he knew of no such instances and claimed, "If you mix in politics, you get what you

Figure 7.1. Catédral de San José, Antigua, Guatemala. (Michael J. Cangemi.)

deserve."[27] By the time the *Time* story was printed in late 1982, ten priests had been murdered in the country since 1976.

Following Casariego's death, the pope named Penados as Guatemala's new archbishop on December 1, 1983. A native of Flores, Petén, Penados was ordained as a priest in 1951 and appointed as an auxiliary bishop in the San Marcos diocese in 1966. Penados was ordained as the diocese's titular bishop in 1971, a title he held until his elevation to archbishop. He was also elected president of the CEG in 1982 and served in that role until 1986. As CEG president, Penados endorsed the council's pastoral letters and public statements on the country's violence, inequality, and repression, which often contrasted sharply with Casariego's outlandish denialism and fealty to the military. Furthermore, as his remarks to the pope suggested, Penados had no intention of moderating his words or actions as archbishop and seemed poised to lead a more cohesive—and assertive—CEG.

After Monasterio's murder, US embassy officials in Guatemala City closely monitored the country's escalating church-state tensions. In a detailed cable to the State Department on November 15, Chapin reported that the country's papal nuncio, Monsignor Oriano Quilici, performed Monestario's funeral mass in Antigua Guatemala the previous week, with more than two hundred priests from across the country in attendance.[28] During the funeral, Quilici declared the slain pastor a "martyr for the faith." Chapin also provided the State Department with a description of subsequent actions taken by both the CEG and the Mejía government: on November 9, Mejía's foreign minister, Fernando Andrade, announced that Mejía had ordered an "exhaustive investigation" into the murder, which he attributed to "unknown assailants . . . attempt[ing] to destabilize the government." The CEG responded with an aggressive statement that was printed in the November 13 edition of the *El Grafico* newspaper, which declared that the Guatemalan church had weathered "the problem of a fanatical evangelical minority that used state resources and the government apparatus to gain its own ends far removed from the true ends of evangelization" and was fully prepared to confront the Mejía regime if necessary.[29]

Mejía's deputy public relations secretary, Ramón Zelada Carrillo, responded on November 17 and called the CEG's statement "anti-Guatemalan" and added, "The Bishops will have to explain their actions because these statements have harmed Guatemala and are part of a defamation campaign . . . adding fuel to the fire of subversion." Interior Minister Gustavo Adolfo López Sandoval also accused the CEG of intentionally denigrating the country with their "distressing, lamentable, and anti-patriotic" statements in a separate announcement that day. Chapin was uneasy about Guatemala's resurgent church-state hostilities, and in a November 17 cable to the State Department, he reported that attacks on Guatemala's Catholics had "reopened the struggle between Church and State" and that the ensuing tension was a considerable diplomatic obstacle.[30] Chapin tempered these remarks by asserting that Zelada and López's remarks had been simple bluster and stressed that the regime's hostile reaction toward the CEG and its statement demonstrated that the Guatemalan church was still an influential voice in national politics.

Chapin also levied a striking charge against the Guatemalan military and dictatorship. According to Chapin, the army, which had been interwoven with politics for decades, retained an understanding of Catholicism that was obsolete by 1983. The army, he argued, "seem unaware of Vatican II, which urged the Church to address contemporary social concerns; they seem unaware of the 1968 Medellín Conference and the 1979 Puebla Conference in which Latin American bishops resolved to work for political and social justice. The Guatemalan Church . . . cannot and will not return to a pre-Vatican II . . . role of the Church [functioning] as the bastion of rightist oligarchy. The [CEG] has made it clear that it, too, is on the side of reform: this inevitably brings it into conflict with a military which sees no necessity for such reform. Time is on the side of the Bishops, for the tide of change is running strong. The force of reaction cannot restrain it."[31]

Chapin was correct. Guatemala's Roman Catholic Church had changed since the 1960s; Guatemala's dictatorship had not. The social activism and ministry that foreign priests like Miller, Rother, Schaffer, and Woods had practiced was part of a deeper shift in political and religious awareness that, for better or worse, changed the way that many Catholics understood their faith. For them, San Lucas Tolimán's coffee cooperative, San Miguel Ixthuacán's wood-frame houses and potable water systems, Huehuetenango's schools, and Santiago Atitlán's Tz'utjuil Bibles and masses were not simply community projects. They were instead examples of a new type of Catholicism in action, examples of the Gospels' teachings at the most local level. Just as importantly, they were collaborative works in which foreign-born missionaries were partners rather than patrons or overseers and were launched as evangelical Protestantism made significant demographic gains in Guatemala. By 1983, the entitlement and deference that Mariano Rossell y Arellano and Mario Casariego expected from clergy and laity had become a relic and, as Chapin astutely noted, was not going to return. Guatemalan Catholicism and, more importantly, many of Guatemala's Catholics—wherever they were from—had changed.

As Guatemala's Catholics changed, the country's army and its dictatorship remained stagnant. Repression and violence had become inextricably woven into Guatemala's political, religious, and social fabrics by the end of 1983: the CEH recorded almost six thousand known human rights abuses—an average of two per day—between 1976 and 1983. These acts fueled and were fueled by the country's extreme right and left alike, leaving a more centrist political path unviable throughout the 1970s and early 1980s. Furthermore, the army and its dictatorships used the country's violence as a pretext to commit even more acts of violence against civilian men, women, and children, the overwhelming majority of whom were poor and Mayan. This had been especially the case during the Lucas and Ríos Montt regimes, as neither saw a difference between pacification and genocide.

Mejía, Pellecer, and Penados met in Guatemala City on November 28. Following the meeting, Mejía informed Chapin that the meeting had been entirely cordial and that he and the bishops had come to a "complete understanding" on their differences. Additionally, Andrade told the US Embassy's chargé d'affaires, Richard Graham, that Mejía "was almost apoplectic" when he had learned of Monasterio's murder and immediately visited Quilici to offer his condolences personally. Andrade also flatly denied the regime had been involved in any way and told Graham that "they would have to be stupid beyond belief . . . to have deliberately ordered the . . . priest killed."[32]

While Mejía claimed the meeting resulted in a complete understanding between both sides, Penados did not. In a post-meeting press conference, Penados said that although the discussions had been "positive," Zelada and López were "a pair of liars" and that questioning the CEG's patriotism was a "slanderous" offense. Penados also downplayed the extent of any progress between the CEG and Mejía following the meeting. He told reporters that he and Pellecer briefed Mejía on the report that the CEG presented the pope during their visit to the Vatican but would not comment on the rest of the meeting.[33] Both Zelada and López publicly apologized for their comments on December 12. According to a US Embassy report, Zelada said that "'as a good Catholic and with humility' he accepted the epithet of 'liar' that . . . Penados had placed upon him."[34] In turn, López claimed that he had "spoken without thinking" and that nobody in the Mejía regime questioned the bishops' patriotism. He also offered to apologize to the bishops in person.

On the same day that Zelada and López apologized to the CEG, seminarian Prudencio Mendoza García was murdered in Aguacatan, Huehuetenango, by a PAC member. In a statement printed in the December 21 edition of *Prensa Libre*, the bishops stated that they shared the Huehuetenango Diocese's pain following Mendoza's "assassination," while army spokesman Lieutenant Colonel Edgar Djalma Dominiquez claimed that the shooting had been an accident but referred to Huehuetenango as a center of subversive activities in the country.[35] The following morning, Maryknoll Father Donald Haren was arrested at an army checkpoint in La Libertad, Petén, after a hand grenade was purportedly found in his car during a search. According to a US Embassy telegram to the State Department, Quilici had informed the embassy that after his detention Haren was interrogated and released when army officers "eventually decided he was harmless."[36]

Haren's detention sparked another clash between the Mejía regime and the CEG. After Haren's release, Bishop Jorge Mario Avila del Aguila said in a press release that the grenade "was obviously placed" in the car and that the responsible party had attempted to "calumniate the Church." Although Avila did not directly implicate the regime or army, he intimated that either they or guerrillas were to blame.[37] In response, Mejía maintained that the army had been justified in searching Haren's vehicle, as the area had experienced a recent spike in violence between the army and guerrillas, and that Haren "had no good reason to be travelling through places where military clashes had recently taken place . . . that had resulted in casualties."[38] Mejía added that he had no intention to defame or slander any priest but rather issued his remarks to set the record straight.

Penados's actions following Haren's arrest and Monasterio and Mendoza's murders showed that he still sought reconciliation and better relations with the Mejía regime but would also continue to criticize it when necessary. In a January 1984 interview with *Prensa Libre*, Penados explicitly stated that he welcomed dialogue with Mejía to find a lasting solution to the country's violence. Penados said that "if [the church and CEG] are in continual communication with the authorities, much harm and danger can be avoided: abuses against priests or other[s], for example." Penados also said the church was spiritually obligated to defend human dignity since "all are created in the image of God" and stressed that when the CEG and priests denounced the country's human rights abuses, they did so to encourage peaceful solutions to Guatemala's crises rather than ascribe blame to any individual or organization. Penados also articulated his vision for the Guatemalan church's role in national politics, calling it an interventionist mission in which the church served as "the messenger of peace and love on behalf of Christ."

Penados also endorsed and joined the National Peace Commission in March 1984. The commission was composed of representatives from the country's universities, labor unions, religious denominations, state officials, and other groups and was intended to facilitate dialogue and negotiations for ending the war. Other commission members, most notably University of San Carlos rector Eduardo Meyer Maldonado, welcomed Penados's decision to join because, they believed, his presence lent the group legitimacy.[39] Penados, however, quickly grew disillusioned with the commission because, according to a US Embassy report, "he discovered that the Commission does not have the necessary support to reestablish [sic] peace and tranquility in the country... that the level of violence [had] increased recently and that human rights [were] being totally forgotten."[40] He also rejected the regime's "insistence" that any public denunciations of human rights abuses be approved in advance by the regime and resigned from the commission in May.[41] Meyer also withdrew from the commission, as did the Guatemalan Press Association and the country's Evangelical Alliance. These withdrawals left the commission composed of various members of the business community and regime.

As the commission sputtered during the spring of 1984, Mejía endured sharp public criticism from a seemingly unlikely source. In February, retired Brigadier General Benedicto Lucas García, who had served as army chief of staff during his brother Fernando's dictatorship, assailed Mejía in a wide-ranging interview with *Prensa Libre* that US Embassy officials described as Lucas's attempt to "chip away" at the regime. During the interview, Lucas explicitly questioned the regime's stability and referred to Mejía's recent decision to appoint his chief of staff, Colonel Rodolfo Lobos Zamora, to the newly created position of deputy head of state as evidence of a "grave crisis" within the regime. Lucas claimed some members of the regime believed a coup was possible "at any moment" and that Lobos's reassignment was a "preventative measure" if Mejía was overthrown.[42] Lucas claimed that talk of another impending coup swirled throughout the country and that while he could not "take a position for or against [another] coup," he believed that a return to democracy was the country's most urgent priority. Lucas also endorsed a legislative assembly with broad powers and general elections before the end of the year and, most importantly, called on the army to extricate itself from all political functions.

Reaction to Lucas's interview was swift and sharp. A Guatemalan army press spokesman, Lieutenant Colonel Edgar Djalma Dominguez, said that Lucas's information about the regime's stability "was coming from Radio Havana or the Voice of Nicaragua" and suggested that Lucas's statements "should be analyzed by a psychologist, not by the army."[43] At the US Embassy, Charge d'Affaires Paul Taylor reported that while Lucas had enjoyed a sterling professional reputation as a consummate soldier, he was using his influence to foment disorder among the army's officers to provoke a coup. Taylor speculated that Lucas sought revenge against the regime for his forced retirement in 1983 and that Lucas's refusal to explicitly condemn any potential coup was, in fact, his way of legitimizing one.

Other US agencies warned that Lucas had enough support within the army to launch a successful coup in a matter of weeks. In a cable to the State Department dated February 21, 1984, the DIA reported Lucas had the backing of multiple officers in both the country's army and air force, several of whom had been instrumental in the coup that overthrew Ríos Montt coup the previous year. Chief among them was Brigadier General Héctor Gramajo, who the cable described as "opportunistic" and having an "insatiable appetite for power." The cable, however, also reported that while a coup might be successful in the short term, its chances for long-term success were, at best, dim. Following his discharge from duty the previous year, Lucas had retired to a ranch in Poptún, which the DIA characterized as "a small army village" whose warm reception of Lucas had skewed his perspective.

The cable also showed a clear frustration with Guatemala's right-wing leaders, who the DIA clearly blamed for the country's woes. In one particularly frank passage, DIA officials argued Guatemala's violence had "result[ed] in the government having to spend its energies and limited resources toward stopping rightist idiots from destabilizing a process that, if left alone, would bring about elections and a civilian head of government" and specifically named Lucas and recalcitrant ultrarightist Leonel Sisniega Otero as two of the "idiots" impeding elections and democratic reforms. Derisively referring to Lucas as "Benny," the cable noted that Lucas kept "a virtual zoo of various animals" on his ranch and speculated that "if there was some way to keep Lucas and . . . Sisniega on the farm talking to the animals, a la Dr. Doolittle, and out of the quest for power, Mejía's chances of pulling off elections would be more probable."[44]

Despite the DIA's concern about a potential Lucas family dynasty in Guatemala, the anticipated coup never materialized. In fact, US policymakers' concerns about the coup seemingly vanished as quickly as they appeared: no agency or administrative documents mention the purported coup after March 1984. Those sparse responses nevertheless offer two valuable insights into US officials and policymakers' views on Guatemala's political crises and leadership throughout the late 1970s and early 1980s. First, multiple US ambassadors and embassy officials, as well as agencies like the CIA, the DIA, and the State Department, had issued a litany of reports and warnings of impending coup attempts dating to the Lucas regime. As early as 1978, then US ambassador Davis Boster cast doubt on Lucas's long-term prospects for remaining in power after the bus fare protests in October of that year, while Lucas's vice president, Villagrán, spoke openly about overthrowing Lucas in 1979. United States officials reported similar rumors in 1980, 1982, and 1983 and again in 1985 and 1988.[45] While some of these rumors proved accurate, most proved overstated or largely unfounded, fueling US officials' lack of urgency in responding to the Lucas rumors in 1984.

Second, the DIA's use of the diminutive "Benny" when referring to Lucas and of terms like "rightist idiots" reflected US officials' longtime perception of Guatemala's political leaders. In some cases, US praise for Guatemalan leaders was blunted by personal observations that were irrelevant and, at times, demeaning. In his diary, for example, Carter referred to Laugerud as "an impressive man" but also as a "Norwegian, whose father came to Guatemala as a sailor, got drunk, the ship left him, he married Laugerud's mother and is still living there."[46] At other times, US policymakers' observations were far sharper and more venomous. Boster's successor, Frank Ortiz, did not hide his antipathy for Lucas when he caricatured the dictator as a plodding buffoon in cables to the State Department. Nor did he hide it in his personal recollections, as noted in chapter 4. On the back of a photograph of Ortiz presenting his diplomatic credentials to Lucas in 1979, he referred to Lucas as "the killer president of Guatemala" in a handwritten inscription (Figure 7.2). Likewise, Embassy officials depicted Ríos Montt as a megalomaniacal and increasingly unstable religious fanatic who both believed that God had led him to the presidency and as little more than another stooge serving at the pleasure of the army's high command.[47] Irrespective of their accuracy, comments like these perpetuated US officials' views of Guatemala's successive dictators as ineffective and, in some cases, inept leaders with political feet of clay that oversaw the disappearance, murder, and torture of tens of thousands of their fellow citizens.

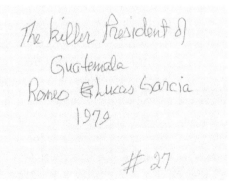

Figure 7.2. Inscription by Ambassador Ortiz on back of the photograph shown in Figure 4.1.

Penados maintained close contact with US Embassy officials during the spring of 1984. He met with the embassy's chargé d'affaires, Paul Taylor, in late May to discuss Guatemala's political climate and the National Assembly elections scheduled for July. Taylor reported that Penados was "generally pessimistic" about the country's political future due to what he described as "an inflexible military mentality" that made dialogue impossible. He also told Taylor that while he and the CEG would endorse the elections and encourage Guatemalans to vote in a forthcoming pastoral letter, he personally believed that "most people were . . . uninterested in the constitutional issues to be decided." Notably, Penados also told Taylor the letter did not include specific criticisms of human rights abuses in order to avoid confrontation with the regime. In his summary of the meeting, Taylor reflected on Penados's demeanor and reported that "throughout this conversation he avoided any expression of bitterness or impatience. He did, however, come across as surprisingly discouraged and frustrated. Possibly his spirit reflects the physical toll of recent extensive dental surgery. In any case, he is proceeding cautiously as he begins what . . . could be a long term of office as leader of the Roman Catholic Church in Guatemala."[48]

During his meeting with Taylor, Penados said he was avoiding conflict with the regime, focusing instead on his pastoral duties and seeking ways to introduce gradual improvements in the country's social inequalities. This included utilizing Catholic rites to push for social and political change, as he did when he led a special mass at the Metropolitan Cathedral on June 2 to pray for the release of Guatemala's disappeared. During his homily, Penados lamented the "common feeling of pain" that so many Guatemalans shared grieving for their missing loved ones and reiterated that the country wanted "the peace of brotherhood, not the peace of the cemetery."[49]

Six days later, the CEG issued a lengthy pastoral letter that addressed several of the country's ongoing crises. The bishops called for immediate solutions to Guatemala's violence, for an end to disappearances, torture, and forced displacement, and for dismantling the country's PACs. They praised the upcoming National Assembly elections as a sign of progress toward a return to civil government and "rejoice[d] deeply and greet[ed] with optimism this opportunity that is presented to Guatemalans at the present time." They also reminded future assembly members that establishing a new national constitution would be among their most important tasks and that the new constitution could be legitimate only if it specifically protected economic, political, and social rights for all citizens. The bishops offered a long list of those rights, including civil rights like freedom of expression and movement, economic rights like a just wage for workers, and greater cultural protection for the country's indigenous majority. They warned that "if these mechanisms are not established . . . we will return to the continual mockery of constitutional principles that has taken place in our country's recent history."[50]

In comments printed in the June 12 edition of the daily newspaper *La Razón*, López praised the pastoral letter as "generally positive" and acknowledged that the PN, which he oversaw in his role as the country's interior minister, had certainly broken the law in the past. According to López, it was "certain that many National Police have violated the law, but they have been subjected to sanctions; some have been discharged, and others, depending on the acts committed, have been arraigned in court."[51] While López's claims about internal accountability were dubious at best, his acknowledgment that the police had committed crimes was notable. USAC rector Eduardo Maldonado Meyer also praised the letter and urged all Guatemalans to "read, study, and analyze" the letter and lauded the church's commitment to human rights advocacy.

Two days later, *El Grafico* reported that Monsignor Rodolfo Quezada Toruño told Catholics in the Zacapa and Chiquimula departments that they were obligated to "vote for change" on July 1 if they wanted the violence to stop.[52] Finally, Penados ordered all Catholic churches in the country to distribute leaflets during the weekend of June 23–24 that "called upon all Christians to exercise their right to elect and decide the destinies of their country and their own community." The pamphlet also proclaimed that citizens had a right to elect their leaders, and asked those elected on July 1 to "complete their work honestly, efficiently, and wisely before God and history."[53]

The 1984 elections were a pivotal moment in Guatemalan history. The army did not intervene in the voting process, and almost two million Guatemalans went to the polls on July 1. Seventeen political parties won assembly seats, with the centrist Unión del Centro Nacional winning twenty-one of the eighty-eight seats and the center-left Christian Democratic Party winning an additional twenty. Christian Democratic candidates dominated the municipal elections, winning 142 of the 322 contests nationwide. They were most successful in the departments that had experienced the greatest violence and anti-Catholic repression since 1978, winning sixty of eighty-six municipalities in the departments of Quetzaltenango, Huehuetenango, and Quiché, and Sololá.[54] On the heels of their strong showing, the party nominated Marco Vinicio Cerezo Arévalo for the 1985 presidential election.

The assembly prioritized human rights in a new constitution that would be ratified the following year. Article I decreed that the state's primary organizational function was to protect the individual for the common national good, and Article II declared the state's primary duty was to safeguard its citizens' rights to "life, liberty, justice, security, peace, and development integral to personal development."[55]

The constitution then articulated a broad range of civil, economic, legal, and social rights to be protected under federal law that included specific protections for Mayan communities, women, and children. In addition to codifying human rights, the new constitution also established laws governing the country's electoral process and defined the roles of the government's executive and legislative branches. The constitution's ratification allowed the presidential election to proceed the following year.

As the assembly completed the ratification process, a US Embassy investigation of alleged human rights abuses in Baja Verapáz yielded surprising results. On June 30, Embassy officials traveled to the town of Rabinal to investigate reports of disappearances and mutilated corpses along the roadside in recent years. The officials met with two local priests who reported that while human rights abuses had been rampant in the area in the past, conditions had "improved markedly" since November 1983. One of the priests noted that "the army was behaving much better toward the civilian population" but also that further improvement was needed.[56]

In the United States, the Catholic press continued reporting on Guatemala's violence and political conditions and served as a means of contact for local activists and groups. In early 1984, the National Catholic News Service printed a page-length story on hunger in Guatemala as part of a special insert titled "Faith Today" that was distributed in diocesan newspapers across the country. It included firsthand accounts from Bishop Lucker and remarks from Monsignor John Egan of the Chicago Archdiocese's Office of Human Relations and Ecumenism, who described missions like San Lucas Tolimán's as a "vision of unity and of responsibility [that] reach[ed] beyond those who are gathered for a particular Mass in a particular place."[57] Clearly written to stir readers to action, the article appealed to Catholic readers specifically as Catholics by linking mission work to spiritual obligation.

In other cases, diocesan newspapers continued to highlight local ties to Guatemala. In February, the *Catholic Messenger* included a story on Sister Miriam Hennessey, a Davenport native who had served as a missionary in Guatemala since the mid-1970s. Hennessey was also a member of the Quad Cities Religious Task Force on Central America, an ecumenical group that coordinated relief packages to Guatemala and public events in the Quad Cities area while also "organizing sanctuary for the few who need it here."[58] The following week's edition recounted the moral transformation within John Volpe, a Davenport man who had resigned his job with the Rock Island Arsenal, a weapons manufacturer. Volpe attended a "peace seminar" with his wife in late 1983 and began to question the morality of his occupation after speaking with a nun at the seminar. According to the article, Volpe and his family attended other meetings and viewed films about Central America's violence in the ensuing months, but, according to his wife, "when we found out that arms found in Guatemala[n] villages had a return address of the Rock Island Arsenal, it really sank in."[59] After being arrested during a peace demonstration at the arsenal in September, Volpe quit his job as a matter of conscience.

Not all local ties were positive. In May, the *Pittsburgh Catholic* reported on two area families who had had relatives kidnapped by repressive governments. The article included the story of Jorge Rosal Paz, the nephew of a Plum Boro family. Eyewitnesses reported that Rosal had been forced into a Jeep at gunpoint near his farm outside Guatemala City the previous August. According to his aunt, Rosal was married and had two children, including a son born after his abduction.[60] The article included information on how readers could address letters to Mejía and to the Guatemalan ambassador to the United States, Jorge Zelaya. The newspaper's editorial staff printed a statement in the edition that asked readers to submit letters to Mejía and Zelaya as well.

Columnists and editorial staffs also continued to bring attention to Guatemala. In addition to the *Pittsburgh Catholic*'s editorial plea for letters supporting Jorge Rosal, Monsignor Rice reflected on the country's upcoming National Assembly elections in his weekly column on June 29. Recalling his visit to the country in 1975, Rice wrote that at the time, he had "commented that a phony election had been held the preceding July; now another phony election is scheduled this July." He explained the circumstances surrounding Monasterio's murder and the United States' deep connections to Guatemala's violence, including the CIA's overthrow of Árbenz in 1954. Rice lamented that little had seemed to change in Guatemala since his visit a decade earlier, stating, "I noted [in 1975] that Guatemala with its natural riches might work out its problems if we were to leave her alone. I expressed no optimism then and express none now."[61] Elsewhere, Catholic college newspapers also included editorials and essays about Guatemala, including the Gonzaga *Bulletin*, Notre Dame's *Observer*, and DePaul University's *DePaulia*.[62]

Ultimately, US policy positions toward Guatemala were somewhat mixed by the end of 1984. On the one hand, State Department officials were encouraged by the election's success and noted that the election had bolstered the country's international image, which, they reported, Mejía sought to leverage for additional foreign military aid to continue fighting the war. A CIA intelligence analysis from November noted that the army's neutrality and noninterference had drawn "widespread praise" and that the regime had successfully resumed diplomatic ties with Spain, which had been broken following the Spanish Embassy massacre in 1980. On the other hand, the analysis noted that Mejía and Andrade, the regime's chief policy architects, continued to pursue a regional foreign policy that drew

Guatemala closer to Mexico than to the United States. This was due in large part to the countries' shared refugee crisis and the United States' attempt to influence the Contadora Group negotiations, a joint initiative of the Colombian, Mexican, Panamanian, and Venezuelan governments to negotiate peaceful settlements to wars in Guatemala, El Salvador, and Nicaragua. The agency predicted that the Mejía regime would attempt to use its position to leverage concessions from the United States by playing the role of a "reluctant partner" in regional crises.[63]

While violence had apparently subsided in places like Rabinal, it persisted elsewhere in 1985. In March, the press reported that approximately thirty people had been murdered in Patzún, Chimaltenango, during January and that the army had been responsible for several of the killings. Additionally, the French press agency Agence France-Presse reported that five hundred soldiers had occupied the town of Xeatxan and killed forty campesinos. Embassy officials visited interviewed witnesses, including local Catholic priests, in March about their experiences. Despite a litany of accounts of disappearances, murders, death threats, and other human rights abuses, new US ambassador to Guatemala Alberto Piedra concluded, "There is no concurrence as to [the] identity, number or dress of those responsible. But it appears that some group did occupy . . . Xeatxan . . . and some persons were killed. In short, the facts are unclear and we are unable to ascertain who the responsible parties were."[64] Other notable instances of violence during early 1985 include the murder of retired General Manuel Sosa and his three-year-old grandson in Guatemala City on March 31, torture and disappearances in Chimaltenango in April, and the torture and murder of Grupo Apoyo Mutual member Hector Gomez Calito in Guatemala City.[65]

In the United States, Catholics' activism continued to take multiple forms throughout 1985. In January, the Davenport Diocese's Lay Council unanimously passed a resolution in support of the Sanctuary Movement. The council's resolution noted in part that "in these times of extreme suffering of our brothers and sisters in Central America, [we] implore the United States government to make an exception and offer these refugees temporary political asylum." The council argued that "the reason [refugees] are considered illegal is that the United States has what are called 'good' relations with El Salvador and Guatemala, and it is a diplomatic insult to those with whom we have 'good' relations if at the same time we listen sympathetically to their citizens when they knock on our doors seeking refuge from brutal treatment at home. . . . In such circumstances, it is a moral obligation to provide refuge, or sanctuary."[66] Likewise, twenty-one members of the Peace and Justice Commission of Saint Thomas Aquinas and Catholic Student Center in Ames, Iowa, wrote a letter to the *Witness* calling on local Catholics to seek all possible forms of nonviolent protest to prevent area refugees from being deported back to Guatemala and El Salvador and to request support for the Overground Railroad's efforts to bring refugees to Canada.[67] Another *Witness* reader, Robert Roethig, asked readers to consider donating to or volunteering with the Iowa City, Iowa, Latin American Human Rights Advocacy Center to "assist *Los Desaprasidos* [sic] of Guatemala."[68]

Dioceses across the country also continued hosting local events to raise awareness about conditions in Guatemala. In Pittsburgh, the Thomas Merton Center and Saint Raphael Elementary School hosted public talks from Garth Cheff and Betsy Larson, two missionaries who had recently spent five months in Guatemala, El Salvador, Honduras, and Nicaragua, and discussed the violent realities facing local catechists and campesinos, while the *Pittsburgh Catholic* continued imploring readers to write Ambassador Zelaya in Washington to demand the safe release of Jorge Rosal, who had been missing for nearly eighteen months by April 1985.[69] In Dubuque, Ron Hennessey discussed his twenty years of mission work in Guatemala with parishioners at churches across the diocese during the summer, and multiple churches in Rochester held daily masses and liturgical readings, educational programs, and community events that promoted greater public awareness of Central America's human rights crises.[70] Public talks, food and medicine drives, and public demonstrations of solidarity occurred in many other dioceses throughout 1985, including Fall River, Massachusetts, Little Rock, Arkansas, and Portland, Oregon, among others.[71]

In Guatemala, rumors of an impending coup arose again in April 1985 amid rising discontent over the country's economic woes. According to US Embassy officials, impending tax increases were an unpopular necessity and the country's currency, the quetzal, had lost value in recent months. These conditions allowed other internal tensions within the regime to rise to the surface, as some of the country's junior officers called for a coup and dissolution of the National Assembly and some senior officers' business investments suffered during the economic downturn.[72] Although neither plot was ultimately launched, they underscore the instability that swirled around the presidential elections in 1985.

Public discontent with the regime also swelled during 1985. In September, the DIA reported that Guatemalan business leaders, with the backing of some retired army officers, had planned a large-scale demonstration to demand the resignations of Mejía and Lobos. The demonstration's organizers condemned Mejía's recent decision to increase municipal workers' salaries and his call for a similar increase in the private sector, despite business owners' preference to increase consumer prices instead. The report also noted that army units in the capital had been placed on alert and that air force leadership had discussed possible scenarios for succession if Mejía resigned.[73]

Amid the coup attempts and public calls for Mejía's ouster, the CEG issued a pastoral letter about the upcoming election on September 14. The bishops praised the newly ratified constitution and the previous year's successful assembly election as positive steps toward a stable peace. More broadly, they viewed these steps as proof that "the spiritual reserves of our people are still strong and capable enough to enable them to advance along the way of dignity and freedom."[74] Finally, after reiterating that voting was a civic and moral responsibility, the letter concluded with an eloquent statement of hope for the future. The bishops wrote, in part, "We should struggle with all our strength to reject every type of violence. We Guatemalans already have a long and painful awareness that violence, whatever its form, leads nowhere and builds nothing. On the contrary, violence destroys everything and impedes the progress of peoples. . . . We hope that the Guatemalan people who on multiple occasions have demonstrated their immense wisdom, courage and responsibility, will show forth their will to bring together every living force in Guatemala in order to build a better homeland."[75] The pastoral letter was the CEG's final public statement prior to the election on November 3.

The URNG also issued a final preelection statement on October 1. The organization's leaders maintained that revolutionary changes were the only viable solution to Guatemala's economic and social problems and warned that whoever won the election "would have to continue facing the insurgence of the grassroots, and the [URNG] has committed itself to our people and to international solidarity not to give up its struggle till it obtains a true democracy, national independence and, finally, our integral development."[76] Despite this warning, State Department officials were largely unconcerned with the prospect of violence at the polls or URNG interference in the electoral process and predicted that any election day problems would "remain within tolerable bounds" and would not be serious enough to discredit the result.[77]

On November 3, 1985, almost two million Guatemalans went to the polls and cast their ballots for one of eight presidential candidates. The Christian Democratic Party (DCG) candidate, Marco Vinicio Cerezo Arévalo, won a 38 percent plurality and forced a runoff vote, scheduled for December 8. A group of twenty observers, led by Indiana senator Richard Lugar, saw no irregularities in the voting process and concluded that the vote had been "fairly and efficiently conducted." A second observer group, led by the Washington Office on Latin America, called the election "as free as it could be, given Guatemala's long history" of rigged votes, and cautiously predicted that the election would be "the first step in Guatemalan progress toward democracy."[78] Cerezo won the runoff handily on December 8 over Jorge Carpio Nicolle, taking nearly two-thirds of all ballots cast (Table 7.1 and Table 7.2). In a moment that would have been unimaginable just three years before, Carpio publicly congratulated Cerezo on his victory and pledged his support "for the good of Guatemala. . . . We will applaud when you are right and criticize when you make mistakes. God save Guatemala and may Guatemala be beginning a period of a series of democratic regimes."[79]

Table 7.1. Guatemalan presidential election, first-round results, November 3, 1985			
Candidate	Party/Parties	Vote Totals	Vote (%)
Marco Vinicio Cerezo Arévalo	Democrática Cristiana Guatemalteco	648,803	38.64
Jorge Carpio Nicolle	Unión del Centro Nacional	339,695	20.23
Jorge Antonio Serrano Elías	Partido Revolucionario-Partido Democrático de Cooperación Nacional	231,423	13.78
Mario Sandoval Alarcón	Movimiento Liberación Nacional-Partido Institucional Democrático	210,966	12.56
Mario David García Velásquez	Central Auténtica Nacionalista	105,540	6.29
Mario Solórzano Martínez	Partido Socialista Democrático	57,368	3.42
Alejandro Maldonado Aguirre	Partido Nacional Renovador	52,949	3.15
Lionel Sisniega Otero	Partido de Unificación Anticomunista-Frente de Unidad Nacional-Movimiento Emergente Concordia	32,256	1.92
Total Valid Ballots		1,679,000	100.00

Table 7.2. Guatemalan presidential election runoff results, December 8, 1985		
Candidate	Vote Totals	Vote (%)
Cerezo	1,133,517	62.96
Carpio	524,306	29.12
Votos nulos	127,913	7.11
Votos en blanco	14,588	0.81
Total	1,800,324	100.00

Major US newspapers applauded Cerezo's victory. A *New York Times* editorial acknowledged the election had been fair and legitimate and that a successful Cerezo presidency would be an anchor for regional democracy. According to the *Times*, "Americans join in hailing his victory, and his promise."[80] Similarly, the *Washington Post* praised Cerezo as "a man of courage and vision" and argued that supporting Guatemala's democracy should be the Reagan administration's top priority in Central America.[81] A *Los Angeles Times* editorial echoed the *Post*'s sentiments and noted that while Cerezo's election was a hopeful sign for the region, it would be more resonant if the Reagan administration increased its economic aid to Guatemala, and that restoring military assistance to the country would be a "mistake."[82] Finally, the *Miami Herald* characterized Cerezo's margin of victory over Carpio as a mandate from Guatemalan voters and a victory for democracy in the region.[83]

United States officials' reaction to Cerezo's victory was somewhat mixed. On the one hand, an embassy cable from Guatemala City lauded Carpio's concession as "an unforeseen . . . gracious demonstration of good faith [that] sealed the legitimacy of the election."[84] Embassy officials also praised UCN party leader Jorge Skinner-Klee, who congratulated Cerezo on his victory and said he was looking forward to working with DCG leaders and Assembly members. The embassy's report concluded that while Guatemalan democracy was still fragile, the election's legitimacy and peace were historic victories. On the other hand, a State Department memorandum to Bush in December 1985 described the new Guatemalan president-elect as "a pragmatic but inexperienced moderate who is friendly to the United States" and informed the vice president that "while Cerezo has a clear political mandate it is unclear what he will be able to do with it."[85]

Catholics in the United States and Guatemala had a somewhat more hopeful outlook about Cerezo. Father Thomas McSherry, who had succeeded Stanley Rother as Santiago Atitlán's parish priest in 1984, was excited about the prospect of a civilian government. He later recalled that "as long as [Cerezo] was elected democratically and not a general or crazy . . . what he wasn't was more important than what he was."[86] In the press, the Catholic News Service reported that Cerezo was committed to seeking economic and social justice for Guatemalans and that he would "try to find the truth" about the country's disappeared.[87] The report also noted Cerezo's desire for greater Mayan participation in politics and for Guatemala to take a leading role in regional peace initiatives. Nationally syndicated Catholic columnist Liz Armstrong took a more optimistic perspective and speculated that Cerezo's presidency could bring "welcome change" to the country, noting that according to the new president-elect, "the real challenge [for Guatemala] is not to have the best army in Central America but the best democracy."[88]

The most hopeful remarks about Guatemala's future, however, came from Cerezo himself. The evening before the runoff election, some Guatemalan Catholics celebrated La Quema del Diablo, a traditional rite in which celebrants burn effigies of Satan in front of their homes to purify them in preparation for the Solemnity of the Immaculate Conception, celebrated annually on December 8. On the evening of December 7, Cerezo spoke confidently about the election the following day and expressed his belief that a new era for the country was imminent. As celebratory fires burned throughout the country, Cerezo remarked, "The devil in Guatemala is the past, the inflexible . . . the one who raises ghosts against freedom and democratic participation. Today we burn the devil, and tomorrow we inaugurate a new era in Guatemala."[89]

Conclusion

"AQUÍ NO LLORÓ NADIE"

Catholic activists were among the most prominent critics of Guatemala's inequality and violence, and the Carter and Reagan administrations' responses to those crises, during the late 1970s and early 1980s. That prominence was rooted in the landmark shifts wrought by Catholic Action and CELAM's Medellín and Puebla conferences, as well as the Second Vatican Council's institutional and liturgical reforms. Just as importantly, Catholic activists sustained their prominence through their broad spectrum of actions. Bill Woods helped organize cooperative markets and delivered supplies to the Ixcán, and San Lucas Tolimán mission workers rescued Mariposa and her siblings from combat zones. James Miller likewise saved Guatemalan boys from serving in PACs, and priests like Hennessey and Rother, bishops like Penados and Roach, and even Pope John Paul II condemned Guatemala's crises and demanded stronger responses from political leaders.

Those condemnations were often published in the US Catholic press, which routinely offered firsthand accounts from the many lay missionaries, nuns, priests, and bishops that traveled between Guatemala and the United States. The *National Catholic Reporter* and wire services like the Catholic News Agency and Religious News Service offered readers in-depth coverage and analysis of Guatemala and Central America that outshone the *New York Times*, the *Washington Post*, and other major newspapers. Simultaneously, diocesan newspapers like the *Pittsburgh Catholic*, the *Catholic Sentinel*, and the *Catholic Messenger*, among many others, emphasized local connections to Guatemala that their national counterparts could not. Ultimately, the US Catholic press's quality reporting and impressive reach allowed readers to stay informed on conditions in Guatemala and understand those conditions in local and, at times, personal contexts.

The Catholic press's consistent coverage of Guatemala was one of several Catholic activist successes during this period. Woods, Schaffer, and Rother helped build and strengthen connections between their home dioceses and missions in the United States and the parishes and communities they served in Guatemala. These connections yielded mission projects like agricultural programs in San Lucas Tolimán and Santiago Atitlán and cooperative markets and housing projects in the Ixcán. Additionally, the CEG's calls for Guatemalans to vote in the early 1980s coincided with increased voter turnout in 1984 and 1985. Meanwhile, Catholic activists in the United States collected and sent tons of desperately needed food, clothing, and medicine to Guatemala and, in some cases, spurred Americans like John Volpe to reconsider and account for their own role in Guatemala's war. Finally, groups like the USCC influenced the Reagan administration's Central American policymaking calculus to such an extent that some administration officials urged "the closest possible cooperation with the Church." While Catholic activists failed to end the war in these years, their successes are nevertheless significant.

Small and mid-sized US cities were a critical reason for these successes. Dioceses like Oklahoma City, New Ulm, and Spokane sponsored missions in Guatemala, and diocesan newspapers in cities like Pittsburgh, Dubuque, and Rochester were important sources of information on local events related to the country. Additionally, dioceses from Ogdensburg, New York, to Portland, Oregon, hosted speaking engagements, talks, letter-writing campaigns, and food and clothing drives while places like San Lucas Tolimán and Santiago Atitlán became important centers of advocacy and activity in Guatemala. In both countries, small and mid-sized cities were essential parts of a broader, distinct TAN shaped by a shared faith and offered Catholic activists from these smaller cities opportunities to facilitate change in Guatemala.

Guatemala returned to civilian rule under Cerezo, but the country's human rights abuses and political upheaval persisted and continued to draw condemnation from Catholics in both countries. In June 1986, a group of parishioners from El Istor, Izabal, wrote Cerezo a letter that "respectfully" criticized "violence we believe to be ultimately derived from social injustice: a plantation system which marginalizes the poor peasant, a lack of employment, and the extreme poverty which scourges the population." Among the many incidents the parishioners cited, approximately eighty people were forcibly displaced from their homes in March, Pataxte finca workers Waldermar Duarte Fernandez and Julián Izaguirre were abducted in April, and soldiers raided the Sepur-Zarco community four times in mid-June. The parishioners also denounced the "anguished suffering, fear and terror" the raids instilled in the parish, urged a full investigation, and demanded the return of all disappeared citizens. They characterized their letter as a matter of religious obligation, citing their "Gospel-inspired mission . . . to promote a peace based on justice" and thanked Cerezo "in the name of Jesus" for his attention.[1]

Penados remained as critical of Guatemala's human rights conditions under Cerezo as he had been under Mejía. Penados spoke in San Francisco, California, in October 1989 and remarked that Catholic activists had "contributed to at least the partial modification of [Guatemala's] dark panorama," but those improvements were minor and remained fragile. He lamented that the Cerezo government had "no real alternative" plan to address Guatemala's poverty, unequal access to resources, or the effects of the country's refugee crisis. Penados also assailed evangelical Protestantism's continued influence on "certain sectors" of Guatemalan society and denounced unnamed evangelical sects for shrouding their politics in Christianity, which he described as "religious piracy." The archbishop asked world leaders and citizens alike to help Guatemala "achieve the peace for which we yearn, that will undoubtedly be the result of respect for . . . human rights leading to the dignification of [all] humans."[2] Weeks later, soldiers kidnapped Ursuline Sister Dianna Ortiz and detained her in a secret jail where they raped and tortured her for twenty-four hours before releasing her.

Finally, organizations like the Maryknoll Fathers and Brothers and the Catholic Social Justice Lobby sponsored and assisted the Guatemala Human Rights Commission (GHRC) in preparing a series of reports that included accounts and photographs of torture that police inflicted on seventeen-year-olds Walter Villatoro and Jovito Josue Castellanos and sixteen-year-old Salvador Sandoval because they witnessed police committing other crimes. Police burned the boys, gouged out their eyes, and cut off their ears and tongues before killing them.[3] In another report, Jose García, a former Guatemalan army cadet, explained how the army trained future torturers by torturing them first. According to García, "little by little, the soldier becomes a walking time bomb, which will eventually explode in a controlled way against any civilian in his path." These eventual explosions included burning civilians with cigarettes, castration, gang rape, and electric shock and reminded human rights activists that although torturers were certainly accountable for the crimes they committed, they were also victims themselves because "torturers are not born but produced."[4] By December 1990, Guatemala's human rights conditions had deteriorated enough that the State Department suspended approximately three million dollars in planned military assistance to Guatemala during the 1991 fiscal year.[5]

Human rights abuses and political crises similarly plagued Cerezo's successor, Jorge Serrano Elías, and his turbulent presidency. On July 14, 1991, the Guatemalan Archdiocese's human rights office released a report that detailed state-sanctioned human rights violations during the Serrano government's first six months in power. The next day, gunmen murdered Julio Quevado Quezada as he walked down a street in Santa Cruz del Quiché with his wife and children. Quevedo was an agronomist for the Catholic relief agency Caritas and was a close associate of Santa Cruz del Quiché bishop Julio Cabrera Ovalle. According to a US

Embassy account of the murder, both Quevedo and Cabrera had "long been considered 'red' by the security forces and Santa Cruz del Quiché is where the rural human rights group CERJ [Council of Ethnic Communities] has its headquarters—a group also considered 'red.'"[6] Both Cabrera and Penados condemned Quevado's murder and predicted Quevado's family would never receive justice for the killing.[7] Indeed, no one was ever arrested or convicted for the crime.

Serrano's presidency also tested Guatemala's fledgling democracy and plunged the country into a constitutional crisis. In late 1992, Serrano authorized the creation of the Gabinete de Seguridad, a secret cabinet-level group that investigated his critics for ties to the URNG.[8] The group's targets included human rights lawyers, Catholic activists, and the CEG, and on November 11, Serrano's defense minister, José Domingo García, charged the archdiocese had URNG ties and that the CEG's activism was rooted in the bishops' desire to delegitimize the Serrano government. Serrano visited the US Embassy the next day and met with Deputy Chief of Mission John Keane, who asserted Serrano's "ignorance—or unwillingness to accept—that his government's human rights performance and his own defensive attitude stand in the way" of improved US-Guatemalan relations and that US officials "ha[d] a long and difficult challenge to educate Serrano ... because he is a poor listener."[9] The embassy's opportunity to educate Serrano, however, proved fleeting. On May 25, 1993, Serrano launched an *autogolpe* ("self-coup") and attempted to suspend the constitution, dissolve the national Congress, and transfer all of Guatemala's legislative and judicial powers to the presidency. Massive public outcry, international condemnation, and a lack of military cooperation foiled Serrano's attempted coup, and Congress forced him to resign in disgrace on June 1.

Although Serrano attempted a coup and his government sanctioned torture, slandered the CEG, and alienated US Embassy officials, his brief presidency was not a total failure. In April 1991, negotiations between representatives from the URNG, the Serrano government, and Guatemala's business, religious, and social sectors in Mexico City led to an agreement to begin formal peace talks "in the shortest possible time."[10] Notably, the army was not invited to participate. They also agreed to a framework for the talks that addressed a multitude of concerns including human rights, strengthening the country's civilian democracy and institutions, recognizing Mayan identity, ethnicity, and rights, and several economic, political, and social reforms. The parties formally signed this agreement in Querétaro, Mexico, during another round of talks in July. The July round of talks included Guatemalan army officers in the Serrano delegation. A subsequent round of talks in Mexico City in October stalled after what the *Washington Post* described as a "clash" over international human rights monitors and monetary compensation to war victims.[11] Quezada met with URNG and government delegates separately to find a middle ground that would allow talks to continue.

Talks resumed in 1992 and continued under Serrano's successor, Ramiro de Léon Carpio. Both sides agreed to include representatives from Mexico, Norway, Spain, and the United States in the peace process in January 1994, and on March 29, 1994, the two sides came to a key agreement on human rights issues that allowed United Nations human rights monitors to collect data unimpeded and authorized the CEH's creation.[12] Additional rounds of talks produced a preliminary agreement on refugee repatriation in June and, in March 1995, the Agreement on the Identity and Rights of Indigenous Peoples. This accord recognized communal land rights, prohibited ethnic discrimination, and called for education reforms that recognized Mayan contributions to Guatemalan history and culture. The accord also specifically called for greater legal protections for Mayan women against sexual harassment and assault.[13] In January 1996, de Léon Carpio's successor, Álvaro Arzú Yrigoyen, dismissed five army generals, ten colonels, four majors, and more than one hundred police officers and commanders for a multitude of crimes, including corruption and human rights abuses. The sides agreed to a cease-fire in March and signed a formal peace agreement in Guatemala City on December 29. After thirty-six years, the war was finally over.

Although the war ended in 1996, one of the era's most notable murders occurred two years later. In April 1998, unidentified assailants murdered Bishop Juan José Gerardi Conedera in his home following the release of the Guatemalan Archdiocese's Human Rights Office's report of the war's violence, *Guatemala: ¡Nunca Más!*, the previous day. In 2001, a Guatemalan court convicted Byron Lima Oliva, an army captain who led a failed coup to overthrow Cerezo in 1988, of Gerardi's murder and sentenced him to twenty years in prison. In 2007, journalist Francisco Goldman implicated several other officers, including General Otto Pérez Molina, in the killing.[14] Molina later served as president of Guatemala from 2012 to 2015, when he and his vice president, Roxanna Baldetti, were removed from office and sentenced to prison for their roles in a multimillion-dollar corruption scandal.[15]

The war's most egregious crime, however, went unpunished. In 2012, Guatemala's Public Ministry indicted José Efraín Ríos Montt on charges of genocide and crimes against humanity, including his culpability in the deaths of 1,771 Ixil Mayans, the forcible displacement of nearly thirty thousand people, torture, rape, sexual assaults, and other depredations. Ríos Montt's trial began on March 19, 2013, with a series of controversial moments that would ultimately upend the trial and its eventual verdict: Ríos Montt fired his entire defense team, leaving Francisco García Gudiel as the disgraced former dictator's only representative. A trial observer, Emi MacLean of the Open Society Justice Initiative, reported that after

Ríos Montt named García Guidel (retained by co-defendant José Mauricio Rodríguez Sánchez, who served as the director of the G-2 intelligence unit under Ríos Montt) as his sole attorney, "García Guidel then proceeded to raise a host of legal challenges, including an effort to delay the start of the trial . . . and a motion to recuse two of the three judges as a result of purported personal conflicts."[16] The trial's three presiding judges expelled García Guidel from the courtroom after introducing several motions and ordered Rodríguez Sánchez's defense team to represent Ríos Montt for the rest of the day. García Guidel and the rest of Ríos Montt's legal team returned to the courtroom on March 20 and consistently sought to undermine trial proceedings, witnesses' credibility, and the trial judges' alleged conflicts of interest in presiding over the trial.

Ríos Montt was convicted of genocide and crimes against humanity on May 10 and sentenced to serve eighty years in prison.[17] Moments after his conviction, members of the courtroom, many of them survivors of Ríos Montt's genocide, cheered, cried, and sang a poem by Guatemalan poet Otto René Castillo: "Aquí no lloró nadie / Aquí solo queremos ser humanos (Here, no one cried / Here, we only want to be human.) On May 20, however, Guatemala's Constitutional Court overturned the verdict in a bitter 3-2 decision, ruling that García Guidel's expulsion from the courtroom on the trial's first day and subsequent occasions had violated Ríos Montt's right to due process. Ríos Montt, who did not serve time in prison, died while under house arrest in Guatemala City in 2018.

Ríos Montt's evasion of justice, Gerardi and Quevado's murders, Ortiz's rape and torture, and repression in places like El Estor underscore that post-dictatorship, postwar Guatemala remained a dangerous place for Catholic activists. Amid these dangers, however, stories of recognition and reunion may still be found. In October 2007, the Oklahoma City Archdiocese opened a Cause for Canonization to begin the lengthy process of sainthood for Rother. The Vatican's Theology Commission of the Congregation for the Cause of Saints named Rother as a martyr of the church and a Servant of God in June 2015. Oklahoma City archbishop Paul Coakley celebrated the announcement and said, "Father Rother laid down his life for Christ and for the people of his parish in Guatemala, whom he dearly loved. It is very encouraging to move one step closer to a formal recognition by the Church of Father Rother's heroic life and death as a martyr for the Gospel."[18] On December 2, 2016, Pope Francis formally recognized Rother as the church's first US-born martyr.

In San Lucas Tolimán, Guatemalan President Óscar Berger Perdomo awarded Schaffer the Order of the Quetzal, the country's highest civilian honor, in October 2007 for his forty-five years of service to the parish. Schaffer was the first US citizen to receive the honor. He served the parish until 2010, when he returned home to Minnesota to undergo cancer treatment and died on May 24, 2012. Thousands of Luqueños attended his funeral mass in San Lucas Tolimán, where Schaffer was laid to rest.

For some, postwar reunions eased the war's psychological burdens. During my interviews with Mariposa, she shared that in 2010, she learned that her father was alive and living in Guatemala City. After their father's abduction, the army tortured him before abandoning him on a road outside their village, but his children had already arrived at Casa Felíz by the time he returned home. He spent years searching for his children in vain, eventually remarried, and resettled in the capital. Shortly after learning their father was alive, Mariposa and Pastor reunited with him, nearly three decades after his disappearance and presumed death.

By any measure, Catholic activists made an unmistakable impact on Guatemala and its relationship with the United States. Although the war's underlying economic and social inequalities still shape Guatemala's politics and relationship with the United States, Catholic activists' influence has greatly receded, as Protestants accounted for nearly half of Guatemala's population by the 2000s.[19] Likewise, evangelical Protestantism's reshaping of American politics, conservative Catholics' ascendancy within the US church, and other significant challenges have similarly diminished Catholic activists' influence in the United States. Their diminution notwithstanding, Catholic activists' methods, structure, and reach made them a resonant voice in politics and policy that advocated for the dignity of all people during the Guatemalan war's bloodiest decade.

NOTES

Introduction

1. Father Stanley Rother, letter to Rev. Archbishop Charles A. Salatka, November 3, 1980. Blessed Stanley Rother Collection, box 10, "Father David Monahan Documents—After Death," Archdiocese of Oklahoma City, Oklahoma.

2. Rother, letter to Salatka, November 3, 1980.

3. "Luqueños" are residents of San Lucas Tolimán.

4. Margaret Keck and Kathryn Sikkink, *Activists Beyond Borders: Advocacy Networks in International Politics* (Ithaca: Cornell University Press, 1998), 1.

5. Jean Quataert, *Advocating Dignity: Human Rights Mobilizations in Global Politics* (Philadelphia: University of Pennsylvania Press, 2009).

6. It is impossible to provide an exact number of deaths directly resultant from the war. Additionally, different quantitative studies of the war's deaths have privileged specific geographic areas or years. For example, the Guatemalan Archdiocese's report, *¡Nunca Más!*, focused predominantly on the country's western departments and deaths reported to government authorities between 1970 and 1985. Further, the ongoing discovery of mass graves, such as one containing approximately five hundred skeletons discovered near Cobán, Alta Verapaz, in January 2013, consistently increase the body count. The estimate of two hundred thousand deaths is taken from the Guatemalan Government's Truth and Reconciliation Committee (Comisión para el Esclarimiento de Histórico [CEH]) report, *Guatemala: Memoria del Silencio*, published in 1998. According to the CEH, Guatemalan state security forces were responsible for 93 percent of all recorded deaths and human rights violations, leftist guerrilla forces were responsible for 3 percent, and the remaining 4 percent were of indeterminate origin. CEH, *Guatemala: Memoria del Silencio, Tomo V: Conclusiones y Recomendaciones* (Guatemala: CEH, 1998), 21–41.

7. Edward T. Brett, *The US Catholic Press on Central America: From Cold War Anticommunism to Social Justice* (Notre Dame, IN: University of Notre Dame Press, 2003).

8. A complete account of this literature is, of course, impossible, but for regional assessments, see Cynthia Arnson, *Crossroads: Congress, the President, and Central America, 1976–1993* (University Park: Penn State University Press, 1993); Thomas Carothers, *In the Name of Democracy: US Policy toward Latin America in the Reagan Years* (Berkeley: University of California Press, 1991); John Coatsworth, *Central America and the United States: The Clients and the Colossus* (New York: Twayne, 1994); Walter LaFeber, *Inevitable Revolutions: The United States in Central America* (New York: Norton, 1983); William M. LeoGrande, *Our Own Backyard: The United States in Central America, 1977–1992* (Chapel Hill: University of North

Carolina Press, 1998); Kathryn Sikkink, *Mixed Signals: U.S. Human Rights Policy and Latin America* (Ithaca: Cornell University Press, 2004); and Christian Smith, *Resisting Reagan: The US Central America Peace Movement* (Chicago: University of Chicago Press, 1996). Notable country-specific studies include Russell Crandall, *The Salvador Option: The United States in El Salvador, 1977–1992* (New York: Cambridge University Press, 2016); Brian D'Haeseleer, *The Salvadoran Crucible: The Failure of US Counterinsurgency in El Salvador, 1979–1992* (Lawrence: University of Kansas Press, 2017); Greg Grandin, *The Last Colonial Massacre: Latin America in the Cold War* (Chicago: University of Chicago Press, 2004); Susanne Jonas, *Of Centaurs and Doves: Guatemala's Peace Process* (Boulder, CO: Westview, 2000); William Michael Schmidli, *The Fate of Freedom Elsewhere: Human Rights and US Cold War Policy toward Argentina* (Ithaca: Cornell University Press, 2013); Donald Schulz and Deborah Sundloff-Schulz, *The United States, Honduras, and the Crisis in Central America* (Boulder, CO: Westview, 1994); and Philip W. Travis, *Reagan's War on Terrorism in Nicaragua: The Outlaw State* (Lanham, MD: Lexington Books, 2017).

9. Multiple US ambassadors wrote about their experiences in Central America during these years. See Jack R. Binns, *The United States in Honduras, 1980–1981: An Ambassador's Memoir* (Jefferson, MO: McFarland, 2000); Frank V. Ortiz Jr., *Ambassador Ortiz: Lessons from a Life of Service* (Albuquerque: University of New Mexico Press, 2005); Robert A. Pastor, *Not Condemned to Repetition: The United States and Nicaragua* (London: Taylor and Francis, 2018); and Lawrence Pezzullo and Ralph Pezzullo, *At the Fall of Somoza* (Pittsburgh: University of Pittsburgh Press, 1993).

10. See Christian G. Appy, "Eisenhower's Guatemalan Doodle: Or, How to Draw, Deny, and Take Credit for a Third World Coup," in *Cold War Constriction: The Political Culture of United States Imperialism, 1945–1966*, ed. Christian G. Appy (Amherst: University of Massachusetts Press, 2000), 183–214; Virginia Garrard-Burnett, *Terror in the Land of the Holy Spirit: Guatemala under General Efraín Ríos Montt, 1982–1983* (New York: Oxford University Press, 2010); Piero Gleijeses, *Shattered Hope: The Guatemalan Revolution and the United States, 1944–1954* (Princeton, NJ: Princeton University Press, 1992); Richard Immerman, *The CIA in Guatemala: The Foreign Policy of Intervention* (Austin: University of Texas Press, 1982); Stephen Schlesinger and Stephen Kinzer, *Bitter Fruit: The Untold Story of the American Coup in Guatemala* (Garden City, NY: Doubleday, 1982).

11. See Arnson, *Crossroads*; John Dumbrell, *The Carter Presidency: A Re-evaluation* (Manchester: Manchester University Press, 1993); Donna Jackson, *Jimmy Carter and the Horn of Africa: Cold War Policy in Ethiopia and Somalia* (Jefferson, MO: McFarland, 2007); Jørgen Jensehaugen, *Arab-Israeli Diplomacy Under Carter: The US, Israel, and the Palestinians* (London: Tauris, 2018); Burton I. Kaufman and Scott Kaufman, *The Presidency of James Earl Carter, Jr.*, 2nd ed. (Lawrence: University of Kansas Press, 1993); Scott Kaufman, *Plans Unraveled: The Foreign Policy of the Carter Administration* (DeKalb: Northern Illinois University Press, 2008); Barbara Keys, *Reclaiming American Virtue: The Human Rights Revolution of the 1970s* (Cambridge, MA: Harvard University Press, 2014); Nancy Mitchell, *Jimmy Carter in Africa: Race and the Cold War* (Stanford: Stanford University Press, 2016); Daniel Sargent, *A Superpower Transformed: The Remaking of American Foreign Relations in the 1970s* (Oxford: Oxford University Press, 2015); David Skidmore, *Reversing Course: Carter's Foreign Policy, Domestic Politics, and the Failure of Reform* (Nashville: Vanderbilt University Press, 1996); Gaddis Smith, *Morality, Reason, and Power: American Diplomacy in the Carter Years* (New York: Hill and Wang, 1986); Robert A. Strong, *Working in the World: Jimmy Carter and the Making of American Foreign Policy* (Baton Rouge: Louisiana State University Press, 2000);

Notes to Chapter 1 / 175

and Salim Yaqib, *Imperfect Strangers: Americans, Arabs, and US-Middle East Relations in the 1970s* (Ithaca: Cornell University Press, 2016).

12. See Cara Burnidge, *A Peaceful Conquest: Woodrow Wilson, Religion, and the New World Order* (Chicago: University of Chicago Press, 2016); Timothy A. Byrnes, *Reverse Mission: Transnational Religious Communities and the Making of US Foreign Policy* (Washington, DC: Georgetown University Press, 2011); Emily Conroy-Krutz, *Christian Imperialism: Converting the World in the Early American Republic* (Ithaca: Cornell University Press, 2015); Sharon Erickson Nepstad, *Convictions of the Soul: Religion, Culture, and Agency in the Central America Solidarity Movement* (New York: Oxford University Press, 2004); Garrard-Burnett, *Terror in the Land of the Holy Spirit*; William Inboden, *Religion and American Foreign Policy, 1945–1960: The Soul of Containment* (New York: Cambridge University Press, 2008); Seth Jacobs, *America's Miracle Man in Vietnam: Ngo Dinh Diem, Religion, Race, and US Intervention in Southeast Asia, 1950–1957* (Durham, NC: Duke University Press, 2004); Theresa Keeley, *Reagan's Gun-Toting Nuns: The Catholic Conflict Over Cold War Human Rights Policy in Central America* (Ithaca: Cornell University Press, 2020); Andrew Preston, *Sword of the Spirit, Shield of Faith: Religion in American War and Diplomacy* (New York: Knopf, 2012); Lauren Frances Turek, *To Bring the Good News to All Nations: Evangelical Influence on Human Rights and US Foreign Relations* (Ithaca: Cornell University Press, 2020).

Chapter 1

1. US Embassy, Guatemala City to State Department, "Political Review #6—April 10, 1976 to April 29, 1976," Confidential Airgram A-45, *Foreign Relations of the United States 1969–1976,* Volume E-11, Part 1, Documents on Mexico, Central America, and the Caribbean 1973–1976, Document 226.

2. Ricardo Falla, SJ, *Massacres in the Jungle: Ixcán, Guatemala, 1975–1982* (Boulder, CO: Westview, 1994), 19.

3. Falla, *Massacres in the Jungle*, 19. In addition to Xalbal, the other four original cooperatives formed were Mayalán, Pueblo Nuevo, Los Angeles, and Cuarto Pueblo. Subsequently, the cooperatives of Samaritano, Zunil, Mónaco, Ixtahuacán Chiquito, Malacatán, Piedras Blancas, and Nueva Comunidad were formed in the Ixcán. (Falla, *Massacres in the Jungle*, 23n6).

4. Falla, *Massacres in the Jungle*, 25.

5. Ron Chernow, "The Strange Death of Bill Woods: Did He Fly Too Far in the Zone of the Generals?" *Mother Jones*, May 1979, 32.

6. Chernow, "The Strange Death of Bill Woods," 41. Woods's associates were correct: a US Embassy telegram dated February 8, 1977, discussed the cost of shipping the engine back to the United States for further investigation and noted, "We doubt anyone would wish [the] engine returned to Guatemala." (Boster, US Embassy, Guatemala, to State Department, "CivAir First Quiché Air Crash," Confidential Telegram 814, February 8, 1977, Digital National Security Archive) (hereafter DNSA).

7. While Rossell issued his letter on April 4, 1954, no archival record of the letter exists. Embassy officials in Guatemala City, however, reported on its content in multiple reports to the State Department that month. See Central Intelligence Agency, "Synthesis of Ambassador Puerifoy's Remarks Relevant to PBSUCCESS Made at a Meeting 21 April 1954," Foreign Relations of the United States, 1952–1954, Guatemala, ed. Susan Holly and David S. Patterson (Washington, DC: Government Printing Office, 2003), Document 131, n3.

176 / Notes to Chapter 1

8. See Gleijeses, *Shattered Hope*; Immerman, *The CIA in Guatemala*; Carlos Sabino, *Guatemala, la historia silenciada Tomo I: Revolución y liberación* (Guatemala: Fondo de Cultura Economica, 2009); Schlesinger and Kinzer, *Bitter Fruit*; and Carlos Rafael Soto Rosales, *El sueño encadenado: El proceso politico guatemalteco, 1944–1999* (Guatemala: Tipografia Nacional, 2002).

9. Mons. Mariano Rossell y Arellano, *Carta pastoral sobre los avances del Comunismo en Guatemala* (Guatemala: Acción Católica Guatemalteca, 1954).

10. Gleijeses, *Shattered Hope*, 198.

11. On Operation PBSUCCESS, see Appy, "Eisenhower's Guatemalan Doodle," in Appy, *Cold War Constructions*; Nick Cullather, *Secret History: The CIA's Classified Account of Its Operation in Guatemala* (Stanford: Stanford University Press, 1999); Gleijeses, *Shattered Hope*; and Immerman, *The CIA in Guatemala*.

12. For a detailed history of the *Cristo Negro* and its significance to Guatemalan Catholics, see Douglass Sullivan-González, *The Black Christ of Esquipulas: Religion and Identity in Guatemala* (Lincoln: University of Nebraska Press, 2016).

13. Sr. Mary Martina Bridgeman, MM, "Diary, June 18, 1954," Maryknoll Sisters Archive, Diaries Collection, H3.2. Maryknoll Mission Archives, Maryknoll, NY.

14. "At Our Doorstep," *Pittsburgh Catholic*, June 24, 1954.

15. "Communists Lowered 'Iron Curtain' in Guatemala Republic," *Courier-Journal* (Rochester, NY), June 25, 1954; Rev. John B. Ebel, "Restrictions on Church Gave Guatemala to Reds," *Catholic Advance* (Wichita, KS), June 25, 1954.

16. "Guatemala Said to Equal Red China in Persecution" and "Communists in Guatemala Plotted Three Times to Exile Archbishop," *Catholic Standard and Times* (Philadelphia, PA), June 25, 1954; "Red Beachhead in the Americas," *Catholic Telegraph-Register* (Cincinnati, OH), June 25, 1954.

17. Richard Pattee, "First Lesson in Guatemala," *St. Louis Register* (MO), July 9, 1954.

18. Ezekiel 37:12. See also "Oración funebre del Arzobispado de Guatemala," *El Imparcial* (Guatemala City, Guatemala), July 8, 1954.

19. "En todo momento el arzobispado estaba listo a dar su sangre por la libertad de Guatemala," *El Imparcial,* July 19, 1954.

20. Henry F. Holland, US Department of State, to John Foster Dulles, "Situation in Guatemala," June 29, 1956, DNSA.

21. In a July 31, 1957, telegram, Acting Secretary of State Christian Herter noted the State Department's position that the "possibility cannot be overlooked that [Castillo Armas's] assassination was [a] rightist plot." (Herter to US Embassy, London, Telegram 714, July 31, 1957, *Foreign Relations of the United States, 1955–1957, Volume VII, The American Republics: Central and South America*, Document 57).

22. Robert Corrigan, US Embassy, Guatemala, "Revolt against Government of Guatemala by Elements [of] Guatemalan Army," Confidential Despatch, November 25, 1960, DNSA.

23. Sabino, *Guatemala: La historia silenciada, Tomo I*, 294.

24. Sabino, *Guatemala: La historia silenciada, Tomo I*, 296.

25. Pope Leo XIII, *Rerum Novarum, Encyclical of Pope Leo XIII on Capital and Labor*, May 15, 1891, sec. 3.

26. Milagros Peña, "Liberation Theology in Peru: An Analysis of the Role of Intellectuals in Social Movements," *Journal for the Scientific Study of Religion* 33, no. 1 (March 1994): 39.

27. Lawrence Elliott, *I Will Be Called John: A Biography of Pope John XXIII* (London: Collins, 1974), 21–22.

Notes to Chapter 1 / 177

28. Elliott, *I Will Be Called John,* 125–171. Quotation from Pope John XXIII, *Letters to His Family* (New York: McGraw-Hill, 1970), 662.

29. Pius XI, *Ubi Arcano dei Consilio, Encyclical Letter on the Peace of Christ in the Kingdom of Christ,* December 23, 1922, sec. 54–55.

30. Pius XI, *Ubi Arcano dei Consilio,* sec. 58.

31. Peña, "Liberation Theology in Peru," 39.

32. Capovilla recounted these events in *Giovanni XXIII: Quindici Letture* (Roma: Edizioni di Storia e Letteratura, 1970), 746.

33. Paul Hoffman, "Pope to Summon Council to Seek Unity," *New York Times,* January 26, 1959.

34. The council was formally summoned to meet in the encyclical *Humanae Salutis,* which was issued on December 25, 1961.

35. Pat Morrison, "Vatican II: Forty Years Later," *National Catholic Reporter* (Kansas City, MO), October 4, 2002.

36. These changes were enumerated in the Apostolic Constitution *Sacrosanctum Concilium,* Apostolic Declaration *Unitatis Reintegratio,* and Apostolic Decree *Perfectae Caritatis.*

37. Second Vatican Council, *Ad Gentes, Apostolic Decree on the Mission Activity of the Church,* December 7, 1965, sec. 24.

38. John XXIII, *Princeps Pastorum, Encyclical Letter on the Missions, Native Clergy, and Lay Participation,* November 28, 1959.

39. Second Vatican Council, *Ad Gentes, Apostolic Decree on the Mission Activity of the Church,* December 7, 1965.

40. John XXIII, *Mater et Magistra, Encyclical of Pope John XXIII on Christianity and Social Progress,* May 15, 1961, sec. 23.

41. John XXIII, *Mater et Magistra,* sec. 171–74.

42. John XXIII, *Mater et Magistra,* sec. 147 and 192.

43. John XXIII, *Pacem in Terris, Encyclical of Pope John XXIII on Establishing Universal Peace in Truth, Justice, Charity, and Liberty,* April 11, 1963, sec. 11–27.

44. John XXIII, *Pacem in Terris,* sec. 80.

45. Leo XIII, *Custodi de Quella Fede, Encyclical of Pope Leo XIII on Freemasonry,* December 8, 1892; Pius XI, *Quadregesimo Anno, Encyclical Letter of Pope Pius XI on Reconstruction of the Social Order,* March 19, 1937, and *Divini Redemptoris, Encyclical Letter of Pope Pius XI on Atheistic Communism,* March 19, 1937.

46. John XXIII, *Pacem in Terris,* sec. 158.

47. For accounts of the plan, see Edward T. Brett, *The U.S. Catholic Press on Central America;* Gerald Costello, *Mission to Latin America: The Successes and Failures of a Twentieth-Century Crusade* (Maryknoll, NY: Orbis Books, 1979); and Ivan Illich, "The Seamy Side of Charity," in Illich, *Celebration of Awareness: A Call for Institutional Revolution* (Garden City, NY: Doubleday, 1970), 53–68.

48. Bruce Calder, *Crecimiento y Cambio de la Iglesia Católica Guatemalteca, 1944–1966* (Guatemala: Seminario de Integración Social Guatemaltecas, Ministerio de Educación, 1970), 19.

49. Carlos Sabino, *Guatemala, la historia silenciada, 1944–1989, Tomo II: El dominó que no cayó* (Guatemala: Fondo de Cultura Económica de Guatemala, 2008), 82–84.

50. Schaffer, Untitled Document, n.d., Msgr. Gregory T. Schaffer Personal Papers, Owatonna, MN, unpublished. This document is a sixteen-page memoir, written by Schaffer, about his earliest years in San Lucas Tolimán. Although the document itself is undated, it can be

estimated that it was written sometime in late 1970: on page 15, Schaffer noted that a Dr. Thelma Gutiérrez, an instructor at the San Carlos University dental school in Guatemala City, "has been assigned to San Lucas for 1971."

51. Schaffer, Untitled Document, n.d. According to Martinka's obituary, published in the St. Paul, Minnesota, *Pioneer Press*, on March 27, 2011, Martinka founded the San Alfonso Mission in Juárez, Mexico, after his discharge from the Air National Guard. Martinka served as that mission's resident pastor for more than thirty years.

52. Schaffer, Untitled Document, n.d., 6.

53. Schaffer, Untitled Document, n.d., 7.

54. Schaffer, Untitled Document, n.d., 11.

55. Schaffer, Untitled Document, n.d., 8.

56. *Gaudium et Spes, Pastoral Constitution on the Church in the Modern World*, December 7, 1965, sec. 2.

57. *Gaudium et Spes*, sec. 29.

58. *Gaudium et Spes*, sec. 88.

59. Paul VI, *Populorum Progressio, Encyclical Letter on the Development of Peoples*, March 26, 1967, sec. 3, 13.

60. Paul VI, *Populorum Progressio*, sec. 47.

61. Paul VI, *Populorum Progressio*, sec. 71.

62. The countries were Argentina, Bolivia, Brazil, Chile, Colombia, Ecuador, El Salvador, Guatemala, Mexico, Nicaragua, Panama, Paraguay, Peru, and Uruguay.

63. Alfred T. Hennelly, ed., *Liberation Theology: A Documentary History* (Maryknoll, NY: Orbis, 1990), 59.

64. Rafael Luciani, "Medellín Fifty Years Later: From Development to Liberation," *Theological Studies* 79, no. 3 (September 2018): 567.

65. John M. Breen, M.M., "Report: The 'Melville Affair,'" n.d., 6. Maryknoll Fathers and Brothers Archive, Central American Collection, box 7, folder 1. Maryknoll Mission Archives, Maryknoll, NY.

66. Breen, "Report: The 'Melville Affair,'" 13.

67. The four Maryknoll missionaries named were the Melville brothers, Bradford, and Sister Marian Pahl.

68. Breen, "Report: The 'Melville Affair,'" 21–22.

69. Breen, "Report: The 'Melville Affair,'" 22. On March 3, 1968, a CIA cable provided a detailed timeline of the Melville group's proposed scheme, which would have culminated with a political takeover of the department of Huehuetenago. See CIA, "Plans of the Melville Brothers' Group for Revolutionary Action against the Guatemalan Government, as Related by an Adherent of the Group," Secret Cable, March 8, 1968.

70. Breen, "Report: The 'Melville Affair,'" 23. It is unclear how Mein was already aware of the Melville plot, nor is it clear who notified the US Embassy. There is no record of anyone reporting the plan to either Mein or US Embassy officials prior to Breen and Guriaran's meeting with Mein on December 12.

71. Breen, "Report: The 'Melville Affair,'" 23–30.

72. According to Maryknoll Mission historian Penny Lernoux, Bradford and Thomas Melville married in January 1968. In May of that year, they, along with seven other protestors, entered the Catonsville, Maryland, Selective Service office and poured homemade napalm on the office's draft files to protest the Vietnam War as well as US policy toward Guatemala and Latin America. Bradford and Melville received one- and two-year prison sentences,

Notes to Chapter 1 / 179

respectively. Penny Lernoux, *Hearts on Fire: The Story of the Maryknoll Sisters* (Maryknoll: Orbis, 1993). For an account of the Catonsville incident, see Shawn Francis Peters, *The Catonsville Nine: A Story of Faith and Resistance in the Vietnam Era* (New York: Oxford University Press, 2012).

73. Breen, "Report: The 'Melville Affair,'" 37–39.

74. Lernoux, *Hearts on Fire*, 153. An undated mission document from the period stated that "the future in Guatemala will always be a delicate one. . . . As long as we are allowed to do something vital and worthwhile for the people, then we should stay. . . . If the day comes where we can not preach the Gospel as we see it as a Group, the better we leave" ("The Present Situation as a Result of the Melville Affair," 44. Maryknoll Fathers and Brothers Archive, Central American Collection, box 7, folder 1, "The Melville Affair." Maryknoll Mission Archives).

75. "Arzobispo Casariego Secuestrado el Sábado," *Prensa Libre*, March 18, 1968; Sabino, *Guatemala, la historia silenciada, 1944–1989, Tomo II*, 107–9.

76. Deputy Chief of Mission Max V. Krebs, US Embassy, Guatemala, to US Department of State, Confidential Telegram, August 28, 1968, *Foreign Relations of the United States, 1964–1968*, Volume XXXI, South and Central America; Mexico, eds. David C. Geyer, David H. Herschler, Edward C. Keefer (Washington, DC: Government Printing Office, 2004), Document 114.

77. Krebs to US Department of State.

78. There was no clear consensus on the facts immediately after the assassination. On August 28, Ortega reported the assassins drove a 1964 Buick and a "small red truck" with an unknown number of people inside. In contrast, a telegram to the State Department dated September 4 contained other eyewitness reports that "the green vehicle may have been a 1968 model Chevy II" and that the truck was "a small red Japanese car." Further, Ortega's account only mentioned a "young man" in olive fatigues and armed with a submachine gun, while the September 4 telegram stated that as many as eight armed men were involved and three of the assassins subsequently fled on foot, while the others left in the red car. See Krebs, US Embassy, Guatemala to US Department of State, "Death of Ambassador: Preliminary Political Assessment," Confidential Telegram 6306, September 4, 1968, *Foreign Relations of the United States, 1964–1968*, Volume XXXI, South and Central America, Document 116.

79. Acting Assistant Secretary of State for Inter-American Affairs Viron Vaky to Secretary of State Dean Rusk, "Assassination of Ambassador Mein," Memorandum, August 29, 1968, *Foreign Relations of the United States, 1964–1968*, Volume 31, South and Central America, Document 115. Although Embassy officials reported on August 29 that the FAR had intended to murder Mein in retaliation for Sanchez's arrest, they amended their conclusions in the September 4 telegram to the State Department to state that the FAR's original intent was to merely kidnap Mein and exchange him for Sanchez. In either case, it is clear the events of August 28 were directly related to Sanchez's arrest.

80. Vaky to Rusk, "Assassination of Ambassador Mein." In January 1969, Guatemalan police and soldiers captured and "neutralized" four of the suspected assassins. See US Embassy, Guatemala to the Department of State, "Internal Security—Chart of Incidents, January 1969," Confidential Airgram A-35, *Foreign Relations of the United States, 1969–1976*, Volume E-10, The American Republics, 1969–1972, Douglas Kraft, James Siekmeier, Edward C. Keefer, eds. (Washington, DC: Government Printing Office, 2009), Document 320.

81. Krebs, "Death of Ambassador: Preliminary Political Assessment."

82. Office of Human Rights, Archdiocese of Guatemala (ODHAG), *Guatemala: ¡Nunca Más!* (Maryknoll: Orbis, 1999), 199.

83. ODHAG, *Guatemala: ¡Nunca Más!*, 200.

84. ODHAG, *Guatemala: ¡Nunca Más!*, 199.

85. See Susanne Jonas, *The Battle for Guatemala: Rebels, Death Squads, and U.S. Power* (Boulder, CO: Westview, 1991), 63.

86. ODHAG, *Guatemala: ¡Nunca Más!*, 200.

87. See Virginia M. Hagen, United States House of Representatives Committee on Foreign Affairs, "Central American Politics: A Brief Survey of the Governments and Politics of Costa Rica, El Salvador, Guatemala, Honduras, Nicaragua, and Panama" (Washington, DC: Government Printing Office, 1970), 9–10.

88. CIA to Latin American Staff, "What to Expect in Guatemala," March 6, 1970, *Foreign Relations of the United States, 1969–1976*, Volume E-10, Document 329.

89. US Embassy, Guatemala to US Department of State, "The Arana Administration: A Preliminary View," Confidential Airgram A-170, *Foreign Relations of the United States, 1969–1976*, Volume E-10, Document 340.

90. CIA, "Information on Guatemalan Government Security Service," n.d., *Foreign Relations of the United States, 1969–1976*, Volume E-10, Document 356.

91. CIA, "Information on Guatemalan Government Security Service." Two other documents corroborate the CIA's claims that Arana personally ordered assassinations. On March 13, 1971, US ambassador to Guatemala Nathaniel Davis reported that during a conversation with Guatemalan Government Minister Jorge Arenales, Arana refused to allow police and death squad members to place Congressman Rene De Leon Schlotter, Guatemala City Mayor Manuel Colom Argueta, and Council of State member Hector Zachrisson on their hit lists. Instead, they were put on what Arenales called "the waiting list." Additionally, the CIA informed State Department officials that "agency information indicated direct participation by President Arana in drawing up death lists." US Embassy, Guatemala to US Department of State, "GOG Reaction to U.S. Warning on Counter-Terror," Confidential Telegram 1083, March 13, 1971, and US Department of State, "Memorandum for the Record: Meeting at Department of State 1620–1820 Hours, 16 August 1971," September 9, 1971, *Foreign Relations of the United States, 1969–1976*, Volume E-10, Documents 350 and 355.

92. Sabino, *Guatemala: La historia silenciada (1944–1989), Tomo II*, 176.

93. Sabino, *Guatemala: La historia silenciada (1944–1989), Tomo II*, 182.

94. Sabino, *Guatemala: La historia silenciada (1944–1989), Tomo II*, 174.

95. Sabino, *Guatemala: La historia silenciada (1944–1989), Tomo II*.

96. Mario Payeras, *Los días de la selva* (Guatemala: Editorial Piedra Santa, 2002), 130. Qtd. in Sabino, *Guatemala: la historia silenciada (1944–1989), Tomo II: El dominió que no cayó*, 185.

97. See Comisión para el Esclarecimiento Histórico (CEH), *Guatemala: Memoria del Silencio, Tomo X: Casos Presentados, Anexo II* (Guatemala: CEH, 1999), 1110–1112, casos 11493; 11634; 925; 20034; 11142, and 11223. While the cases account for thirty known victims, case 11223 also notes an "undetermined" number of unidentified people.

98. CEG, "Mensaje del Episcopado de la Provincía Eclesiastica de Guatemala dirigido al pueblo con motiv de la difícil situación de violencia por la que atreviesa el país actualmente," February 5, 1971, *Al Servicio de la vida, la justicia y la paz* (Guatemala: Conferencia Episcopal de Guatemala, 1997), 95–98.

99. CEG, "Comunicado de prensa de la Conferencia Episcopal de Guatemala," April 5, 1974, *Al Servicio de la vida, la justicia y la paz*, 102–4.

100. Schaffer, Untitled Document, n.d., Msgr. Gregory T. Schaffer Personal Papers.

Notes to Chapter 2 / 181

101. Donna Whitson Brett and Edward T. Brett, *The Bill Woods Story: Maryknoll Missionary in Guatemala* (Maryknoll, NY: Orbis, 1988), 14.

102. Brett and Brett, *The Bill Woods Story*, 17.

103. Brett and Brett, *The Bill Woods Story*, 18.

104. Ron Chernow, "The Strange Death of Bill Woods," 32.

Chapter 2

1. Office of the White House Press Secretary, "Remarks of the President at the Commencement Exercises of Notre Dame University," May 22, 1977. Chief of Staff Files [Butler] box 101, Hospital Cost Containment, 1/24/79–10/29/79 [CF, O/A 561] through ILO [International Labor Organization], 3/16/77–9/12/77 [CF, O/A 8,] folder 7, "Human Rights in Latin America, 4/30/77–8/19/77," Jimmy Carter Library (hereafter JCL), 1.

2. See, for example, "Rhodesian White Bishop Gets 10 Years in Prison," *Arizona Daily Star* (Tucson, AZ), October 2, 1976; Bruce W. Sumner, "A Bishop Is a Martyr to Human Freedom," *Los Angeles Times*, November 26, 1976; "Bishop Lamont Has No Regrets, Brother Fears For Those in Rhodesia," *Catholic Advance*, April 14, 1977; Keyes Beech, "18 Koreans Sentenced for Defying Park," *Lincoln Journal Star* (Lincoln, NE), August 28, 1976; Paul Shin, "South Korea Opposition Leaders Get Jail Term," *Daily Courier* (Connellsville, PA), August 28, 1976; "Church Fights Park Decrees in S. Korea," *Saint Louis Post-Dispatch* (St. Louis, MO), April 18, 1977; Leonard Greenwood, "Brazil Bishops Oppose Transfer of Cardinal," *Los Angeles Times*, March 19, 1973; Jack Anderson, "U.S. Tax Dollars Help Sustain Torture," *Asbury Park Press* (Asbury Park, NJ), June 17, 1973; "Brazilian repression continues," *Brandon Sun* (Brandon, MB), November 14, 1975; and Agostino Bono, "Only the bishops remain against the Latin Military," *Baltimore Sun* (Baltimore, MD), July 24, 1977.

3. Office of the White House Press Secretary, "Remarks of the President at the Commencement Exercises of Notre Dame University."

4. Office of the White House Press Secretary, "Remarks of the President at the Commencement Exercises of Notre Dame University."

5. Office of the White House Press Secretary, "Remarks of the President at the Commencement Exercises of Notre Dame University."

6. For analyses of the Carter administration's understanding of the connection between human rights and foreign policymaking, see, for example, Michael J. Cangemi, "Frank Ortiz and Guatemala's 'Killer President,' 1976–1980," *Diplomatic History* 42, no. 4 (2018): 613–39; Kaufman and Kaufman, *The Presidency of James Earl Carter, Jr.*, 2nd ed.; Christian Peterson, *Globalizing Human Rights: Private Citizens, the Soviet Union, and the West* (New York: Taylor and Francis, 2012); Sargent, *A Superpower Transformed*; Schmidli, *The Fate of Freedom Elsewhere*; David F. Schmitz and Vanessa Walker, "Jimmy Carter and the Foreign Policy of Human Rights: The Development of a Post-Cold War Foreign Policy," *Diplomatic History* 28, no. 1 (2004): 113–43; and Strong, *Working in the World*.

7. For comprehensive analyses of Nicaragua's Sandinista Revolution and the Carter administration's response, see Derek Buckaloo, "Carter's Nicaragua and other Democratic Quagmires" in *Rightward Bound: Making America Conservative in the 1970s*, **ed.** Bruce Schulman and Julian Zelizer (Cambridge, MA: Harvard University Press, 2008); María Dolores Ferrero Blanco, *La Nicaragua de los Somoza: 1936–1979* (Managua: Instituto de Historico de Nicaragua y Centroamérica de la Universidad Centroaméricana, 2012); Robert Kagan, *A Twilight Struggle: American Power and Nicaragua, 1977–1981* (New York: Free Press, 1996);

Gerardo Sánchez Nateras, "The Sandinista Revolution and the Limits of the Cold War in Latin America: The Carter Administration and the Nicaraguan Crisis, 1977–1981," *Cold War History* 18, no. 2 (2018): 66–86, and William Michael Schmidli, "'The Most Sophisticated Intervention We Have Seen': The Carter Administration and the Nicaraguan Crisis, 1978–1979," *Diplomacy and Statecraft* 23, no. 1 (2012). For analyses of El Salvador, see Erik Ching, *Stories of Civil War in El Salvador: A Battle over Memory* (Chapel Hill: University of North Carolina Press, 2016); Crandall, *The Salvador Option*; D'Haeseleer, *The Salvadoran Crucible*; Jeffrey L. Gould, *Solidarity under Siege: The Salvadoran Labor Movement, 1970–1990* (New York: Cambridge University Press, 2019); Mario Lungo, *El Salvador en los años 80: Contrainsurgencia y revolución* (San José: Facultad Latinoamericana de Ciencias Sociales, 1990); Tommie Sue Montgomery, *Revolution in El Salvador: From Civil Strife to Civil Peace* (Boulder, CO: Westview, 1995); and William D. Stanley, *The Protection Racket State: Elite Politics, Military Extortion, and Civil War in El Salvador* (Philadelphia: Temple University Press, 1996).

8. Sarah Snyder, "'A Call for U.S. Leadership': Congressional Activism on Human Rights," *Diplomatic History* 37, no. 2 (April 2013): 372–97.

9. John Maffre, "New Leaders, Staff Changes Stimulate House Foreign Affairs Committee," *National Journal*, June 19, 1971, qtd. in Snyder, "A Call for U.S. Leadership," 372.

10. Mary Stuckey, *Jimmy Carter, Human Rights, and the National Agenda* (College Station, TX: Texas A&M University Press, 2008), 108. Additionally, Snyder notes that Congress held no human rights hearings in 1972. Snyder, "A Call for U.S. Leadership," 372n2.

11. International Financial Institutions Act, P.L. 95–118, 22 U.S.C. 262(d), 95th Cong., 1st Sess. (1977).

12. Jimmy Carter, "Address to the Chicago Council on Foreign Relations," Chicago, IL, March 15, 1976, "Foreign Policy" folder, box 247, Vickie Mongiardo Urban Ethnic Affairs Subject Files, JCL, 4.

13. Carter, "Relations Between the World's Democracies," New York, June 23, 1976, "Foreign Policy" folder, box 247, Vickie Mongiardo Urban Ethnic Affairs Subject Files, JCL, 2.

14. Amnesty International, Briefing Paper No. 8, "Guatemala," December 1976.

15. See René de Leon Schlotter's testimony, US Congress, House of Representatives, Subcommittee on International Organizations, *Human Rights in Nicaragua, Guatemala, and El Salvador: Implications for U.S. Policy*, 94th Cong., 2nd Sess., June 8 and 9, 1976 (Washington, DC: Government Printing Office, 1976), 52.

16. Gen. Kjell Eugenio Laugerud García, "Discurso del Gen. Kjell Eugenio Laugerud García, Presidente de la República ante el honorable congreso en su tercer año de gobierno," July 1, 1977 (Guatemala City: Tipografía Nacional, 1977), 15.

17. Subcommittee on International Organizations, *Human Rights in Nicaragua, Guatemala, and El Salvador*, 132.

18. United Nations General Assembly Official Records, 15th Plenary Meeting, 32nd Session, A/32/PV.15 (September 30, 1977), 242.

19. Memorandum, Carter to National Security Council, "Presidential Review Memorandum NSC-17, Review of United States Policy toward Latin America," [hereafter PRM NSC-17] March 12, 1977, National Security Council Institutional Files, 1977–1981, box 60, "PRC 008 Latin America, 3/21/77" folder, JCL.

20. PRM NSC-17.

21. PRM NSC-17.

22. PRM NSC-17, 12–13. The PRC report shows that the committee listed a potential policy shift that would "Take [a] forthcoming posture in North-South dialogue. Move to

Notes to Chapter 2 / 183

repeal Harkin, re-examine our negative position on the U.N. Charter on Economic Rights and Duties and 'collective economic security' in the OAS Charter Reform. Pressure governments politically to eliminate torture and assure habeas corpus and due process." However, nothing in the report details to what extent the committee considered this direction.

23. PRM NSC-17, 1–2.

24. PRM NSC-17, 12.

25. Uruguay was the first Latin American country to make such a refusal on February 28, 1977, followed by Argentina and Brazil on March 3 and 5, respectively, and El Salvador on March 17. See Juan de Onis, "Argentina and Uruguay Reject U.S. Assistance Linked to Human Rights," *New York Times,* March 2, 1977, 10; "Brazil Cancels Military Aid Treaty Over U.S. Report on Human Rights," *New York Times,* March 12, 1977, 1; Lee Leseaze, "Guatemala Rejects Aid, Cites Rights Criticism," *Washington Post,* March 18, 1977, 14, "El Salvador Rejects U.S. Arms Aid," *Washington Post,* March 18, 1977, 12.

26. "Guatemala es el quinto país que rechaza la ayuda militar de EE.UU. condicionada," *Prensa Libre,* March 18, 1977.

27. Soto Rosales, *El sueño encadenado,* 105.

28. "214 casos de secuestro de enero a noviembre de 1977: Mayoría de ellos intereso a campesinos y agricultores de San Marcos, Chiquimula y Santa Rosa," *El Grafico* (Guatemala City, Guatemala), December 19, 1977.

29. Mario Sandoval Alarcón, "God, Fatherland, and Liberty," *Proceedings; 10th WACL conference, Theme: Freedom Forces Unite Against Communist Tyranny!, Taipei, Taiwan, Republic of China, April 18–22, 1977* (Taipei: WACL, 1977).

30. See Instituto de Estudios Políticos para América Latina y Africa, *Guatemala, un futuro próximo* (Madrid, IEPALA, 1980), 198.

31. Romero biographer and contemporary Jon Sobrino described Grande's murder as the moment that "the scales fell from [Romero's] eyes.... His response was to make an option for the *campesinos*—to be converted and transformed into their defender, to become the voice of the voiceless." See Scott Wright, *Oscar Romero: Communion of the Saints* (Maryknoll, NY: Orbis Books, 2009), 51.

32. "Murdered Priest Knew the Risk of Preaching Christ," *Catholic Messenger* (Davenport, IA), April 28, 1977.

33. CEG, "Comunicado de los Obispos de Guatemala," May 4, 1977. See CEG, *Al Servicio de la vida, la justicia y la paz* (Guatemala: Conferencia Episcopal de Guatemala, 1997), 161–64.

34. "Walk from Guatemala to Aid Quake Victims," *Pittsburgh Catholic,* September 9, 1977.

35. "Childhood Head Sees Need in Guatemala," *Pittsburgh Catholic,* August 26, 1977.

36. "St. Monica Society Celebrates Tenth Anniversary," *Prairie Catholic* (New Ulm, MN), June 1977; "Here and There Around the Diocese," *Guardian* (Little Rock, AR), December 2, 1977.

37. Members of Guatemala's military and police forces were convicted of Andrade's murder in 1979 and López's murder in 1984.

38. Ciencia y Tecnología para Guatemala, A.C., *El Movimiento sindical en Guatemala, 1975–1985* (Mexico DF: Ciencia y Tecnología para Guatemala A.C., 1989), 57.

39. CEH, *Guatemala: Memoria del Silencio, Tomo VI: Casos Illustrativos, Annexo I* (Guatemala: Oficina de Servicios para Proyectos de las Naciones Unidas, 1999), 107. The report submitted to the CEH identified the getaway car as a red Datsun 120Y.

40. CEH, *Guatemala: Memoria del Silencio, Tomo VI.* For the "official" police account of

184 / Notes to Chapter 2

López's murder, see Policía Nacional de Guatemala, "Informe de investigación atentado, Lic. Mario López Larrave," June 8, 1977, GT PN 50 S010, Departamento de Investigaciones Criminológicas, Expedientes de juzgados de instancia ramo criminal, document number (11.0427.0852) 1452, Archivo Histórico de la Policía Nacional (AHPN), Guatemala City, Guatemala.

41. CEH, *Guatemala: Memoria del Silencio, Tomo VI*, 108.

42. Roberto Valdevellano, "Mario López Larrave: Hombre honesto, revolucionario y luchador," *Voz Universitaria Informativa* (May/June 1977), Centro de Investigaciones Regionales de Mésoamerica, Anigua Guatemala, Guatemala.

43. Confidential Cable, Davis L. Boster, US Embassy, Guatemala City, to State Department, Washington, DC, "Political Violence: Increased Concern," Confidential Cable 3987, June 24, 1977, DNSA.

44. "MLN rechaza nexos con nueva entidad secreta," *Prensa Libre*, June 24, 1977.

45. Boster, "Political Violence: Increased Concern."

46. Secretaría de la Paz, "Jornadas de agosto de 1977" (Guatemala: Secretaría de la Paz, Gobierno de Guatemala, 2009), 21.

47. Heather Vrana, "Revolutionary Transubstantiation in 'The Republic of Students': Death Commemoration in Urban Guatemala from 1977 to the Present," *Radical History Review* 114 (Fall 2012): 69–70.

48. Amaru Barahona Portocarrero, *Estudio sobre la historia conemporánea de Nicaragua* (San Pedro de Montes de Oca, San Juan, Costa Rica: Instituto de Investigaciones Sociales, Facultad de Ciencias Sociales, Universidad de Costa Rica, 1977). See also Vrana, "Revolutionary Transubstantiation in 'The Republic of Students': Death Commemoration in Urban Guatemala from 1977 to the Present," n16.

49. Vrana, "Revolutionary Transubstantion in 'The Republic of Students.'"

50. Cyrus Vance, US Department of State, to US Embassy, Guatemala, "Draft Human Rights Evaluation Report Prepared by ARA/CEN," July 13, 1977, Confidential Cable 162645, DNSA. Mention of "heavy-handed tactics in Northern Guatemala" refers to the military's operations in Ixcán and murder of Maryknoll Mission priest Father Bill Woods, detailed in chapter 1.

51. Vance, "Draft Human Rights Evaluation Report Prepared by ARA/CEN."

52. Memorandum, Christine Dodson to Standing Consultative Commission, "SCC Meeting on Central America," July 19, 1979, "RAC 20 Staff Files" folder, NLC 20–25–1–1–0, JCL.

53. US Embassy, Guatemala, to Department of State, "Monthly Report on Political Violence and Human Rights: September 1977," Confidential Airgram A-107, October 19, 1977, DNSA.

54. Belize did not gain independence until 1981. It was officially known as British Honduras until 1973 and was the subject of lengthy debate between Britain and Guatemala. In 1978, US policymakers believed Laugerud was willing to go to war with Britain over its Belizean claims; the Holy See's mediation relaxed these tensions considerably.

55. CEG, "Catequisis de los obispos de Guatemala al pueblo Cristiano sobre fe y política," February 1978, *Al Servicio de la vida, la justicia y la paz*, 171.

56. CEG, "Catequisis de los obispos de Guatemala al pueblo Cristiano sobre fe y política," 178.

57. Paul VI, *Octogesima Adveniens, Apostolic Letter of Pope Paul VI*, May 14, 1971. Specifically, the bishops quoted the pope's contention that "political power must know how to stand aside from [its] particular interests in order to view its responsibility with regard to the good

Notes to Chapter 3 / 185

of all men, even going beyond national limits." For the bishops' use of the term "critical conscience," see sec. 702.

58. CEG, "Catequisis de los obispos de Guatemala al pueblo Cristiano sobre fe y política," 178.

59. CEG, "Exhortación de los Obispos de Guatemala," March 1978, 179.

60. Soto Rosales, *El sueño encadenado*, 85.

61. US Embassy, Guatemala City, Guatemala, to US Department of State, Washington, DC, "Post-Election Furor: Some Perspectives through the Haze," Confidential Cable 1476, March 9, 1978, DNSA.

62. Marlise Simons, "Army Killings in Indian Village Shock Guatemala," *Washington Post*, June 24, 1978.

63. Grandin, *The Last Colonial Massacre*, 1.

64. "Guerrilleros y religiosos responsables de la tragedia en Panzós, dice el ministro Spiegeler," *Prensa Libre*, June 1, 1978.

65. CEG, "Boletin de Prensa," June 2, 1978, *Al Servicio de la vida, la justicia y la paz*, 182–83.

66. CEG, "Comunicado de la Conferencia Episcopal de Guatemala," June 15, 1978, *Al Servicio de la vida, la justicia y la paz*, 184.

67. "Obispo de las Verapazes repudia los sucesos de Panzós," *Prensa Libre*, June 2, 1978.

68. US Embassy, Rome, Italy, to US Department of State, Washington, DC, "The Vatican and the Massacre of 'Campesinos' in Guatemala," Confidential Cable 11626, June 22, 1978, DNSA.

69. "34 Are Reported Killed in Guatemalan Violence," *New York Times*, May 31, 1978; "Guatemalan Troops Hunt Peasant Revolt Leaders," *Chicago Tribune*, May 31, 1978; Simons, "Army Killings in Indian Village Shock Guatemala"; "Peasants Clash with Military Troops," *Statesman Journal* (Salem, OR), May 31, 1978; "Machete Fight Kills 43 Guatemalans," *Billings Gazette* (Billings, MT), May 31, 1978; "Landowners Kill 38 Peasants," *Oshkosh Northwestern* (Oshkosh, WI), May 30, 1978.

70. See, for example, "Peasant Uprising in Guatemala," *Catholic Advance*, June 8, 1978; "Bishops Condemn Guatemala Massacre," *Globe* (Sioux City, IA), June 15, 1978; and *Witness* (Dubuque, IA), June 16, 1978; "Guatemalan Church Leaders Charge Government with 'Genocidal Violence,'" *Courier-Journal*, June 21, 1978; "Indians Massacred," *Catholic Messenger*, June 22, 1978.

71. Grandin, *The Last Colonial Massacre*.

72. US Embassy, Guatemala City, to US Department of State, Washington, DC, "Seventeen Soldiers Dead in Panzós Reprisal," Confidential Cable 3526, June 15, 1978, DNSA.

73. US Embassy, Guatemala City, to US Department of State, Washington, DC, "Monthly Report on Violence and Human Rights," June 1978, Airgram A-78, August 24, 1978, DNSA.

74. Multiple Catholic newspapers across the United States reported on López's murder. See, for example, "'A Willingness to Die,'" *Denver Catholic Register* (Denver, CO), July 19, 1978; "Priest Termed 'Martyr,'" *Pittsburgh Catholic*, July 21, 1978; "Martyred Priest," *Witness*, July 27, 1978; "Murder of Pastor Leads to March," *Catholic Advance*, August 3, 1978; and "Priest's Murder Stirs Guatemala Protest," *Arkansas Catholic* (Little Rock, AR), August 4, 1978.

Chapter 3

1. After resigning as defense minister, Lucas was replaced by General Otto Guillermo Spiegler Noriega, who had falsely accused the church of instigating the Panzós massacre in May 1978.

186 / Notes to Chapter 3

2. "Paul VI Is Praised Around the World," *New York Times*, August 8, 1978.

3. The Fourteen Families were El Salvador's Llach, De Sola, Hill, Dueñas, Regalado, Wright, Salaverria, García Prieto, Quiñones, Guirola, Borja, Sol, Daglio, and Meza Ayau families. By 1980, the Salaverria, Dueñas, and Regalado families enjoyed a combined net worth of over 350 million dollars; in comparison, the average agricultural worker earned less the four dollars per day. Paul Heath Hoeffel, "The Eclipse of the Oligarchs," *New York Times*, September 6, 1981.

4. These totals include abuses committed by non-state forces, including guerrillas and civilians.

5. Boster, US Embassy, Guatemala to US Department of State, "The Lucas Victory: Implications," March 14, 1978, Confidential Cable 001476, DNSA.

6. CEH, *Guatemala: Memoria del Silencio, Tomo VIII: Casos Presentados, Anexo II* (Guatemala: Oficina de Servicios para Proyectos de las Naciones Unidas, 1999), 65, caso 9413.

7. CEH, *Guatemala: Memoria del Silencio, Tomo VIII*, 135, caso 9397.

8. Boster later reported that one potential explanation for Lucas's sluggish response was "sensitivity to U.S. opinion" and the regime's hopes that a more cautious approach to the protests would facilitate reinstatement of US military aid to the country. See Boster, US Embassy, Guatemala, to US Department of State, "U.S. Goals and Objectives," December 19, 1978, Confidential Cable 7398, DNSA.

9. Boster, US Embassy, Guatemala, to US Department of State, "Student Leader Assassinated," October 23, 1978, Confidential Cable 6243, DNSA.

10. CEH, *Guatemala: Memoria del Silencio, Tomo II*, 81–82.

11. CEH, *Guatemala: Memoria del Silencio, Tomo II*. In 2014, the Sixth Command Unit's director, Pedro García Arredondo, was convicted in a Guatemalan court for the unit's role in the Spanish Embassy Massacre of 1980.

12. Amnesty International, "The Human Rights Year in Guatemala: A Calendar of Abuses" (London: Amnesty International, 1979).

13. CEH, *Guatemala: Memoria del Silencio, Tomo VIII, 361*, caso 20002.

14. CEH, *Guatemala: Memoria del Silencio, Tomo X*, 1112–1113, caso 16709.

15. Boster, US Embassy, Guatemala to US Department of State, "Lucas's First Five Months," December 5, 1978, Confidential Cable 7172, DNSA.

16. Boster, US Embassy, Guatemala to US Department of State, "Developments Relating to Castañeda Killing and ESA," October 30, 1978, Confidential Cable 6426, DNSA.

17. John Bennett, US Embassy, Guatemala to US Department of State, "EGP Activities on South Coast," Telegram 0913, February 8, 1979, DNSA.

18. Bennett, US Embassy, Guatemala to US Department of State, "Vice President Villagrán Kramer: Golpe in Guatemala?" March 29, 1978, Confidential Cable 2046, DNSA. Boster retired from the foreign service in January 1979, and Bennett assumed ambassadorial duties until Ortiz's appointment later in the year.

19. CIA, "Alberto Fuentes Mohr, Manuel Colom Argueta, and Comando Seis," Secret Cable, March 15, 1980, DNSA.

20. CIA, "Manuel Colom Argueta Assassinated," March 22, 1979, DNSA.

21. CEH, *Guatemala: Memoria del Silencio, Tomo VIII*, 169, casos 8033 and 708.

22. CEH, *Guatemala: Memoria del Silencio, Tomo VIII*, 297, caso 20035.

23. Cyrus Vance, US Department of State to US Embassy Guatemala, "IMET for Guatemala," March 22, 1979, Confidential Cable 71549, DNSA.

24. Bennett, US Embassy Guatemala to US Department of State, "IMET Vote Reaction," March 27, 1979, Confidential Cable 1953, DNSA.

Notes to Chapter 3 / 187

25. CEH, *Guatemala: Memoria del Silencio, Tomo X*, 1012, caso 15493.

26. Guatemala News and Information Bureau (GNIB), "Report on Violence in Northern Quiché, Guatemala," Princeton University, Civil War, Society, and Political Transition in Guatemala: The Guatemala News and Information Bureau Archive, hereafter GNIBA.

27. CEH, *Guatemala: Memoria del Silencio, Tomo X*, 689, caso 20012.

28. GNIB, "Trabajadores ocupan iglesia," ¡*Guatemala!*ˆ, November/December 1979, GNIBA.

29. GNIB, "Trabajadores ocupan iglesia."

30. John Paul I, *Urbi et Orbi*, August 27, 1978. The term *Urbi et Orbi* ("to the City and World") denotes a special pontifical address to mark a solemn occasion; it is typically associated with a new pope's initial address to Catholics following his election. For attendance estimates, see Frederic Hill, "Cardinal Luciani Is Elected Pope," *Baltimore Sun*, August 27, 1978.

31. John Paul I, *Urbi et Orbi*.

32. John Paul II, "To Members of the Third General Conference of the Latin American Episcopate," Puebla, Mexico, January 28, 1979.

33. John Paul II, "To Members of the Third General Conference of the Latin American Episcopate."

34. See, for example, Ratzinger's "Instruction on Certain Aspects of the 'Theology of Liberation,'" and "Instruction on Christian Freedom and Liberation."

35. John Paul II, "Meeting with Mexican *Indios*," Culiapán, Mexico, January 29, 1979.

36. John Paul II, "Meeting with Mexican *Indios*." The pope's reference to *Mater et Magistra* specifically focused on the encyclical's third part, which addressed, among other issues, economic and material inequality, the global common good, wealthy nations' obligation to the poor, and "disinterested" aid to the developing world.

37. CELAM, *La evangelización en el presente y en el futuro de América Latina* (Lima, Peru: Labrusa, 1982), 132–36.

38. CELAM, *La evangelización en el presente y en el futuro de América Latina*, 83–84.

39. Jerry Filteau, "'Three Popes' in Mexico?" *Pittsburgh Catholic*, February 9, 1979.

40. Frederic M. Lilly, "Pope Didn't Speak from 'Both Sides of Mouth,'" *Denver Catholic Register*, February 7, 1979.

41. "Puebla Will Affect U.S. Church," *Anchor* (Fall River, MA Diocese), February 15, 1979; "U.S. Church Leaders Support Puebla Vision," *Catholic Sentinel* (Portland, OR), February 23, 1979.

42. CEG, "Comunicado de la Conferencia Episcopal de la Iglesia Católica de Guatemala," March 2, 1979, *Al Servicio de la vida, justicia, y la paz*, 187–89.

43. See Alarcón, "God, Fatherland, and Liberty."

44. National Catholic News Service, "Guatemalan Bishops Deny Charges of Marxism," May 17, 1977.

45. "Salvador Priests Ban," *Catholic Herald* (London), December 16, 1977.

46. Catholic News Service, June 27, 1979.

47. Father John Goggin, interview with author, San Lucas Tolimán, Sololá, Guatemala.

48. Frank V. Ortiz, Jr., US Embassy, Guatemala, to US Department of State, "The Villagrán Kramer Saga: The Final Chapter Begins?" Confidential Cable 000648, January 29, 1980, DNSA.

49. Ortiz, "The Villagrán Kramer Saga."

50. Oficina de Derechos Humanos del Arzobispado de Guatemala (ODHAG), *Guatemala: Never Again!* (Maryknoll, NY: Orbis, 1999), 225.

188 / Notes to Chapter 3

51. Ortiz used the term "siege mentality" to describe Lucas's state of mind in a cable dated January 30, 1980. See Ortiz, US Embassy, Guatemala to US Department of State, "President Lucas Comments on the Current Situation," Confidential Cable 00673, DNSA.

52. CEH, *Guatemala: Memoria del Silencio, Tomo VI*, 164.

53. According to the CEH's account of the Spanish Embassy Massacre, the Chajúl massacre occurred on December 6, 1979. However, no record of this massacre exists in the CEH's exhaustive, 350-page list of massacres and other human rights violations from the Quiché department during the war. A massacre dated March 1979 is recorded in Chajúl (caso 11120), as well as the murder of Tomás Anay, a suspected guerrilla (caso 16763). See CEH, *Guatemala: Memoria del Silencio, Tomo X*, 810–11, 1012.

54. Embassy occupations were not unheard of in Latin America at the time. The most notable example of this occurred later in 1980, when Cubans' occupation of the Peruvian Embassy in Havana resulted in the Mariél Boatlift between April and October of that year. One of the best accounts of this event is María Cristina García's *Havana, USA: Cuban Exiles and Cuban-Americans in South Florida, 1959–1994* (Berkeley: University of California Press, 1997).

55. Sabino, *Guatemala, la historia silenciada, Tomo II*, 202.

56. Parts of this footage were included in filmmaker Pamela Yates's 1983 documentary *When the Mountains Tremble*.

57. CEH, *Guatemala: Memoria del Silencio, Tomo VI*, 172.

58. Diocese of Quiché, "Communique of the Diocese of Quiché on the Massacre in the Spanish Embassy 31-1-1980." The diocese's statement was reprinted in the *Iglesia Guatemalteca en el Exilio*'s *Boletin* newsletter in May 1987. See *Iglesia Guatemalteca en el Exilio, Boletin* 7, no. 1 (May 1987): 60, GNIBA.

59. CIA, "Alberto Fuentes Mohr, Manuel Colom Argueta, and Commando Seis."

60. CEH, *Guatemala: Memoria del Silencio, Tomo VIII*, 132, caso 10288.

61. CEH, *Guatemala: Memoria del Silencio, Tomo I*, 191.

62. CEH, *Guatemala: Memoria del Silencio, Tomo VIII*, 143, caso 2269.

63. CEH, *Guatemala: Memoria del Silencio, Tomo VIII*, 143, caso 16186.

64. CEH, *Guatemala: Memoria del Silencio, Tomo X*, 1274–1275, casos 3268, 3278, 12074, 15109, and 2949.

65. To protect survivors' privacy, I have changed their names.

66. Interview with author, January 2, 2015.

67. Interview with author, January 3, 2015.

68. Father David Roney, "Dominga, New Orphans, New Problems," Diocese of New Ulm Newsletter, vol. XI, no. 1, August 1981. Diocese of New Ulm Archive, New Ulm, MN.

69. See "Priest Termed 'Martyr,'" *Pittsburgh Catholic*, July 21, 1978; "Stop Genocide . . . and Persecution," *Witness*, June 28, 1979; and Catholic News Agency, "Assailants Machine-gun Belgian Priest in Guatemala," May 14, 1980.

70. Peggy Scherer, "Pentagon Tour," *Catholic Worker*, March 3, 1981.

71. Lauri Wahl, "Fr. Buechele: Guatemala Presents Dilemma to Church," *Catholic Messenger*, October 4, 1979.

72. "Good Luck, Mr. President!" *Witness*, April 3, 1980.

73. "Human Rights Emphasis Seen in Question," *Courier-Journal*, December 17, 1980.

74. "Friendship Force to Visit Guatemala," *Witness*, February 22, 1979.

75. "Women Religious Discuss Social Justice May 1–2," *South Texas Catholic* (Corpus Christi, TX), May 17, 1979.

Notes to Chapter 4 / 189

76. ODHAG, *Testigos de la fe por paz: Vidas ejemplares de la Iglesia Católica de Guatemala* (Guatemala: ODHAG, 2003), 58. Haren gave his account in a homily in Guatemala City on June 30, 2000, as part of the country's Day of Martyrs ceremonies.

77. ODHAG, *Testigos de la fe por paz*, 20.

78. *El Grafico*, January 16, 1980.

79. Public Relations Secretariat of the Presidency, "The Right of Response to a Publication Which Appeared on January 16 on Page 22: The Right to Clarification," *El Grafico*, January 17, 1980.

80. Jesuit Conference of the United States, "Jesuits in Guatemala Threatened with Death," January 29, 1980, GNIBA.

81. CEH, *Guatemala: Memoria del Silencio, Tomo III*, 1053–54, caso 2768.

82. Amnesty International, "Guatemala: A Government Program of Political Murder" (London: Amnesty International Publications, 1981), AMR 34/02/81.

Chapter 4

1. Davis L. Boster, US Embassy, Guatemala, to US Department of State, "Background for Our Human Rights Speeches," Confidential Cable 004230, July 18, 1978, DNSA.

2. "Guatemalan General Named New Leader," *San Bernardino County Sun* (San Bernardino, CA), July 2, 1978.

3. "Guatemala 'Under Siege' for Inauguration," *Lincoln Journal Star*, July 2, 1978.

4. "We'll Punish Abuse, Carter Tells Latin Leaders," *Miami Herald* (Miami, FL), June 22, 1978.

5. Boster, "Background for Our Human Rights Speeches."

6. Richard Feinberg, US Department of State, Washington, DC, to Jennone Walker, "Direction of Human Rights in Guatemala," confidential memorandum, September 1, 1978, DNSA.

7. According to Boster, Villagrán made his remarks on August 11, while Lucas met with Boster on August 15 and Castillo on August 17. See Viron P. Vaky to Stephen Cohen, "Tear Gas for Guatemala," August 19, 1978, *Foreign Relations of the United States, 1977–1980*, Volume 15, Central America, 1977–1980, ed. Nathaniel L. Smith (Washington, DC: Government Printing Office, 2010), Document 28, n2.

8. DIA, "Military Intelligence Summary (MIS), Volume VIII—Latin America," September 1980, DNSA.

9. See, for example, "Missioner Protests Reported Israeli Arms Sale to Nicaragua," *National Catholic Reporter*, March 16, 1979; "Priest: 'U.S. Must Vow No More Nicaraguan Aid,'" *National Catholic Reporter*, April 20, 1979; and "Christians Rap Arms Shipments to El Salvador," *National Catholic Reporter*, November 7, 1980.

10. General Accounting Office, "Military Sales: The United States Continuing Munition Supply Relationship with Guatemala," Report to the Chairman, Subcommittee on Western Hemisphere Affairs, Committee on Foreign Affairs, House of Representatives (Washington: Government Printing Office), 1986. The specific sections referred to in the GAO report are 50 U.S.C. app. 2401, et. seq. and 22 U.S.C. 2751, et. seq. for the Export Administration Act of 1979 and the Arms Export Control Act, respectively.

11. According to a report from the National Security Council, a license application for the sale of five thousand tear gas canisters from an "unknown supplier" was received on August 17, 1978, and approved five days later. See "SCC Meeting on Central America," JCL.

12. See Schmidli, *The Fate of Freedom Elsewhere*, 129–39.

13. Frank M. Tucker, Jr., US Embassy, San Salvador, to US Department of State, "Nicaraguan Situation Report No. 2—11:00 a.m. June 10," Confidential Cable 02553, June 10, 1979, DNSA.

14. For in-depth analyses of the FSLN, Sandinista Revolution, and US-Nicaraguan relations, see Michael Dodson and Laura Nuzzi O'Shaughnessy, *Nicaragua's Other Revolution: Religious Faith and Political Struggle* (Chapel Hill: University of North Carolina Press, 1990); Dennis Gilbert, *Sandinistas: The Party and the Revolution* (New York: Blackwell, 1988); Jeffrey L. Gould, *To Lead as Equals: Rural Protest and Political Consciousness in Chinandega, Nicaragua, 1912–1979* (Chapel Hill: University of North Carolina Press, 1990); Roger Lancaster, *Thanks to God and the Revolution: Popular Religion and Class Consciousness in the New Nicaragua* (New York: Columbia University Press, 1988); Robert A. Pastor, *Condemned to Repetition: The United States and Nicaragua* (Princeton, NJ: Princeton University Press, 1987); Pezzullo and Pezzullo, *At the Fall of Somoza*; Margaret Randall, *Sandino's Daughters: Testimonies of Nicaraguan Women in Struggle* (Vancouver: New Star Books, 1981); Margaret Randall, *Sandino's Daughters Revisited: Feminism in Nicaragua* (New Brunswick: Rutgers University Press, 1994); and Matilde Zimmerman, *Sandinista: Carlos Fonseca and the Nicaraguan Revolution* (Durham, NC: Duke University Press, 2001).

15. Frank J. Devine, US Embassy, San Salvador, to US Department of State, "Initial Coup Proclamation," Confidential Cable 05890, October 16, 1979, DNSA.

16. For in-depth analyses of the FMLN, Salvadoran Civil War, and the country's church-state relations during this period, see Arnson, *Crossroads*; Mark Danner, *The Massacre at El Mozote: A Parable of the Cold War* (New York: Vintage Books, 1994); Martha Doggett, *Death Foretold: The Jesuit Murders in El Salvador* (Washington, DC: Georgetown University Press, 1993); Erickson Nepstad, *Convictions of the Soul*; Montgomery, *Revolution in El Salvador*; Courtney Prisk, ed., *The Commandante Speaks: Memoirs of an El Salvadoran Guerrilla* (Boulder, CO: Westview, 1991); Jon Sobrino, SJ, *Monseñor Romero* (San Salvador: UCA Editores, 1989); and Molly Todd, *Beyond Displacement: Campesinos, Refugees, and Collective Action in the Salvadoran Civil War* (Madison: University of Wisconsin Press, 2010).

17. Meeting minutes, "Presidential Review Committee," PRC 111 Central America, 6/11/79 folder, box 76, National Security Council Institutional Files, 1977–1981, JCL.

18. US Department of State, "Press Briefing," July 12, 1979, Frank V. Ortiz Collection, box 5, folder 5, Fray Angélico Chavez History Library, Palace of the Governors, Santa Fe, NM.

19. Ortiz, US Embassy, Guatemala to US Department of State, "A View from Guatemala," September 4, 1979, Classified Telegram 005839, Frank V. Ortiz Collection, box 5, folder 5.

20. Ortiz, "A View from Guatemala."

21. John Bushnell, US Department of Defense, letter to Ortiz, US Embassy, Guatemala, October 13, 1979, Frank V. Ortiz Collection, box 5, folder 5.

22. Letter, Bushnell to Ortiz, October 13, 1979.

23. Letter, Bushnell to Ortiz, October 13, 1979.

24. James Mack, US Department of State, letter to Ortiz, US Embassy, Guatemala, October 19, 1979, Frank V. Ortiz Collection, box 5, folder 5.

25. Section 116 of the Foreign Assistance Act stated, "No assistance may be provided under this part to the government of any country which engages in consistent pattern of gross violations of internationally recognized human rights, including torture or cruel, inhuman, or degrading treatment or punishment, prolonged detention without charges, or other flagrant denial of the right to life, liberty and the security of the person, unless such assistance

will directly benefit the needy people in such country" (P.L. 94–161, Foreign Assistance Act of 1974, 22 U.S.C. 2151).

26. Ortiz Jr., *Ambassador Ortiz*, 129.

27. Ortiz, US Embassy, Guatemala to US Department of State, "The Villagrán Kramer Saga: Final Chapter Begins?" January 29, 1980, Confidential Cable 000648, DNSA, 9.

28. Ortiz, US Embassy, Guatemala to US Department of State, "Vice President Villagrán Kramer's Future in the Government of Guatemala," November 27, 1979, Confidential Telegram, Ambassador Frank Ortiz Collection, box 5, folder 5.

29. See Ortiz, US Embassy, Guatemala, to John Bushnell, US Department of Defense, February 21, 1980, Ambassador Frank Ortiz Collection, box 5, folder 8, Fray Angélico Chavez History Library. See also "Politica erratica: Inconsecuencia de EE.UU con paises amigos," and "Agresion económica," *El Imparcial*, February 8, 1980.

30. Msgr. James B. Flynn, "Meanwhile in Guatemala," *Interchange*, August 7, 1979, GNIBA.

31. Archbishop James Casey, "A Statement of Policy Regarding Investments for the Archdiocese," *Denver Catholic Register*, August 2, 1978.

32. Casey, "A Statement of Policy Regarding Investments for the Archdiocese.".

33. Msgr. Charles Owen Rice, "The Nicaraguan Tragedy," *Pittsburgh Catholic*, July 6, 1979.

34. Heather Foote, "Statement of Heather Foote, Washington Office on Latin America," Human Rights and the Phenomenon of Disappearances, Hearings Before the Subcommittee on International Organizations of the Committee of Foreign Affairs, House of Representatives, 96th Cong., 1st Sess., September 25, 1979 (Washington, DC: GPO, 1979), 246–87.

35. See appendix 16, "Human Rights and the Phenomenon of Disappearances," 606–10.

36. Donald J. Pease, "Violence in Guatemala," *Congressional Record, Extensions of Remarks*, May 7, 1980 (Washington, DC: GPO), 10413–14.

37. Ortiz, US Embassy, Guatemala to US Department of State, "Pertinent Comments on the Situation in Guatemala," June 20, 1980, Confidential Cable 003936, Ambassador Frank Ortiz Collection, box 5, folder 8, 1.

38. Ortiz, "Pertinent Comments on the Situation in Guatemala," 2.

39. Council on Hemispheric Affairs, Press Release, May 29, 1980, Ambassador Frank Ortiz Collection, box 5, folder 8.

40. Letter, Tom Harkin, US House of Representatives, to Carter, June 10, 1980, "Ortiz, Frank, State Dept., Guatemala, 12/79–6/80" folder, box 30, Special Assistant to the President—Torres File, White House Central Files Collection, JCL.

41. Letter, Ortiz, US Embassy, Guatemala, to Harkin, US House of Representatives, June 26, 1980, Ambassador Frank Ortiz Collection, box 5, folder 8.

42. Graham Hovey, "Envoy Losing Post after Policy Clash," *New York Times*, June 28, 1980.

43. US Embassy, Guatemala Press Briefing, July 3, 1980, Ambassador Frank Ortiz Collection, box 5, folder 8.

44. "Causa extrañeza posible cambio de embajador de EUA" and "'El embajador Ortiz ha hecho un buen papel,'" *La Tarde*, July 3, 1980; "Ortiz, Frank, State Dept., Guatemala, 7/3/80–7/25/80" folder, box 30, Special Assistant to the President—Torres File, White House Central Files Collection, JCL.

45. "Maquinación consumada en el despido del embajador Ortiz," *Prensa Libre*, July 4, 1980; "Ortiz, Frank, State Dept., Guatemala, 7/3/80–7/25/80" folder, box 30, Special Assistant to the President—Torres File, White House Central Files Collection, JCL.

46. Celia Dugger, "U.S. Changing Latin American Envoys," *Washington Post*, July 20, 1980.

47. For Ortiz's comments on Guatemala, see his memoir, *Ambassador Ortiz*, 124.

48. Committee of Santa Fe, *A New Inter-American Policy for the Eighties* (Washington, DC: Council for Inter-American Security, 1980), 1.

49. The committee's members were L. Francis Bouchey, executive vice president of the Council for Inter-American Security and author of *Guatemala: A Promise in Peril*; Fontaine; Dr. David C. Jordan, a member of the Institute for Foreign Policy Analysis and professor of government and foreign affairs at the University of Virginia; Lt. General Gordon Sumner, Jr. (Ret.), special adviser to the assistant secretary of state for Inter-American Affairs; and Dr. Lewis Tambs, a history professor at Arizona State University and former petroleum contractor in Venezuela.

50. Committee of Santa Fe, *A New Inter-American Policy for the Eighties*, 21.

51. Committee of Santa Fe, *A New Inter-American Policy for the Eighties*, 22.

Chapter 5

1. Alice Feinstein, "Spokane Diocese Missionaries to Guatemala Work in Danger," *Spokane Daily Chronicle* (Spokane, WA), January 16, 1981.

2. National Catholic News Service, "Spokane Bishop Finds Suffering 'Extreme' in Left-Right Conflict," January 23, 1981. The wire report was also published in the January 29 edition of the *Catholic Advance* and the January 30 edition of the *Catholic Sentinel*.

3. Guatemala Solidarity Committee of Minnesota, "An Open Letter to President Reagan," *Minneapolis Tribune* (Minneapolis, MN), January 20, 1981.

4. Guatemala Solidarity Committee of Minnesota, "An Open Letter to President Reagan."

5. Letter, Richard Allen to William Wilson, June 25, 1981. William A. Wilson Papers, box 1, folder 4, Georgetown University Library, Washington, DC. The United States did not establish full, formal diplomatic relations with the Holy See until 1984, when Wilson was named the first United States ambassador to the Holy See. Before that, the president's personal representative to the Holy See fulfilled diplomatic obligations and tasks, but without the official title of ambassador. Among the most notable studies on US relations with the Holy See are Luca Castagna, *A Bridge Across the Ocean* (Washington, DC: Catholic University of America Press, 2014); P. Peter Sarros, *U.S.-Vatican Relations, 1975–1980: A Diplomatic Study* (Notre Dame, IN: University of Notre Dame Press, 2020).

6. For the Reagan administration's early positions on arms traffic through Honduras, see CIA, "Central American Arms Trafficking: The Comayagua Cache," intelligence report, February 28, 1981, DNSA, and William P. Clark, Jr., US Department of State, to US Embassy, Managua, Nicaragua, "Arms Trucked through Honduras," Secret Cable 101392, April 21, 1981. For its positions on the country's refugee crisis, see Joint Chiefs of Staff Message Center, Department of Defense, to DIA, "300 Salvadorans Blocked From Entering Ho[nduras]," Unclassified Cable, February 5, 1981; Jack Binns, US Embassy, Tegucigalpa, Honduras, to US Department of State, "1981 World Refugee Report to Congress," Unclassified Cable 03253, May 11, 1981, DNSA, and US Embassy, Tegucigalpa, to US Department of State, "Update on the Miskito Refugees," Confidential Cable 04987, July 10, 1981, DNSA.

7. US Department of State, "Interagency Options for El Salvador," February 23, 1981, folder "NSC 00004, February 27, 1981, [Poland, Caribbean Basin, F-15, El Salvador]," box 91282, Executive Secretariat: Meeting File, Ronald Reagan Library (hereafter RRL). For a

Notes to Chapter 5 / 193

comprehensive and in-depth analysis of the Reagan administration's policy approaches to El Salvador during this period, see Gail E. S. Yoshitani, *Reagan on War: A Reappraisal of the Weinberger Doctrine, 1980–1984* (College Station: Texas A&M University Press, 2012).

8. LeoGrande, *Our Own Backyard*, 82.

9. Yoshitani, *Reagan on War*, 37.

10. National Security Council, "Strategy Toward Cuba and Central America," Washington, DC, November 10, 1981, "NSC 00024, November 10, 1981, Strategy toward Cuba and Central America" folder, NSC NSPG Meeting Minutes and Presidential Memos Collection, RRL.

11. LeoGrande, *Our Own Backyard*, 81.

12. LeoGrande, *Our Own Backyard*, 84.

13. LeoGrande, *Our Own Backyard*, 88.

14. Jim Lackey, "Church Groups Protest 'Lethal' Supplies Included in New Aid to El Salvador," *Pittsburgh Catholic*, January 23, 1981.

15. "No New Prisons, Senate Advises," *Catholic Sentinel*, February 27, 1981.

16. Father J. Bryan Hehir, "Testimony of Rev. J. Bryan Hehir," Hearings before the Subcommittee of Foreign Operations and Agencies, US House of Representatives Appropriations Committee, 97th Cong., 1st Sess., February 25, 1981 (Washington, DC: GPO), 241.

17. Haig made his remarks during a House Foreign Affairs Committee hearing on funding for El Salvador on March 18. See United States House of Representatives, *Foreign Assistance Legislation for Fiscal Year 1982, Part I* (Washington, DC: GPO, 1981), 163.

18. See "Excerpts from Haig's Replies Before House Panel," *New York Times*, March 19, 1981; "Soviets Have a 'Hit List,' Haig Charges," *Miami Herald*, March 19, 1981; "4 Women Not Shot in Cold blood?" *Indianapolis Star*, March 19, 1981; and "Haig Concerned Over Weapons to Nicaragua," *Los Angeles Times*, March 20, 1981.

19. "Slain Nuns' Families Charge U.S. 'Smear,'" *San Francisco Examiner*, March 19, 1981.

20. "Salvadorans Assail Haig on 'Soviet Peril,'" *Arizona Republic* (Phoenix, AZ), March 20, 1981.

21. "Haig Backs Off on How Nuns Might Have Died," *San Francisco Examiner*, March 19, 1981.

22. Melvin E. Sinn, US Embassy, Guatemala City, to US Department of State, "Meeting with President Lucas," Confidential Cable 0001469, March 9, 1981. DNSA.

23. Sinn, "Meeting with President Lucas."

24. CEH, *Guatemala: Memoria del Silencio, Tomo II*, 401–2, caso 13255.

25. Other responsible state forces included local military commissions and auxiliary patrols.

26. CEH, *Guatemala: Memoria del Silencio, Tomo VIII*, 46–47, caso 11063.

27. "Gunmen in Guatemala Kill 4 Convicts in Raid," *New York Times*, February 12, 1981; "14 Guatemalans Are Found Dead; Marks On Bodies Indicate Torture," February 16, 1981; "Behind the Killings in Guatemala," February 17, 1981; and "Guatemala Leader Accused by Rights Group in Killings," February 18, 1981. See also "15 Die in Guatemala Strife," *Chicago Tribune*, January 24, 1981; "Eight Guatemalan Men Reportedly Strangled," *Los Angeles Times*, February 12, 1981; "Raiders Kill 36 in Guatemalan Village," *Washington Post*, June 3, 1981.

28. See "Oklahoma Priest Murdered in Guatemala," August 14, 1981; "No News on Priest's Death in Guatemala," October 9, 1981; and "Priest Killed in Guatemala," July 17, 1981. See also Lernoux, "The Struggle for Central America," September 25, 1981; Hebblethwaite,

"Central America's Problems Appraised," July 3, 1981; and Drinan, "Haig's Remarks 'Ambiguous, Send Ominous Cloud,'" February 6, 1981.

29. See "Davenport Native Tours U.S." and "A New Man Settles in at SVC," *Catholic Messenger*, September 9, 1982, and August 5, 1982.

30. "Profound Faith Only Hope of Church," *Denver Catholic Register*, November 4, 1981.

31. See, for example, Gordon Oliver, "Nun Who Visited El Salvador Asks Halt to U.S. Aid," *Catholic Sentinel*, January 23, 1981; "No to Guatemala," *Witness*, September 12, 1982, and Stephen Karlinchak, "Ex-Area Nun Headed for Troubled Guatemala," *Pittsburgh Catholic*, October 9, 1981.

32. "Children Reach Out to Hurting Families," *Catholic Messenger*, April 1, 1982.

33. Sinn, US Embassy, Guatemala City, to Haig, US Department of State, "Guatemala Policy Review Input," Confidential Cable 3083, February 20, 1981, folder "Guatemala [7], box RAC 8, Roger Fontaine Files, RRL.

34. Roger W. Fontaine and Robert L. Schweitzer, National Security Council, to Richard Allen, National Security Council, "Central America: Biting the Bullet," Secret memorandum, folder "Guatemala [7], box RAC 8, Roger Fontaine Files," RRL.

35. Sinn, US Embassy, Guatemala City, to Haig, "The Roman Catholic Church as a Factor in Guatemalan Politics," Secret Airgram 267913, folder "Guatemala [5]," box RAC 8, Roger Fontaine Files, RRL.

36. The six priests were Father Coronado de la Crúz, murdered May 1, 1980, in Guatemala City; Walter Voordeckers, May 12, 1980, in Escuintla; José María Gran Cirera, June 5, 1980, in Quiché; Juan Alonzo Fernandez, February 16, 1981, in Quiché; Carlos Gálvez Galindo, May 14, 1981, in Tecpán; and Faustino Villanueva Villanueva, July 10, 1981, in Quiché.

37. Sinn, "The Roman Catholic Church as a Factor in Guatemalan Politics," 14.

38. Sinn, "The Roman Catholic Church as a Factor in Guatemalan Politics," 10. According to Sinn, Lucas made the remark "while addressing an anti-Communist rally" on September 7, 1980. The statement was also reported as a threat to "throw" priests out instead of "carry" them out.

39. Sinn, "The Roman Catholic Church as a Factor in Guatemalan Politics," 16.

40. Sinn, "The Roman Catholic Church as a Factor in Guatemalan Politics," 18.

41. Sinn, "The Roman Catholic Church as a Factor in Guatemalan Politics," 17.

42. Archbishop Charles Salatka, interview with Father David Monahan, Oklahoma City, OK, August 30, 1994, interview 35. Blessed Stanley Rother Collection (hereafter BSRC), box 9, Father David Monahan Interviews, "Interviews for Second Book," Archdiocese of Oklahoma City, Oklahoma. According to Salatka, the mission's four principal initiatives were worship, evangelization via its *Voz de Atitlán* radio station, building and operating a medical clinic, and improved agricultural production.

43. Diego and Andrea Ixbalan Tacaxoy interview with Monahan, Oklahoma City, OK, August 30, 1994, interview 8. BSRC, box 9, Father David Monahan Interviews, "Interviews for Second Book."

44. Father Adan García, interview, interview with Monahan, Santiago Atitlán, Sololá, July 27, 1989, interview 5. BSRC, box 9, Father David Monahan Interviews, "Interviews for Second Book."

45. Bishop Angelico Melotto, interview with Monahan, Guatemala City, July 1990, interview 16. BSRC, box 9, Father David Monahan Interviews, "Interviews for Second Book."

46. Father Stanley Rother, letter to Sam Leven, July 9, 1980, BSRC, box 10, "Father David

Notes to Chapter 5 / 195

Monahan Documents—After Death."

47. For more information on the attack on Voz de Atitlán's offices and Culán's disappearance, see "The 'Voice of Atitlán' Silenced," *Palm Beach Post* (West Palm Beach, FL), February 22, 1981.

48. Rother, letter to Sam Leven, November 20, 1980, BSRC, box 10, "Father David Monahan Documents—After Death."

49. Rother, letter to Salatka, September 22, 1980, BSRC, box 10, "Father David Monahan Documents—After Death."

50. Rother, letter to Sister Bertha Sánchez, November 20, 1980, BSRC, box 10, "Father David Monahan Documents—After Death."

51. Rother, letter to Sánchez, November 20, 1980.

52. Rother, letter to Archbishop Charles A. Salatka, November 4, 1980, Blessed Stanley Rother Collection, box 10, Father David Monahan Documents—After Death.

53. Rother, letter to Leven, November 20, 1980. Rother's mention of "cofrades" in this letter refers to the town's *cofradias*, local religious organizations by and for the area's Mayan population that celebrated both Catholic and traditional Mayan rites in their worship. Rother had long enjoyed a cordial relationship with the local cofradias and continued to do so until his murder.

54. Melvin E. Sinn, US Embassy, Guatemala City, to US Department of State, "Campesino Deaths in Santiago Atitlán," Confidential Cable 000226, January 14, 1981. DNSA.

55. Cocales is approximately thirty miles south of Santiago Atitlán, while San Andres Senetabaj is approximately twenty-five miles northeast of Santiago Atitlán, due east of the town of Panajachel.

56. Sinn, "Campesino Deaths in Santiago Atitlán."

57. Father Stanley Rother, letter, January 5, 1981, Msgr. Gregory Schaffer papers, unpublished.

58. Sinn, "Campesino Deaths in Santiago Atitlán."

59. Sinn, "Campesino Deaths in Santiago Atitlán."

60. Interview with Father John Goggin, San Lucas Tolimán, January 2015.

61. Sinn, "Campesino Deaths in Santiago Atitlán."

62. Melvin E. Sinn, US Embassy, Guatemala City, to US Department of State, "Situation in Santiago Atitlán: Further Developments," Confidential Telegram 000391, January 21, 1981, DNSA.

63. John Rosengren, "Father Stan Rother: American Martyr in Guatemala," *St. Anthony Messenger* (Cincinnati, OH) (July 2006).

64. Don White, letter to Salatka, March 22, 1981, BSRC, box 10, Father David Monahan Documents—After Death.

65. White, letter to Embassy of Guatemala, Washington DC, March 23, 1981, BSRC, box 10, Father David Monahan Documents—After Death. Although White did not sign this version of his letter, there is little doubt about its author. The letter's content, in spots, is identical to White's letter to Salatka, identifies the writer as having attended Saint John the Baptist for the homily, and registered the same complaints about Rother's remarks.

66. CEG, "Carta pastoral colectiva del episcopado guatemalteco el hombre, su dignidad y derechos. Misión de la iglesia y sus miembros en el momento actual," April 8, 1981, *Al Servicio de la vida, justicia y la paz*, 238.

67. Francisco Bocel, unaddressed letter, December 12, 1981. BSRC, box 10, "Father David Monahan Documents—After Death."

68. Schaffer, interview with Monahan, July 24, 1989, San Lucas Tolimán, Guatemala, BSRC.

69. CIA, Guatemala City Station, Guatemala, "[Murder of American Priest; Highly Excised]," August 1981, DNSA.

70. A copy of Bocel's statement to police is archived at the AHPN. See GT PN 35–03 S003, Archivo General, Solicitud, F32664.

71. "Guatemalan Police Charges Three with Death of U.S. Priest," August 4, 1981, GNIBA.

72. Letter, Archbishop Charles Salatka, to Ronald Reagan, July 28, 1982, WHORM 82, folder 09500–119999, RRL.

73. Religious Task Force on Central America, National Network in Solidarity with the People of Guatemala, "Call to Commemorate the Life of Fr. Stanley Rother," n.d., GNIBA.

74. "Call to Commemorate the Life of Fr. Stanley Rother."

75. "Calls for 'Full Investigation,'" *Anchor*, October 22, 1981.

76. Collins, "Heart of a Martyr."

77. Rep. Ron Paul, Letter to Guatemalan Ambassador to the United States Doroteo Monterroso, November 6, 1981, GT PN 35–03 S003, Archivo General, Solicitud, F32658, Document 882, AHPN.

78. See GT PN 35–03 S003, Archivo General, Solicitud, F32659, Document 872, AHPN.

79. Rosengren, "Father Stan Rother: American Martyr in Guatemala."

80. USCC, "Statement on Central America," November 19, 1981.

81. CEG, "Crisis Profunda de Humanismo," June 13, 1980, *Al Servicio de la vida, justicia, y la paz*, 209–12.

82. USCC, "Statement on Central America."

83. Interview with author, San Lucas Tolimán, Sololá, Guatemala, January 3, 2015.

84. Interview with author, January 3, 2015.

85. Interview with author, January 3, 2015.

86. Interview with author, January 3, 2015.

87. Interview with author, March 12, 2021. For privacy, I have used the pseudonym "Señor Ortiz."

88. Interview with author, March 12, 2021.

89. "Archbishop Road Reiterates Opposition to Guatemalan Aid," *Catholic Voice* (Omaha, NE), February 26, 1982.

90. Frederic L. Chapin to United States Department of State, "Murder of James A. Miller of La Salle Brothers Order: Background on Possible Motives or Attackers," Confidential Cable 1053, February 15, 1982, DNSA.

91. Report, Richard C. Brown, "The Challenge to the U.S. of Liberation Theology in Latin America," "Liberation Theology in Latin America (1)" folder, RAC box 006, Alfonso Sapia Bosch Files, WHORM: Alpha File, Ronald Reagan Library. Brown served the State Department at postings in Spain, Vietnam, Brazil, and Mauritius. He was also special assistant to the assistant secretary of the Bureau of Inter-American Affairs from 1969 to 1972, a National Security Council staff member from 1978 to 1979, and the deputy director of the Office of Central American Affairs from 1979 to 1981.

92. Brown, "The Challenge to the U.S. of Liberation Theology in Latin America," vii.

93. Brown, "The Challenge to the U.S. of Liberation Theology in Latin America," 16.

94. Brown, "The Challenge to the U.S. of Liberation Theology in Latin America," 19.

Notes to Chapter 6 / 197

95. Brown, "The Challenge to the U.S. of Liberation Theology in Latin America," 45.

96. Brown, "The Challenge to the U.S. of Liberation Theology in Latin America," 52.

Chapter 6

1. The Ixil Triangle is an area of Quiché between the towns of Santa Maria Nebaj, San Juan Cotzal, and San Gaspar Chajul. The area's significant Ixil population, as well as its level of guerrilla activity, made it the site of the war's worst violence during this period.

2. Morton Blackwell, Special Assistant to the President, Memorandum to Faith Ryan Whittlesey, Office of Public Liaison, US Department of State, "Letter to Monsignor Hoye of the U.S. Catholic Conference," September 9, 1983, "Central America VII (2)" folder, box 55, Morton Blackwell Files, RRL.

3. Frank V. Ortiz, Jr., to United States Department of State, "A Human Rights Strategy for Guatemala," March 10, 1980, Confidential Cable 001620, DNSA.

4. Jennifer Schirmer, *The Guatemalan Military Project: A Violence Called Democracy* (Philadelphia: University of Pennsylvania Press, 1998), 19. For US perspectives on the issue, see CIA, "Guatemala: Officers Disgruntled," Top Secret Analysis, March 27, 1982, DNSA.

5. Soto Rosales, *El sueño encadenado*, 93–94.

6. CIA, "Guatemala: Prospects for the Guevara Administration," Top Secret analysis, March 22, 1982, DNSA.

7. General Anibal Guevara Rodríguez, "The Road to Peace, Well-Being and Progress for All Guatemalans," October 1981, "1982 Elections (Guevara)" folder, box 90502, Jacqueline Tillman Files, Ronald Reagan Library, 1.

8. Guevara, "The Road to Peace, Well-Being and Progress for All Guatemalans," 4.

9. Guevara, "The Road to Peace, Well-Being and Progress for All Guatemalans," 8.

10. Frederic L. Chapin, US Embassy, Guatemala, to US Department of State, "General Arana Views the Election Scene," January 14, 1982, Confidential Cable 000302, DNSA.

11. URNG, "Guatemala, the People Unite! Unitary Statement from the Guatemalan National Revolutionary United—URNG: Declaration of the Guatemalan Patriotic Unity Committee" (San Francisco: Solidarity Publications, April 1982), GNIBA.

12. CIA, "Guatemala: Election Prospects," March 5, 1982, DNSA.

13. Chapin, US Embassy, Guatemala, to US Department of State, "Guatemalan Elections: The Status as of March 10," March 10, 1982, Confidential Cable 001757, DNSA.

14. Chapin, US Embassy, Guatemala, to US Department of State, "Guatemalan Post-election Issues," March 11, 1982, Secret Cable 008149, DNSA.

15. CIA, "Guatemala: Prospects for the Guevara Administration," Top Secret analysis, March 22, 1982, DNSA.

16. US Department of State, Washington, DC, to Thomas O. Enders, "Guatemalan Coup," secret memorandum, March 25, 1982, DNSA.

17. Chapin, US Embassy, Guatemala to US Department of State, "Coup Sitrep No. 13," March 23, 1982, Confidential Cable 002115, DNSA.

18. DIA, "Coup Sitrep No. 2," Confidential Cable, March 25, 1982, DNSA.

19. United States Army Intelligence and Security Command, "Brigadier General José Efraín Ríos Montt," January 1972, DNSA.

20. Sabino, *Guatemala, la historia silenciada, Tomo II*, 129.

21. William Bowdler, US Embassy, Guatemala City, to US Department of State, "Biweekly Political Review, June 21–July 4, 1972," Airgram A-121, July 5, 1972, DNSA.

198 / Notes to Chapter 6

22. Turek, *To Bring the Good News to All Nations*, 127.

23. Turek, *To Bring the Good News to All Nations*, 133.

24. Garrard-Burnett, *Terror in the Land of the Holy Spirit*, 57. Other accounts of Ríos Montt's role in the coup contradict Verbo's official version: in a private meeting between Chapin and Leonel Sisniega Otero on March 24, Sisniega told Chapin that he had been the "intellectual organizer" of the coup and that he had been in contact with Ríos Montt, who had been aware of "his role" as early as March 22, the day before the coup. See Chapin, US Embassy, Guatemala City, to US Department of State, "Coup Sitrep 15," Secret Cable 2118, March 24, 1982, DNSA.

25. URNG, "Coup in Guatemala, a reactionary maneuver by the Reagan government, by the genocidal army and by the ruling class," March 24, 1982, GNIBA.

26. Chapin, US Embassy, Guatemala, to US Department of State, "Ma[r]yknoll Order Delivers Document of Army Atrocities and Pre and Po[s]t-Coup of March 23," April 22, 1982, Confidential Cable 008758, DNSA.

27. *Guardian*, "Where God Is Forced to Take Sides," April 12, 1982.

28. CEG, "Carta de la CEG a la junta militar de gobierno," March 31, 1982, *Al Servicio de la vida, justicia, y la paz* (Guatemala: CEG, 1997), 291.

29. CEG, "Exhortación pastoral," March 31, 1982, *Al Servicio de la vida, justicia, y la paz*, 296. Penados's mention of Jesus's command at the Last Supper was a reference to John 15:12, in which Jesus told his disciples, "Love each other as I have loved you."

30. Chapin, US Embassy, Guatemala to US Department of State, "Guatemalan Coup Developments: Thunder on the Right, Dissatisfaction by Young Officers," March 25, 1982, Confidential Cable 002193. See also CIA, "Guatemalan Officers Disgruntled," March 29, 1982, and DIA, "New Guatemal[a] Junta: More of the Same?" March 29, 1982, DNSA.

31. Chapin, US Embassy, Guatemala to US Department of State, "Coup Developments and Relations with Guatemala," March 29, 1982, Confidential Cable 002264, DNSA.

32. Chapin, US Embassy, Guatemala to US Department of State, Washington, DC, "Ambassador's Conversation with President Ríos Montt," April 8, 1982, Secret Cable 008595, DNSA.

33. DIA, "A Junior Officer's Comments on the Coup—Before, During and After," Confidential Cable, March 27, 1982, DNSA.

34. Falla, *Massacres in the Jungle*, 125–40.

35. CEH, *Guatemala: Memoria del Silencio, Tomo VII*, 65–72.

36. Schirmer, *The Guatemalan Military Project*, 90.

37. CEH, *Guatemala: Memoria del Silencio, Tomo VII*, 115–22.

38. Schirmer, *The Guatemalan Military Project*, 91.

39. CEH, *Guatemala: Memoria del Silencio, Capítulo segundo: Las violaciones de los derechos humanos y los hechos de violencia*, 31.

40. CEH, "Caso ilustrativo No. 107: La masacre de la comunidad de Acul," Guatemala: Memoria del Silencio, Tomo VII, 115–22.

41. Stephen Kinzer, "Efraín Ríos Montt, Guatemalan Dictator Convicted of Genocide, Dies at 91," *New York Times*, April 1, 2018.

42. Stephen Bosworth, "Statement of Hon. Stephen W. Bosworth," US Congress, Senate, Committee on Foreign Relations, *U.S. Policy in the Western Hemisphere*, 97th Cong., 2nd Sess., April 20, 1982 (Washington, DC: GPO, 1982), 56.

43. Bosworth, "Statement of Hon. Stephen W. Bosworth," 58.

44. CEH, *Guatemala: Memoria del Silencio, Tomo VII*, 149.

Notes to Chapter 6 / 199

45. CEH, *Guatemala: Memoria del Silencio, Tomo VII*, 150.

46. CEG, "La iglesia condena masacre de campesinos," May 27, 1982, 1074.

47. "Guatemalan Refugees Flood Mexico," *New York Times*, August 18, 1982.

48. Chapin to US Department of State, "Ríos Montt Declares State of Siege," July 1, 1982, Confidential Cable 004814, DNSA.

49. "Guatemala Enlists Religion in Battle," *New York Times*, July 18, 1982.

50. "Plan de campana 'Victoria '82,'" Guatemala General Orders Collection, National Security Archive, George Washington University, Washington, DC.

51. DIA, "Additional Information on Operations Plan 'Victoria 82,'" Confidential Cable, July 30, 1982, DNSA.

52. "Plan de campana 'Victoria '82,'" 29.

53. "Plan de campana 'Victoria '82,'" 29.

54. "Plan de campana 'Victoria '82,'" 39.

55. CEH, *Guatemala: Memoria del Silencia, Tomo VII*, 41–52; *Tomo I*, 507, caso 776; *Tomo VIII*, 505, caso 6119, 512, caso 6320, and 771, caso 8376.

56. CEH, *Guatemala: Memoria del Silencio, Tomo III*, 340–41, casos 3082 and 3452.

57. CEH, *Guatemala: Memoria del Silencio, Tomo III*, 202.

58. CEH, *Guatemala: Memoria del Silencio, Tomo III*, 205, caso 12018.

59. CEH, *Guatemala: Memoria del Silencio, Tomo III*, 205, caso 16517.

60. "The Testimony of a Kekchi-Protestant Pastor," Religious Task Force on Central America and Mexico, Series 3, Guatemala, box 41, folder 5, Maryknoll Mission Archives.

61. "The Testimony of a Kekchi-Protestant Pastor."

62. "Archbishop Roach to Guatemalan Bishops," July 28, 1982, GNIBA.

63. Paul Taylor, US Embassy, Guatemala to US Department of State, "Congressional Hearing on Guatemala," August 2, 1982, Cable 005665, DNSA.

64. US Department of State, Bureau of Intelligence and Research, "Inter-American Highlights: Human Rights in Guatemala," August 13, 1982, Secret Analysis, DNSA.

65. See, for example, "Allegations of Government Violence," August 3, 1982, Confidential Cable 005673, and "More Alleged Government of Guatemala Atrocities," September 16, 1982, Confidential Cable 006921, DNSA.

66. Chapin to US Department of State, "Alleged April Massacre by Army of 100 in Péten Disputed," September 24, 1982, Confidential Cable 007192; and "Father Ronald Hennessey's Allegations of Army Violence in Huehuetenango," October 4, 1982, Confidential Cable 007473, DNSA.

67. Chapin to US Department of State, "More Alleged Government of Guatemala Atrocities," "Government of Guatemala Army Response to Embassy Query on Alleged Army Massacres—Part II," October 15, 1982, Confidential Cable 007775, "Embassy Attempt to Verify Alleged Massacres in Huehuetenango," October 21, 1982, Confidential Cable 006921, DNSA.

68. Chapin to US Department of State, "Further on Choatalun," October 28, 1982, Confidential Cable 008150, DNSA. No record of this massacre exists in the CEH's report.

69. Francis J. McNeil, US Embassy, Costa Rica, to US Department of State, "President-Elect Monge Affirms Non-Intervention in Nicaragua; More Reaction to Pastora Statement," April 20, 1982, Cable 002691, "Nicaragua: the Making of U.S. Policy, 1978–1990," DNSA.

70. Steven. R. Harper, "U.S. Assistance to Honduras: Foreign Aid Facts," June 12, 1985, DNSA.

200 / Notes to Chapter 6

71. Council on Hemispheric Affairs, "Congressman Clarence D. Long Assails Guatemalan Regime," April 14, 1983, GNIBA.

72. Frank Fromherz, "U.S. Aid to Guatemalan Regime Questioned," *Catholic Sentinel*, August 20, 1982.

73. Daniel Halloran, "Cry for Justice," *Evangelist* (Albany, NY), September 2, 1982, and Sr. Cecilia Holbrook, "Swinging the Spotlight," *Evangelist*, August 5, 1982.

74. See *Witness*, April 4, 1982; *Denver Catholic Register*, April 14, 1982, and "Meddling in Guatemala," *Pittsburgh Catholic*, December 27, 1982.

75. "Priests Group Backs Harboring Refugees," *Pittsburgh Catholic*, December 24, 1982.

76. Janet Dolphin, SVM, "Azucena Blossoms in Adopted Culture," *Witness*, May 2, 1982; James Fiedler, "Guatemala Refugees in Mexico," *Denver Catholic Register*, December 14, 1983.

77. "Diocesans Promote Campaign for Peace in Central America," *Courier-Journal*, March 9, 1983; "Abbey Readies for Peace, Justice Series," *Catholic Sentinel*, November 19, 1982.

78. See *Catholic Voice*, June 4, 1982; and "Roncalli High School Students Give $1,000 to Missions," March 4, 1983.

79. "Priest Serving in Guatemala Charges Atrocities by Army," *Des Moines Register*, September 12, 1982.

80. "Bishops Hit Reagan on Guatemala," *Chicago Tribune*, November 6, 1982.

81. Richard Meislin, "Pope to Visit Salvador Next Year; Other Stops in the Area Expected," *New York Times*, November 29, 1982.

82. John Paul II, Angelus, March 7, 1982.

83. Alfonso Sapia-Bosch, Memorandum to William Clark, "Letter to You from Senator Jepsen Suggesting 'A Working Meeting' Between Guatemalan President Ríos Montt and President Reagan," September 22, 1982, box 90127 (RAC box 8), "Guatemala (2)" folder, Roger Fontaine Files, RRL.

84. US Embassy, Guatemala, to US Department of State, "Meeting between President Reagan and President Ríos Montt," Confidential Cable 008703, November 18, 1982, DNSA.

85. US Embassy, Guatemala, "Meeting between President Reagan and President Ríos Montt."

86. Foreign Minister Eduardo Castillo Arriola was not present at the meeting and did not vote; Chapin reported that had he attended, he would have likely voted against attending. See US Embassy, Guatemala, "Meeting between President Reagan and President Ríos Montt."

87. US Embassy, Guatemala City, to US Department of State, "Next Steps for Guatemala," Confidential Cable 000334, January 13, 1983, DNSA.

88. "Reagan Denounces Threats to Peace in Latin America," *New York Times*, December 5, 1982.

89. US Embassy, Guatemala, "Next Steps for Guatemala."

90. US Embassy, Guatemala, "Next Steps for Guatemala."

91. CEH, "Caso ilustrativo No. 31, Masacre de la Dos Erres," *Guatemala: Memoria del Silencio, Tomo VI*, 399.

92. CEH, *Guatemala: Memoria del Silencio, Tomo I*, 61.

93. CEH, *Guatemala: Memoria del Silencio, Tomo I*, 61.

94. Council on Hemispheric Affairs, "COHA Report Marks Shameful Reagan-Ríos Montt Meeting," December 4, 1982, GNIBA.

95. Msgr. Charles Owen Rice, "'Meddling' in Guatemala," *Pittsburgh Catholic*, December 24, 1982.

Notes to Chapter 6 / 201

96. Archbishop Charles Salatka, letter to Secretary of State George Shultz, January 27, 1983, BSRC, box 10.

97. Letter, Salatka to Shultz, January 27, 1983.

98. US Embassy, Guatemala, to US Department of State, "Apostolic Delegate Comments on Executions and Pope's Visit to Guatemala," Confidential Telegram 001716, March 3, 1983, Guatemala General Orders Collection, National Security Archive, George Washington University, Washington, DC.

99. Council on Hemispheric Affairs, "Guatemalan Executions: An Intended Affront to the Pope," GNIBA.

100. John Paul II, "Ceremonia de Bienvenida a Guatemala," March 6, 1982.

101. John Paul II, "Celebración de la Palabra en el Campo de Marte, Homilía del Santo Padre Juan Pablo II," March 7, 1983.

102. John Paul II, "Discurso del Santo Padre Juan Pablo II a los Indígenas," March 7, 1983.

103. John Paul II, "Discorso di Giovanni Paolo II ai Giudici della Corte Interamericana dei Diritti Umani," San José, Costa Rica, March 3, 1983.

104. US Embassy, Managua, to US Department of State, "Pope's Visit to Nicaragua," Confidential Cable 00935, March 5, 1982, DNSA.

105. John Paul II, "Homilía del Santo Padre Juan Pablo II," San Salvador, El Salvador, March 6, 1983.

106. Garrard-Burnett, *Terror in the Land of the Holy Spirit*, 75.

107. José Efraín Ríos Montt, "Los protagonistas del futuro," *Mensajes del presidente de la república, general José Efraín Ríos Montt* (Guatemala: Tipográfia Nacional, 1982).

108. Ríos Montt, "No hemos aprendido a ser Guatemala," *Mensajes del presidente de la república, general José Efraín Ríos Montt.*

109. CEG, "Comunicado de la Conferencia Episcopal de Guatemala al terminar la visita apostólica de Su Santidad Juan Pablo II," March 9, 1983, *Al Servicio de la vida, justicia, y la paz*, 312.

110. CEG, "Mensaje de la Conferencia Episcopal de Guatemala," April 22, 1983, 318.

111. United States Department of Defense, "Brigadier General Ríos Montt Vulnerable and Under Attack," Department of Defense Cable, June 14, 1983, DNSA.

112. "Brigadier General Ríos Montt Vulnerable and Under Attack."

113. Paul Taylor, US Embassy, Guatemala to US Department of State, "General Echeverría's Letter Part of a Coup Plot," Confidential Cable 004560, June 7, 1983, DNSA.

114. Taylor, "General Echeverría's Letter Part of a Coup Plot." According to Castañeda, the five officers were Colonel Jaime Hernández Méndez, Colonel Edilberto Letona Linares, Colonel José Benedicto Ortega Gómez, Colonel Otto Erick Ponce Morales, and Colonel Mario Roberto García Catalán.

115. Taylor, US Embassy, Guatemala to US Department of State, "First Assessment of the June 29 Political Crisis," Confidential Cable 005272, June 29, 1983, DNSA.

116. Taylor, US Embassy, Guatemala to US Department of State, "Disturbances of June 29: Sitrep 6," Unclassified Cable 05268, June 29, 1983, DNSA.

117. Taylor, US Embassy, Guatemala to US Department of State, "The State of Government—A Week and a Half after the Crisis Broke into the Open," Confidential Cable 005514, July 8, 1983, DNSA.

118. Chapin, US Embassy, Guatemala, to US Department of State, "Presidential Advisors' Comments on Current Political Situation," Confidential Cable 006156, July 28, 1983, DNSA.

202 / Notes to Chapter 7

119. Chapin, US Embassy, Guatemala, to US Department of State, "Comments by Former Presidential Advisors on the Events of August 8 and their Aftermath," Confidential Cable 007131, August 25, 1983, DNSA.

Chapter 7

1. "Discurso de Mejía Victores," *Prensa Libre*, August 9, 1983.

2. US Embassy, Guatemala City, to US Department of State, "Summary of Latest Decrees," Telegram 06886, August 15, 1983, Guatemala Revolutionary Organization Collection, National Security Archive.

3. "U.S. Cautious On New Ruler in Guatemala," *St. Louis Post-Dispatch*, August 9, 1983.

4. Henry Trewhitt, "Washington Reacts Cautiously to Coup in Guatemala; Few Changes Expected," *Baltimore Sun*, August 9, 1983.

5. Philip Taubman, "U.S. Hails Remarks by New Guatemala Chief," *New York Times*, August 10, 1983.

6. DIA, "8 August 83 Coup," Secret Cable, August 15, 1983, DNSA.

7. "U.S. Cautious on New Ruler in Guatemala," *St. Louis Post-Dispatch*, August 9, 1983.

8. Philip Taubman, "U.S. Wary on Coup Implications; Says It Hopes for Democratic Rule," *New York Times*, August 9, 1983.

9. Mary Hanneman, "Bishops Report No One Is Safe in Guatemala," *Witness*, September 4, 1983.

10. Despite Ham's assertions, there is no record of a massacre of this size occurring on July 29, 1983, listed in the CEH's report, Embassy or CIA communiques, or any press account other than the *Witness*.

11. Rice, "More on Central America," *Pittsburgh Catholic*, August 5, 1983; "Another Vietnam," October 7, 1983.

12. Frank Fromherz, "United States Is Making a Big Mistake in Guatemala," *Catholic Sentinel*, October 7, 1983. The *Our Sunday Visitor* editorial was reprinted in the September 2, 1983, edition of the *Pittsburgh Catholic*.

13. Organization of American States, Comisión Interamericana de Derechos Humanos, "Informe de 1984" (Washington, DC: OAS), 102.

14. For survivor and witness accounts of the Quetzaltenango abuses, see CEH, *Guatemala: Memoria del Silencio, Tomo V*, 422–23, casos 8186, 8131, 8035, and 8213. For Alta Verapáz abuses, see *Tomo VIII*, 116, caso 9083. For abuses in Chimaltenango, *Tomo VIII*, 210 caso 15308. For abuses in San Marcos, see *Tomo XI*, 1520, caso 7139. For abuses in Totonicapan, see *Tomo XI*, 1660, caso 8124. For Quiché, see *Tomo X*, 958, caso 11347.

15. CEH, *Guatemala: Memoria del Silencio, Tomo VIII*, 2514, caso 10115.

16. CEH, *Guatemala: Memoria del Silencio, Tomo VIII*, 963, caso 13318.

17. CEH, *Guatemala: Memoria del Silencio, Tomo VIII*, 2542, caso 9229.

18. CEH, *Guatemala: Memoria del Silencio, Tomo VIII*, 2767, caso 13356.

19. Iglesia Guatemalteca en Exilio, *Boletin*, January 1984, Colección de Robert H. Trudeau sobre Politica de Guatemala, GT-CIRMA-AH-018, CIRMA.

20. CEH, *Guatemala: Memoria del Silencio, Tomo VIII*, 3811, caso 2816; 3809, caso 16035.

21. An *Ad Limina Apostolorum* visit is an episcopate's visit to Rome to meet with the pope, as required by Catholic law.

22. IGE, "Guatemala: Lessons of History," *Boletin*, May 1987, Colección de Robert H. Trudeau sobre Politica de Guatemala, CIRMA.

Notes to Chapter 7 / 203

23. IGE, "Guatemala: Lessons of History."

24. Chapin, "Funeral of Father Augusto Ramírez Monasterio—and Further Comment," Confidential Cable 009906, November 15, 1983, DNSA.

25. "Central America's only cardinal dies," *Catholic Advance*, June 23, 1983; "Cardinal Casariego Dies, *Witness*, June 26, 1983.

26. IGE, *Boletin* 7, no. 1 (May 1987), Colección de Robert H. Trudeau sobre Politica de Guatemala, CIRMA.

27. "The New Missionary," *Time*, December 27, 1982.

28. A papal nuncio is the Holy See's diplomatic envoy and the pope's personal representative to a country.

29. Chapin, "Funeral of Father Augusto Ramírez Monasterio—and Further Comment."

30. Chapin, US Embassy, Guatemala, to US Department of State, "GOG and the Church: The War of Words Escalates," November 17, 1983, Confidential Cable 010000, DNSA.

31. Chapin, "GOG and the Church."

32. Richard Graham, US Embassy, Guatemala, to US Department of State, "Meeting with Chief of State Mejia," November 29, 1983, Secret Cable 010357, DNSA.

33. Graham, US Embassy, Guatemala, to US Department of State, "President of Episcopal Conference Meets with General Mejia," November 29, 1983, Secret Cable 010352, Guatemala General Orders Collection.

34. Graham, US Embassy, Guatemala, to US Department of State, "GOG Officials Apologize to Bishops," December 12, 1983, Secret Cable 10448, Guatemala General Orders Collection.

35. Taylor, US Embassy, Guatemala, to US Department of State, "Guatemalan Episcopal Conference Protests Death of Seminarian," December 23, 1983, Secret Telegram 11077, Guatemala General Orders Collection.

36. Accounts of Haren's arrest were unclear as to the actual items found. According to the US Embassy, one published account of the incident reported that a grenade was found in Haren's car, while another reported that only a grenade pin was found. See Taylor, US Embassy, Guatemala, to US Department of State, "Detention of Maryknoll Priest Donald Joseph Haren," December 27, 1983, Secret Telegram 11094, Guatemala General Orders Collection, National Security Archive.

37. Taylor, US Embassy, Guatemala, to US Department of State, "Official Church Reaction to Brief Detention of Maryknoll Priest Donald Joseph Haren," December 28, 1983, Secret Telegram 11194, Guatemala General Orders Collection.

38. Taylor, "Official Church Reaction to Brief Detention of Maryknoll Priest Donald Joseph Haren."

39. Taylor, US Embassy, Guatemala, to US Department of State, "The National Peace Commission Falters," June 6, 1984, Confidential Cable 05621, DNSA.

40. Taylor, US Embassy, Guatemala, to US Department of State, "Archbishop Withdraws the Catholic Church from National Peace Commission," May 24, 1984, Confidential Telegram 05183, Guatemala General Orders Collection. See also Taylor, "San Carlos University Rector Resigns from National Peace Commission," May 24, 1984, Confidential Cable 00516, Guatemala General Orders Collection.

41. Taylor, US Embassy, Guatemala, to US Department of State, "Archbishop of Guatemala Comments on the Political Outlook," May 21, 1984, Confidential Cable 05009, DNSA.

42. Taylor, US Embassy, Guatemala, to US Department of State, "Benedicto Lucas Chips Away at Government," March 14, 1984, Confidential Cable 02594, DNSA.

43. Taylor, "Benedicto Lucas Chips Away at Government."

44. DIA, "Coup Plotting Continues," February 21, 1984, Cable, DNSA.

45. See Boster, "Lucas' First Five Months"; Bennett, "Vice President Villagrán Kramer: 'Golpe in Guatemala?'"; Ortiz, "The Villagrán Kramer Saga: Final Chapter Begins?" US Department of State, "Guatemala: Threats to Ríos Montt Government," Secret Report, August 26, 1982, DNSA; DIA, "Coup Reportedly Set for 12–18 Sep[tember] 82," Confidential Cable, September 10, 1982, DNSA; Chapin, "Sisniega and Roca Issue Warning to Mejía"; DIA, "Recent Coup Rumors in Guatemala City," Secret Cable, April 11, 1985, DNSA; and Directorate of Intelligence, CIA, "Guatemala: Potential for a Coup," September 12, 1988, DNSA.

46. Jimmy Carter, *White House Diary* (New York: Picador, 2010), 92–93.

47. See, for example, Chapin, US Embassy, Guatemala City, to US Department of State, "Piedra/Carbaugh Visit: Impressions of President Ríos Montt," Confidential Cable 003591, May 19, 1982, DNSA; and "Congressional Staff Del Ofnwoodard [*sic*], Ross and Cameron Have Dinner Meeting with Junta President Ríos Montt and Aides Bianchi and Contreras," Confidential Cable 003640, May 20, 1982, DNSA.

48. Chapin, "Piedra/Carbaugh Visit: Impressions of President Ríos Montt."

49. Taylor, US Embassy, Guatemala City, to US Department of State, "Archbishop Holds Special Mass for Missing Persons," Confidential Telegram 005662, June 6, 1984, Guatemala General Orders Collection.

50. CEG, "Para construir la paz," June 10, 1984, *Al Servicio de la vida, justicia, y la paz*, 360.

51. Graham, US Embassy, Guatemala City, to US Department of State, "Reaction to Pastoral Letter," Confidential Cable 006045, June 15, 1984, Guatemala General Orders Collection.

52. Graham, "Reaction to Pastoral Letter."

53. Taylor, US Embassy, Guatemala City, to US Department of State, "Archbishop of Guatemala Urges Catholics to Vote July 1 and Calls for Prayers for Peace and Reconciliation." Confidential Cable 006394, June 25, 1984, Guatemala General Orders Collection.

54. Soto Rosales, *El sueño encadenado*, 151.

55. *Constitución Política de la República de Guatemala* (Guatemala, 1985).

56. Taylor, US Embassy, Guatemala, to US Department of State, "Investigation of Human Rights Abuses in Rabinal, Baja Verapaz," July 7, 1984, Confidential Cable 06810, DNSA.

57. Katharine Bird, "'The Eucharist Is Linked to Ordinary Hunger.' Really," *Faith Today* 1, no. 3., National Catholic News Service, Washington, DC. A copy was included in the February 17, 1984, edition of the *Pittsburgh Catholic*.

58. "She's Looking for Sanctuaries," *Catholic Messenger*, February 9, 1984.

59. Kathy Hovey, "Life Makes Sense for the Volpes Since He Quit Making Armaments," *Catholic Messenger*, February 16, 1984.

60. William Fodiak, "Area Families Make Pleas, Ask for Release of Relatives," *Pittsburgh Catholic*, May 4, 1984.

61. Rice, "Guatemala," Pittsburgh Catholic, June 29, 1984.

62. See "Reagan's Jingoism Must End," Bulletin, January 9, 1984; "The Monroe Doctrine Is Not an Excuse to Go In," *Observer* (South Bend, IN), November 28, 1984; "Fire on the Doorstep," *DePaulia* (Chicago, IL), May 11, 1984.

63. Central Intelligence Agency, "Guatemala: Reluctant Partner," November 23, 1984, DNSA.

64. Alberto Piedra, US Embassy, Guatemala, to US Department of State, "Accounts of Violence in Patzún Region of Chilmaltenango [*sic*]," March 8, 1985, Confidential Cable 006969, DNSA.

Notes to Chapter 7 / 205

65. Piedra, US Embassy, Guatemala, to US Department of State, "Retired General and Grandson Assassinated in Guatemala City," April 1, 1985, Cable 03117, DNSA; CEH, *Guatemala: Memoria del Silencio, Tomo VIII*, 239, caso 24; 240, caso 49; 339, caso 243.

66. "The Lay Council Pays Attention to an Important Issue," *Catholic Messenger*, February 7, 1985.

67. "Central America," *Witness*, February 10, 1985.

68. "Guatemalans Vote," *Witness*, November 3, 1985.

69. "Couple Speak Out on El Salvador," *Pittsburgh Catholic*, March 15, 1985; Phil Taylor, "Area Relatives Seek Word about Family in Guatemala," *Pittsburgh Catholic*, April 5, 1985. The newspaper would again call for readers to request information on Rosal in its August 16, 1985, edition.

70. "Maryknoll Missionaries Relate Service in Central America," *Witness*, June 9, 1985; "Parishes Join Central America Week Events," *Courier-Journal*, March 13, 1985.

71. See, for example, Pat McGowan, "10-mile Peace Statement," *Anchor* (Fall River, MA), July 19, 1985; "Vincentian Priests Come to Diocese of Little Rock," *Guardian* (Little Rock, AR), January 18, 1985; "Florida Church Feeds Many," *Guardian*, August 16, 1985, and "Sanctuary Caravan Passes Through Oregon," *Catholic Sentinel*, July 12, 1985. See also Father Jerome Beat, "Reflections on My Trip to Central America," *Catholic Advance*, December 12, 1985.

72. See Piedra, US Embassy, Guatemala City, to US Department of State, "Guatemala Beset with Coup Rumors; Chief of State Cancels Trip to the Vatican and Schedules Address to Nation," Confidential Cable 003486, April 11, 1985; and DIA, "Recent Coup Rumors in Guatemala City," Secret Cable, April 11, 1985, DNSA.

73. DIA, "A Call for Resignations," Secret Cable, September 6, 1985, DNSA.

74. CEG, "La verdad os hará libres," September 14, 1985, *Al Servicio de la vida, justicia, y la paz*, 391.

75. CEG, "La verdad os hará libres," 395.

76. URNG, "Present Situation and Outlook in Guatemala: Vision of the Guatemalan Revolutionary National Unity (URNG)," October 1, 1985, GNIBA.

77. US Department of State, Bureau of Intelligence and Research, "Guatemala's November 1985 Elections: Transition to Civilian Rule," Secret Analysis 1190-AR, October 31, 1985, DNSA.

78. Stephen Kinzer, "Christian Democrat takes Big Lead in Guatemala," *New York Times*, November 5, 1985.

79. Kinzer, "Centrist Wins Big in Guatemala Vote," *New York Times*, December 10, 1985.

80. "New Chance in Guatemala," *New York Times*, December 12, 1985.

81. "Reengaging in Guatemala," *Washington Post*, December 19, 1985.

82. "Guatemala's Message," *Los Angeles Times*, December 10, 1985.

83. "Hope in Guatemala," *Miami Herald*, December 11, 1985.

84. Roger R. Gamble, US Embassy, Guatemala, to US Department of State, "Guatemalan Elections End on a Note of Reconciliation and Civility," Confidential Cable 003175, December 11, 1985, "Cables—Guatemala" folder, box 90681, Constantine Menges Files, RRL.

85. Nicholas Platt, US Department of State, Washington, DC, "Vice President's Meeting with Vinicio Cerezo, President-Elect of Guatemala," December 14, 1985, Secret Memorandum, DNSA.

86. Father Thomas McSherry, interview with author, July 10, 2014.

87. "Social Justice to Be Sought in Guatemala," *Pittsburgh Catholic*, December 20, 1985.

206 / Notes to Conclusion

88. Liz Armstrong, "Civilian Government Could Bring Change," *Witness*, January 5, 1986.

89. Marjorie Miller, "Military Rule Ending; 'New Era' Seen: 'Guatemala Devil' Dead, President-Elect Pledges," *Los Angeles Times*, December 10, 1985.

Conclusion

1. Parroquia San Pedro, San Izabal, Guatemala, "Letter to President Cerézo from Members of the Catholic Church in El Estor, Izabál, Asking for End of Violence," GNIBA.

2. Archbishop Prospero Penados del Barrio, "Message from Msgr. Prospero Penados del Barrio, Metropolitan Archbishop of Guatemala, to the Representatives of Institutions Defending Human Rights in San Francisco, California," October 12, 1989, GNIBA.

3. Guatemala Human Rights Commission (GHRC), "Guatemalan Street Children: Kidnapping and Extrajudicial Execution," June 1990. Guatemala Human Rights Commission Collected Papers, Swarthmore College Peace Collection, Swarthmore, PA.

4. GHRC, "Who Is the Torturer?" Guatemala Human Rights Commission Collected Papers.

5. This dollar amount is cited in the State Department briefing paper "President's Meeting with Guatemalan President Jorge Serrano Elias," September 27, 1991, DNSA.

6. Stroock, US Embassy, Guatemala, to US Department of State, "Catholic Lay Activist Killed: Rights Ombudsman Calls It Political; Archbishop Links It to Mack Murder," Confidential Cable 007065, July 17, 1991, DNSA.

7. Stroock, US Embassy, Guatemala, to US Department of State, "Catholic Lay Activist Killed: Rights Ombudsman Calls It Political; Archbishop Links It to Mack Murder," Confidential Cable 007065, July 17, 1991, DNSA. See also W. George Lovell, *A Beauty That Hurts: Life and Death in Guatemala* (Austin: University of Texas Press, 1995).

8. John F. Keane, US Embassy, Guatemala, to US Department of State, "Serrano Administration Lashes Out on Human Rights: Critics Be Damned," Confidential Cable 012066, November 13, 1992, DNSA. *Gabinete* members included Defense Minister José Domingo García, General Otto Pérez Molina, Foreign Minister Gonzalo Menendez Park, Interior Minister Francisco Perdomo, and Manuel Conde, one of the Serrano government's representatives at peace talks with the URNG.

9. John F. Keane, US Embassy, Guatemala, to US Department of State, Washington, DC, "Serrano: 'Let's Mend Relations,'" Confidential Cable 012071, November 16, 1992, DNSA.

10. United Nations General Assembly, *The Situation in Central America: Threats to International Peace and Security and Peace Initiatives*, A/46/713 (December 2, 1991).

11. Shelley Emling, "Guatemalan Peace Prospects Sag as Talks Dealock," *Washington Post*, November 26, 1991.

12. The most comprehensive account of Guatemala's peace process is Jonas, *Of Centaurs and Doves*.

13. United Nations General Assembly, *Agreement on Identity and Rights of Indigenous People*, A/49/882 (April 10, 1995).

14. Francisco Goldman, *The Art of Political Murder: Who Killed the Bishop?* (New York: Grove Press, 2007).

15. Azam Ahmed and Elisabeth Malkin, "Otto Pérez Molina of Guatemala Is Jailed Hours After Resigning Presidency," *New York Times*, September 3, 2015.

16. Emi MacLean, *Judging a Dictator: The Trial of Guatemala's Rios Montt*.

17. Rodriguez Sánchez was acquitted "as the court found he did not have command

responsibility, and that his responsibility for and involvement in the crimes had not been sufficiently established" (Maclean, *Judging a Dictator*, 12).

18. Carla Hinton, "Okarche Priest Moves Step Closer to Sainthood," *Oklahoman*, June 24, 2015.

19. Todd Hartch, *The Rebirth of Latin American Christianity* (New York: Oxford University Press, 2014), 30.

BIBLIOGRAPHY

ARCHIVAL SOURCES

Archivo Histórico de la Policía Nacional, Guatemala City, Guatemala
Blessed Stanley Rother Collection, Archdiocese of Oklahoma City, Oklahoma
Centro de Investigaciones Regionales de Mesoamérica (CIRMA), Antigua, Guatemala, Sacatepéquez, Guatemala
Digital National Security Archive
Frank V. Ortiz Collection, Fray Angélico Chavez History Library, Palace of the Governors, Santa Fe, NM
Guatemala News and Information Bureau Archive, Princeton, NJ
Jimmy Carter Library, Atlanta, GA
Maryknoll Fathers and Brothers Archive, Maryknoll Mission Archives, Maryknoll, NY
Maryknoll Sisters Archive, Maryknoll Mission Archives, Maryknoll, NY
National Security Archive, George Washington University, Washington, DC
Ronald Reagan Library, Simi Valley, CA
Swarthmore College Peace Collection, Swarthmore, PA
William A. Wilson Papers, Georgetown University Library, Washington, DC

CATHOLIC NEWSPAPERS AND PERIODICALS

Arkansas Catholic (Little Rock, AR)
Bulletin (Managua, Nicaragua)
The Catholic Advance (Wichita, KS)
Catholic Herald (London)
The Catholic Messenger (Davenport, IA)
Catholic News Service (Washington, DC)
The Catholic Standard and Times (Philadelphia, PA)
The Catholic Telegraph-Register (Cincinnati, OH)
The Catholic Voice (Omaha, NE)
Courier-Journal (Rochester, NY)
Denver Catholic Register (Denver, CO)
The DePaulia (Chicago, IL)
Diocese of New Ulm Newsletter (New Ulm, MN)
The Evangelist (Albany, NY)
The Guardian (Little Rock, AR)
National Catholic Reporter (Kansas City, MO)
The Observer (South Bend, IN)

The Pittsburgh Catholic
The Prairie Catholic (New Ulm, MN)
St. Anthony Messenger (Cincinnati, OH)
The Witness (Dubuque, IA)

NON-CATHOLIC NEWSPAPERS AND PERIODICALS

Arizona Daily Star (Tucson, AZ)
Arizona Republic (Phoenix, AZ)
Asbury Park Press (Asbury Park, NJ)
The Baltimore Sun
The Billings Gazette (Billings, MT)
The Brandon Sun (Brandon, MB)
Chicago Tribune
The Daily Courier (Connellsville, PA)
Des Moines Register
The Globe (Sioux City, IA)
El Grafico (Guatemala City, Guatemala)
The Guardian (Manchester, UK)
El Imparcial (Guatemala City, Guatemala)
Indianapolis Star
Lincoln Journal Star (Lincoln, NE)
Los Angeles Times
The Miami Herald (Miami, FL)
Minneapolis Tribune (Minneapolis, MN)
Mother Jones
New York Times
The Oklahoman (Oklahoma City, OK)
The Oshkosh Northwestern (Oshkosh, WI)
The Palm Beach Post (West Palm Beach, FL)
Pioneer Press (St. Paul, MN)
Prensa Libre (Guatemala City, Guatemala)
The St. Louis Register
Saint Louis Post-Dispatch (St. Louis, MO)
The San Bernardino County Sun (San Bernardino, CA)
San Francisco Examiner
Spokane Daily Chronicle (Spokane, WA)
Statesman Journal (Salem, OR)
Time

GOVERNMENT DOCUMENTS, ORGANIZATIONS' PUBLICATIONS, AND PRIMARY SOURCES

Alarcón, Mario Sandoval. "God, Fatherland, and Liberty," *Proceedings; 10th WACL Conference, Theme: Freedom Forces Unite Against Communist Tyranny!, Taipei, Taiwan, Republic of China, April 18–22, 1977.* Taipei: WACL, 1977.

Amnesty International. Briefing Paper No. 8, "Guatemala." London: Amnesty International, 1976.

———. "Guatemala: A Government Program of Political Murder." London: Amnesty International Publications, 1981.

Bibliography / 211

———. "The Human Rights Year in Guatemala: A Calendar of Abuses." London: Amnesty International, 1979.

Comisión para el Esclarecimiento Histórico (CEH). *Guatemala: Memoria del Silencio, Tomo I*. Guatemala: Oficina de Servicios para Proyectos de las Naciones Unidas, 1999.

———. *Guatemala: Memoria del Silencio, Tomo II*.

———. *Guatemala: Memoria del Silencio, Tomo III*.

———. *Guatemala: Memoria del Silencio, Tomo VI: Casos Illustrativos, Annexo I*.

———. *Guatemala: Memoria del Silencio, Tomo VIII: Casos Presentados, Anexo II*.

———. *Guatemala: Memoria del Silencio, Tomo X: Casos Presentados, Anexo II*.

———. *Guatemala: Memory of Silence: Report of the Commission for Historical Clarification, Conclusions and Recommendations*. Guatemala: CEH, 1998.

Conferencia Episcopal de Guatemala. *Al Servicio de la vida, la justicia y la paz*. Guatemala: Conferencia Episcopal de Guatemala, 1997.

General Accounting Office. *Report to the Chairman, Subcommittee on Western Hemisphere Affairs, Committee on Foreign Affairs, House of Representatives*. Washington, DC: Government Printing Office, 1986.

Gobierno de Guatemala. *Constitución Política de la República de Guatemala*. Guatemala, 1985.

Hagen, Virginia. *Central American Politics: A Brief Survey of the Governments and Politics of Costa Rica, El Salvador, Guatemala, Honduras, Nicaragua, and Panama*. Washington, DC: Government Printing Office, 1970.

Instituto de Estudios Políticos para América Latina y Africa. *Guatemala, un futuro próximo*. Madrid, IEPALA, 1980.

International Financial Institutions Act, P.L. 95–118, 22 U.S.C. 262(d), 95th Cong., 1st Sess. Washington, DC: Government Printing Office, 1977.

Laugerud García, Kjell Eugenio, General. "Discurso del Gen. Kjell Eugenio Laugerud García, Presidente de la República ante el honorable congreso en su tercer año de gobierno," July 1, 1977. Guatemala City: Tipografía Nacional, 1977.

Organization of American States, Comisión Interamericana de Derechos Humanos. "Informe de 1984." Washington, DC: Organization of American States, 1984.

Pope John XXIII. *Mater et Magistra, Encyclical of Pope John XXIII on Christianity and Social Progress*, May 15, 1961.

———. *Pacem in Terris, Encyclical of Pope John XXIII on Establishing Universal Peace in Truth, Justice, Charity, and Liberty*, April 11, 1963.

———. *Princeps Pastorum, Encyclical Letter on the Missions, Native Clergy, and Lay Participation*, November 28, 1959.

Pope John Paul I. *Urbi et Orbi*, August 27, 1978.

Pope John Paul II. "Celebración de la Palabra en el Campo de Marte, Homilía del Santo Padre Juan Pablo II." March 7, 1983.

———. "Ceremonia de Bienvenida a Guatemala." March 6, 1982.

———. "Discorso di Giovanni Paolo II ai Giudici della Corte Interamericana dei Diritti Umani." San José, Costa Rica, March 3, 1983.

———. "Discurso del Santo Padre Juan Pablo II a los Indígenas." March 7, 1983.

———. "Homilía del Santo Padre Juan Pablo II." San Salvador, El Salvador, March 6, 1983.

———. "Meeting with Mexican *Indios*." Culiapán, Mexico, January 29, 1979.

———. "To Members of the Third General Conference of the Latin American Episcopate." Puebla, Mexico, January 28, 1979.

Pope Leo XIII. *Custodi de Quella Fede, Encyclical of Pope Leo XIII on Freemasonry*, December 8, 1892.

———. *Rerum Novarum, Encyclical of Pope Leo XIII on Capital and Labor*, May 15, 1891.

Pope Paul VI. *Populorum Progressio, Encyclical Letter on the Development of Peoples*, March 26, 1967.

———. *Octogesima Adveniens, Apostolic Letter of Pope Paul VI*, May 14, 1971.

Pope Pius XI. *Divini Redemptoris, Encyclical Letter of Pope Pius XI on Atheistic Communism*, March 19, 1937.

———. *Quadregesimo Anno, Encyclical Letter of Pope Pius XI on Reconstruction of the Social Order*, March 19, 1937.

———. *Ubi Arcano dei Consilio, Encyclical Letter on the Peace of Christ in the Kingdom of Christ*, December 23, 1922.

Rossell Arellano, Mariano, Monseñor. *Carta pastoral sobre los avances del Comunismo en Guatemala*. Guatemala: Acción Católica Guatemalteca, 1954.

Second Vatican Council. *Ad Gentes, Apostolic Decree on the Mission Activity of the Church*. December 7, 1965.

———. *Gaudium et Spes, Pastoral Constitution on the Church in the Modern World*. December 7, 1965.

United Nations General Assembly. *The Situation in Central America: Threats to International Peace and Security and Peace Initiatives*, A/46/713. New York: United Nations, 1991.

———. Official Records, 15th Plenary Meeting, 32nd Session, A/32/PV.15. New York: United Nations, 1977.

United States Conference of Catholic Bishops. "Statement on Central America," November 19, 1981.

US Congress. *Congressional Record, Extensions of Remarks*. May 7, 1980. Washington, DC: Government Printing Office.

———. House. Committee on Foreign Affairs. *Foreign Assistance Legislation for Fiscal Year 1982, Part I. Hearings Before the Committee on Foreign Affairs*. 97th Cong., 1st Sess., March 13, 18, 19, and 23, 1981.

———. House. Committee on Foreign Affairs. *Foreign Assistance Legislation for Fiscal Year 1982, Part I. Hearings Before the Committee on Foreign Affairs*. 97th Cong., 1st Sess., March 13, 18, 19, and 23, 1981.

———. House. Subcommittee on Foreign Operations and Agencies. *Hearings before the Subcommittee on Foreign Operations Appropriations*. 97th Cong., 1st Sess., February 25, 1981.

———. House. Subcommittee on International Organizations. *Human Rights and the Phenomenon of Disappearances, Hearings Before the Subcommittee on International Organizations of the Committee of Foreign Affairs*. 96th Cong., 1st Sess., September 25, 1979.

———. House. Subcommittee on International Organizations. *Human Rights in Nicaragua, Guatemala, and El Salvador: Implications for U.S. Policy*. Washington, DC: Government Printing Office, 1976.

———. Senate. Committee on Foreign Relations. *U.S. Policy in the Western Hemisphere*. 97th Cong., 2nd Sess., April 20, 1982.

US Department of State. *Foreign Relations of the United States, 1955–1957, Volume VII, The American Republics: Central and South America*. Washington, DC: Government Printing Office, 1987.

———. *Foreign Relations of the United States, 1964–1968, Volume XXXI, South and Central

America; Mexico. Washington, DC: Government Printing Office, 2004.

_____. *Foreign Relations of the United States, 1969–1976, Volume E-10, The American Republics, 1969–1972.* Washington, DC: Government Printing Office, 2009.

_____. *Foreign Relations of the United States 1969–1976, Volume E-11, Part 1, Documents on Mexico; Central America; and the Caribbean 1973–1976.* Washington, DC: Government Printing Office, 2015.

_____. *Foreign Relations of the United States, 1977–1980, Volume XV, Central America, 1977–1980.* Washington, DC: Government Printing Office, 2010.

Secondary Sources

Appy, Christian G. "Eisenhower's Guatemalan Doodle: or: How to Draw, Deny, and Take Credit for a Third World Coup." In *Cold War Constructions: The Political Culture of United States Imperialism, 1945–1966,* ed. Christian Appy. Amherst: University of Massachusetts Press, 2000.

Arnson, Cynthia. *Crossroads: Congress, the President, and Central America, 1976–1993.* University Park: Penn State University Press, 1993.

Bouchey, Francis. *Guatemala: A Promise in Peril.* Washington, DC: Council for Inter-American Security, 1980.

Binns, Jack R. *The United States in Honduras, 1980–1981: An Ambassador's Memoir.* Jefferson, MO: McFarland, 2000.

Brett, Donna Whitson, and Edward T. Brett. *The Bill Woods Story: Maryknoll Missionary in Guatemala.* Maryknoll, NY: Orbis, 1988.

Brett, Edward T. *The US Catholic Press on Central America: From Cold War Anticommunism to Social Justice.* Notre Dame, IN: University of Notre Dame Press, 2003.

Buckaloo, Derek. "Carter's Nicaragua and Other Democratic Quagmires." In *Rightward Bound: Making America Conservative in the 1970s,* edited by Bruce Schulman and Julian Zelizer, 246–64. Cambridge, MA: Harvard University Press, 2008.

Burnidge, Cara. *A Peaceful Conquest: Woodrow Wilson, Religion, and the New World Order.* Chicago: University of Chicago Press, 2016.

Byrnes, Timothy A. *Reverse Mission: Transnational Religious Communities and the Making of US Foreign Policy.* Washington, DC: Georgetown University Press, 2011.

Calder, Bruce. *Crecimiento y Cambio de la Iglesia Católica Guatemalteca, 1944–1966.* Guatemala: Seminario de Integración Social Guatemaltecas, Ministerio de Educación, 1970.

Cangemi, Michael J. "Frank Ortiz and Guatemala's 'Killer President,' 1976–1980." *Diplomatic History* 42, no. 4 (2018): 613–39.

Capovilla, Loris, Monsignor. *Giovanni XXIII: Quindici Letture.* Roma: Edizioni di Storia e Letteratura, 1970.

Carothers, Thomas. *In the Name of Democracy: US Policy toward Latin America in the Reagan Years.* Berkeley: University of California Press, 1991.

Carter, Jimmy. *White House Diary.* New York: Picador, 2010.

Castagna, Luca. *A Bridge Across the Ocean: The United States and the Holy See between the Two World Wars.* Washington, DC: Catholic University of America Press, 2014.

Consejo Episcopal Latinoamericano y Caribeño. *La evangelización en el presente y en el futuro de América Latina.* Lima, Peru: Labrusa, 1982.

Ching, Erik. *Stories of Civil War in El Salvador: A Battle over Memory.* Chapel Hill: University of North Carolina Press, 2016.

Ciencia y Tecnología para Guatemala, A.C. *El Movimiento sindical en Guatemala, 1975–1985.* Mexico DF: Ciencia y Tecnología para Guatemala A.C., 1989.

Coatsworth, John. *Central America and the United States: The Clients and the Colossus.* New York: Twayne, 1994.

Committee of Santa Fe. *A New Inter-American Policy for the Eighties.* Washington, DC: Council for Inter-American Security, 1980.

Conroy-Krutz, Emily. *Christian Imperialism: Converting the World in the Early American Republic.* Ithaca, NY: Cornell University Press, 2015.

Costello, Gerald. *Mission to Latin America: The Successes and Failures of a Twentieth-Century Crusade.* Maryknoll, NY: Orbis Books, 1979.

Crandall, Russell. *The Salvador Option: The United States in El Salvador, 1977–1992.* New York: Cambridge University Press, 2016.

Cullather, Nick. *Secret History: The CIA's Classified Account of its Operation in Guatemala.* Stanford: Stanford University Press, 1999.

D'Haeseleer, Brian. *The Salvadoran Crucible: The Failure of US Counterinsurgency in El Salvador, 1979–1992.* Lawrence: University of Kansas Press, 2017.

Danner, Mark. *The Massacre at El Mozote: A Parable of the Cold War.* New York: Vintage Books, 1994.

Dodson, Michael, and Laura Nuzzi O'Shaughnessy. *Nicaragua's Other Revolution: Religious Faith and Political Struggle.* Chapel Hill: University of North Carolina Press, 1990.

Doggett, Martha. *Death Foretold: The Jesuit Murders in El Salvador.* Washington, DC: Georgetown University Press, 1993.

Dumbrell, John. *The Carter Presidency: A Re-evaluation.* Manchester: Manchester University Press, 1993.

Elliott, Lawrence. *I Will Be Called John: A Biography of Pope John XXIII.* London: Collins, 1974.

Erickson Nepstad, Sharon. *Convictions of the Soul: Religion, Culture, and Agency in the Central America Solidarity Movement.* New York: Oxford University Press, 2004.

Falla, Ricardo, SJ. *Massacres in the Jungle: Ixcán, Guatemala, 1975–1982.* Boulder, CO: Westview, 1994.

Ferrero Blanco, María Dolores. *La Nicaragua de los Somoza: 1936–1979.* Managua: Instituto de Historico de Nicaragua y Centroamérica de la Universidad Centroaméricana, 2012.

García, María Cristina. *Havana, USA: Cuban Exiles and Cuban-Americans in South Florida, 1959–1994.* Berkeley: University of California Press, 1997.

Garrard-Burnett, Virginia. *Terror in the Land of the Holy Spirit: Guatemala under General Efraín Ríos Montt, 1982–1983.* New York: Oxford University Press, 2010.

Gilbert, Dennis. *Sandinistas: The Party and the Revolution.* New York: Blackwell, 1988.

Gleijeses, Piero. *Shattered Hope: The Guatemalan Revolution and the United States, 1944–1954.* Princeton, NJ: Princeton University Press, 1992.

Goldman, Francisco. *The Art of Political Murder: Who Killed the Bishop?* New York: Grove Press, 2007.

Gould, Jeffrey L. *To Lead as Equals: Rural Protest and Political Consciousness in Chinandega, Nicaragua, 1912–1979.* Chapel Hill: University of North Carolina Press, 1990.

———. *Solidarity under Siege: The Salvadoran Labor Movement, 1970–1990.* New York: Cambridge University Press, 2019.

Grandin, Greg. *The Last Colonial Massacre: Latin America in the Cold War.* Chicago: University of Chicago Press, 2004.

Hartch, Todd. *The Rebirth of Latin American Christianity*. New York: Oxford University Press, 2014.

Hennelly, Alfred T., ed. *Liberation Theology: A Documentary History*. Maryknoll, NY: Orbis, 1990.

Illich, Ivan. *Celebration of Awareness: A Call for Institutional Revolution*. Garden City, NY: Doubleday, 1970.

Immerman, Richard. *The CIA in Guatemala: The Foreign Policy of Intervention*. Austin: University of Texas Press, 1982.

Inboden, William. *Religion and American Foreign Policy, 1945–1960: The Soul of Containment*. New York: Cambridge University Press, 2008.

Jackson, Donna. *Jimmy Carter and the Horn of Africa: Cold War Policy in Ethiopia and Somalia*. Jefferson, MO: McFarland, 2007.

Jacobs, Seth. *America's Miracle Man in Vietnam: Ngo Dinh Diem, Religion, Race, and US Intervention in Southeast Asia, 1950–1957*. Durham, NC: Duke University Press, 2004.

Jensehaugen, Jørgen. *Arab-Israeli Diplomacy Under Carter: The US, Israel, and the Palestinians*. London: Tauris, 2018.

Jonas, Susanne. *The Battle for Guatemala: Rebels, Death Squads, and U.S. Power*. Boulder, CO: Westview, 1991.

————. *Of Centaurs and Doves: Guatemala's Peace Process*. Boulder, CO: Westview, 2000.

Kagan, Robert. *A Twilight Struggle: American Power and Nicaragua, 1977–1981*. New York: Free Press, 1996.

Kaufman, Burton I., and Scott Kaufman. *The Presidency of James Earl Carter, Jr.*, 2nd ed. Lawrence: University of Kansas Press, 1993.

Kaufman, Scott. *Plans Unraveled: The Foreign Policy of the Carter Administration*. DeKalb: Northern Illinois University Press, 2008.

Keck, Margaret E., and Kathryn Sikkink. *Activists Beyond Borders: Advocacy Networks in International Politics*. Ithaca, NY: Cornell University Press, 1998.

Keeley, Theresa. *Reagan's Gun-Toting Nuns: The Catholic Conflict Over Cold War Human Rights Policy in Central America*. Ithaca, NY: Cornell University Press, 2020.

Keys, Barbara. *Reclaiming American Virtue: The Human Rights Revolution of the 1970s*. Cambridge, MA: Harvard University Press, 2014.

LaFeber, Walter. *Inevitable Revolutions: The United States in Central America*. New York: Norton, 1983.

Lancaster, Roger. *Thanks to God and the Revolution: Popular Religion and Class Consciousness in the New Nicaragua*. New York: Columbia University Press, 1988.

LeoGrande, William M. *Our Own Backyard: The United States in Central America, 1977–1992*. Chapel Hill: University of North Carolina Press, 1998.

Lernoux, Penny. *Hearts on Fire: The Story of the Maryknoll Sisters*. Maryknoll, NY: Orbis, 1993.

Lovell, W. George. *A Beauty That Hurts: Life and Death in Guatemala*. Austin: University of Texas Press, 1995.

Luciani, Rafael. "Medellín Fifty Years Later: From Development to Liberation." *Theological Studies* 79, no. 3 (September 2018): 566–89.

Lungo, Mario. *El Salvador en los años 80: Contrainsurgencia y revolución*. San José: Facultad Latinoamericana de Ciencias Sociales, 1990.

Mitchell, Nancy. *Jimmy Carter in Africa: Race and the Cold War*. Stanford: Stanford University Press, 2016.

Montgomery, Tommie Sue. *Revolution in El Salvador: From Civil Strife to Civil Peace.* Boulder, CO: Westview, 1995.

Office of Human Rights, Archdiocese of Guatemala (ODHAG). *Guatemala: ¡Nunca Más!* Maryknoll, NY: Orbis, 1999.

———. *Testigos de la fe por paz: Vidas ejemplares de la Iglesia Católica de Guatemala.* Guatemala: ODHAG, 2003.

Ortiz, Frank V., Jr. *Ambassador Ortiz: Lessons from a Life of Service.* Albuquerque: University of New Mexico Press, 2005.

Pastor, Robert A. *Condemned to Repetition: The United States and Nicaragua.* Princeton, NJ: Princeton University Press, 1987.

———. *Not Condemned to Repetition: The United States and Nicaragua.* London: Taylor and Francis, 2018.

Payeras, Mario. *Los días de la selva.* Guatemala: Editorial Piedra Santa, 2002.

Peña, Milagros. "Liberation Theology in Peru: An Analysis of the Role of Intellectuals in Social Movements." *Journal for the Scientific Study of Religion* 33, no. 1 (March 1994): 34–45.

Peters, Shawn Francis. *The Catonsville Nine: A Story of Faith and Resistance in the Vietnam Era.* New York: Oxford University Press, 2012.

Peterson, Christian. *Globalizing Human Rights: Private Citizens, the Soviet Union, and the West.* New York: Taylor and Francis, 2012.

Pezzullo, Lawrence, and Ralph Pezzullo. *At the Fall of Somoza.* Pittsburgh: University of Pittsburgh Press, 1993.

Pope John XXIII. *Letters to His Family.* New York: McGraw-Hill, 1970.

Portocarrero, Amaru Barahona. *Estudio sobre la historia contemporánea de Nicaragua.* San Pedro de Montes de Oca, San Juan, Costa Rica: Instituto de Investigaciones Sociales, Facultad de Ciencias Sociales, Universidad de Costa Rica, 1977.

Preston, Andrew. *Sword of the Spirit, Shield of Faith: Religion in American War and Diplomacy.* New York: Knopf, 2012.

Prisk, Courtney, ed. *The Commandante Speaks: Memoirs of an El Salvadoran Guerrilla.* Boulder, CO: Westview, 1991.

Quataert, Jean. *Advocating Dignity: Human Rights Mobilizations in Global Politics.* Philadelphia: University of Pennsylvania Press, 2009.

Randall, Margaret. *Sandino's Daughters: Testimonies of Nicaraguan Women in Struggle.* Vancouver: New Star Books, 1981.

———. *Sandino's Daughters Revisited: Feminism in Nicaragua.* New Brunswick, NJ: Rutgers University Press, 1994.

Ríos Montt, José Efraín, Brigadier General. *Mensajes del presidente de la república, general José Efraín Ríos Montt.* Guatemala: Tipográfia Nacional, 1982.

Sabino, Carlos. *Guatemala, la historia silenciada Tomo I: Revolución y liberación.* Guatemala: Fondo de Cultura Economica, 2009.

———. *Guatemala, la historia silenciada, 1944–1989, Tomo II: El dominó que no cayó.* Guatemala: Fondo de Cultura Economica, 2009.

Sánchez Nateras, Gerardo. "The Sandinista Revolution and the Limits of the Cold War in Latin America: The Carter Administration and the Nicaraguan Crisis, 1977–1981." *Cold War History* 18, no. 2 (2018): 66–86.

Sargent, Daniel. *A Superpower Transformed: The Remaking of American Foreign Relations in the 1970s.* Oxford: Oxford University Press, 2015.

Bibliography / 217

Sarros, Peter. *U.S.-Vatican Relations, 1975–1980: A Diplomatic Study*. Notre Dame, IN: University of Notre Dame Press, 2020.

Schirmer, Jennifer. *The Guatemalan Military Project: A Violence Called Democracy*. Philadelphia: University of Pennsylvania Press, 1998.

Schlesinger, Stephen, and Stephen Kinzer. *Bitter Fruit: The Untold Story of the American Coup in Guatemala*. Garden City, NY: Doubleday, 1982.

Schmidli, William Michael. *The Fate of Freedom Elsewhere: Human Rights and US Cold War Policy toward Argentina*. Ithaca, NY: Cornell University Press, 2013.

———. "'The Most Sophisticated Intervention We Have Seen': The Carter Administration and the Nicaraguan Crisis, 1978–1979." *Diplomacy and Statecraft* 23, no. 1 (2012): 66–86.

Schmitz, David F., and Vanessa Walker. "Jimmy Carter and the Foreign Policy of Human Rights: The Development of a Post-Cold War Foreign Policy." *Diplomatic History* 28, no. 1 (January 2004): 113–43.

Schulz, Donald, and Deborah Sundloff-Schulz. *The United States, Honduras, and the Crisis in Central America*. Boulder, CO: Westview, 1994.

Secretaría de la Paz. "Jornadas de agosto de 1977." Guatemala: Gobierno de Guatemala, 2009.

Sikkink, Kathryn. *Mixed Signals: U.S. Human Rights Policy and Latin America*. Ithaca, NY: Cornell University Press, 2004.

Skidmore, David. *Reversing Course: Carter's Foreign Policy, Domestic Politics, and the Failure of Reform*. Nashville, TN: Vanderbilt University Press, 1996.

Smith, Christian. *Resisting Reagan: The US Central America Peace Movement*. Chicago: University of Chicago Press, 1996.

Smith, Gaddis. *Morality, Reason, and Power: American Diplomacy in the Carter Years*. New York: Hill and Wang, 1986.

Snyder, Sarah. "'A Call for U.S. Leadership': Congressional Activism on Human Rights." *Diplomatic History* 37, no. 2 (April 2013): 372–97.

Sobrino, Jon, SJ. *Monseñor Romero*. San Salvador: UCA Editores, 1989.

Soto Rosales, Carlos Rafael. *El sueño encadenado: El proceso político guatemalteco, 1944–1999*. Guatemala: Tipografia Nacional, 2002.

Stanley, William D. *The Protection Racket State: Elite Politics, Military Extortion, and Civil War in El Salvador*. Philadelphia: Temple University Press, 1996.

Strong, Robert A. *Working in the World: Jimmy Carter and the Making of American Foreign Policy*. Baton Rouge: Louisiana State University Press, 2000.

Stuckey, Mary. *Jimmy Carter, Human Rights, and the National Agenda*. College Station: Texas A&M University Press, 2008.

Sullivan-González, Douglass. *The Black Christ of Esquipulas: Religion and Identity in Guatemala*. Lincoln: University of Nebraska Press, 2016.

Todd, Molly. *Beyond Displacement: Campesinos, Refugees, and Collective Action in the Salvadoran Civil War*. Madison: University of Wisconsin Press, 2010.

Travis, Philip W. *Reagan's War on Terrorism in Nicaragua: The Outlaw State*. Lanham, MD: Lexington Books, 2017.

Turek, Lauren Frances. *To Bring the Good News to All Nations: Evangelical Influence on Human Rights and US Foreign Relations*. Ithaca, NY: Cornell University Press, 2020.

Valdevellano, Roberto. "Mario López Larrave: Hombre honesto, revolucionario y luchado." *Voz Universitaria Informativa* (May/June 1977).

Vrana, Heather. "Revolutionary Transubstantiation in 'The Republic of Students': Death

Commemoration in Urban Guatemala from 1977 to the Present." *Radical History Review* 114 (Fall 2012): 66–90.

Wright, Scott. *Oscar Romero: Communion of the Saints.* Maryknoll, NY: Orbis Books, 2009.

Yaqib, Salim. *Imperfect Strangers: Americans, Arabs, and US-Middle East Relations in the 1970s.* Ithaca, NY: Cornell University Press, 2016.

Yoshitani, Gail E. S. *Reagan on War: A Reappraisal of the Weinberger Doctrine, 1980–1984.* College Station: Texas A&M University Press, 2012.

Zimmerman, Matilde. *Sandinista: Carlos Fonseca and the Nicaraguan Revolution.* Durham, NC: Duke University Press, 2001.

INDEX

Aguilar Urizar, Yolanda de la Luz, 57–58, 67

Aircraft Armaments, Inc., 44–45, 51, 74. *See also* munitions sales, private

Ajpuac, Geronimo, 65

Alta Verapáz (department), 50–54, 63–64, 71, 94, 118, 145. *See also* Panzós massacre

Andrade, Fernando, 148–49, 157–58

Angelo Giuseppe Roncalli See John XXIII (pope)

ARA (Bureau of Inter-American Affairs, US Department of State), 74–75, 77, 78

Arana Osorio, Carlos, 26–27, 29, 119–20, 180n91

Árbenz Guzmán, Jacobo, 6, 13, 43

Archdiocese of Guatemala Human Rights Office, 26

Archila, Miguel, 57

Arenas Barrera, José Luis, 28

Arévalo Bermejo, Juan José, 13, 14

Arns, Paulo Evaristo, 32

Arzú Yrigoyen, Álvaro, 169

Asturias, Rodrigo, 27

Baldetti, Roxanna, 169

Beagle Channel, 89. *See also* John Paul II (pope)

Belize, Guatemala's dispute over, 45, 72, 184n54

Bennett, John T., 56

Berger Perdomo, Óscar, 170

Birns, Larry, 82

bishops in Guatemala. *See* CEG

Blackwell, Morton, 117

Bocel, Francisco, 104–6

Bocel, Pedro, 2, 10, 100, 103–4

Boster, Davis, 41, 53–56, 72–73, 153, 186n8. *See also* Ortiz Jr., Frank V.

Bosworth, Stephen W., 125

Bowdler, William, 78, 83, 122

Bradford, Marjorie, 23, 178n72. *See also* Melville affair

Breen, John M., 23

Breve historia del movimiento syndical guatemalteco (Mario López Larrave), 43

Bridgeman, Mary Martina, 14, 30

Brockmann, Miguel d'Escoto, 53. *See also* Nicaragua

Brown, Richard, 111–14, 117, 196n91

Brzezinski, Zbigniew, 37, 83

Buechele, Thomas, 66

Bush, George H. W., 144

Bushnell, John, 77–78

Caballeros Ramírez, Aníbal Leonel, 41, 43

Cáceres Lehnhoff, Eduardo, 62

CACIF (Comité Coordinador de Asociaciones Agrícolas, Comerciales, Industriales y Financieras), 41, 44, 50. *See also* ESA

Cajal, Máximo, 61–62

Calder, Bruce, 20

Calderón, Jorge, 18

campesinos: EGP recruiting, 27; impressment into PACs or military, 50, 124–25, 139; John Paul II's remarks to, 59; labor organizing, 28, 49; and land ownership, 28, 49, 119; and Óscar Romero, 183n31; as targets of abuse, 28, 49–50, 127, 129, 158–59. *See also* CUC; land reform; Panzós massacre

CAN (Central Auténtica Nacionalista party), 119, *120*

Cancinos, David, 56

Capovilla, Loris, 18

Cardenal, Ernesto, 72

Cardenal, Fernando, 72

220 / Index

Carpio Nicolle, Jorge, 160–*61*, 162, 169

Carter administration's human rights-based foreign policy: criticism of before US election, 83–84; deemed counterproductive by PRC (1977), 36–37; denounced as imperialist by Laugerud and Lucas, 34–35, 71–72; goals and record in Central America, 7, 8, 33; increased congressional influence in 1970s, 34, 56–57, 82; as increasing human rights abuses, 33, 36; limits of and undercutting of US influence, 7, 43–44, 50–51, 81; tenets of, 7–8, 31–33, 35–37, 51, 181n6. *See also* Boster, Davis; Laugerud and Lucas regimes and conditional US military aid; munitions sales, private; PRC (1977); PRC (1978)

Casa Indigena, 110

Casariego y Acevedo, Mario: death, 143, 146; denialism and alignment with far right, 60, 146–47; denunciation of activism and priests' political involvement, 39, 60, 146; kidnapping of, 25; rift with CEG, 39, 51, 53, 69, 72; unpopularity with clergy, subtle expressions of, 98

Casey, William, 91

Castañeda de León, Oliverio, 54–55, 184n50

Castillo, Otto René, 170

Castillo Armas, Carlos, 13–16, 176n21

Cathedral de San José (Antigua, Guatemala), 146, *147*

Catholic Action: bolstered by Vatican II's doctrine on laity, mission work, and human dignity, 17–18, 22, 58, 165; as bulwark against Marxism, 17–18; fostering liberation theology in Latin America, 12–13; growth in Latin America, 16, 18; influence on John XXIII, 13, 17; murder or abduction of members, 55, 68, 145–46; origins in nineteenth-century anti-poverty discourses, 13, 16; and prominence of Catholic activists in 1970s and 1980s, 165; students, workers, and farmers, 44. See also *Rerum Novarum* (Leo XIII)

Catholic activists after Ríos Montt: dangers faced in postwar Guatemala, 170; diminished influence in US, 171; local and global human rights advocacy, 143, 159, 166. *See also* US Catholic press; US Catholic press, diocesan newspapers; *and specific activists*

Catholic activists before Reagan: direct intervention in abuses, 8, 64–65, 109, 113–14; diverse methods of activism, 8, 64–67, 79, 80–81; diversity of, 3; exposing violence and inequities, 3–4, 7–8, 53, 66–67, 72, 79–80; importance of smaller US cities and dioceses for, 3–5; increased prominence under Laugerud, 34; strengthening transnational connections, 5, 61; testimonies in US parishes, 39–40, 109; viewed as political threat in Guatemala, 53, 60–61, 69–70, 84–85. *See also* US Catholic press; US Catholic press, diocesan newspapers; *and specific activists*

Catholic activists under Reagan: Brown's suspicion of and advice on neutralizing, 111–13; congressional testimony, 90, 92, 114, 117; demonized as Marxist sympathizers in US, 84–85, 89–90; importance of human rights reportage for, 87–88, 113–14, 117; importance of smaller US cities and dioceses for, 166; relationship with Reagan administration, 87–88, 117; urging investigation of Rother's murder, 8, 106, 114. *See also* Haig, Alexander; US Catholic Press; US Catholic press, diocesan newspapers; USCC; *and specific activists*

Catholic churches: closing or occupation of, 69; as sites of atrocities, 9. *See also individual churches*

Catholic faith, shifts in understandings of due to social activism: Guatemalan church out of sync with, 148–49; major causes, 138, 148–49. *See also* Miller, James; Rother, Stanley; Schaffer, Gregory; Woods, Bill

Catholic press. *See* US Catholic press

Catholic understandings of human dignity, statements on: CEG 1978 catechesis on temporal government and common good, 45–46; *Gaudium et Spes* and Vatican II's commitment to human rights, 21–22, 39, 46; industrialized nations' obligations to poor, 22, 59; influence of *Populorum Progressio*, 22–23; *Mater et Magistra* and *Pacem in Terris* (John XXIII) and welfare of poor, 19–20; need for missionaries to the poor, 19–20; Paul VI on social and economic justice, 22, 46, 58. *See also* CELAM; John Paul II (pope)

CEG (Conferencia Episcopal de Guatemala): 1978 catechesis and shift to assertive criticism, 51; 1978 statement on politics and common good, 45–46; cautious reception of junta, 123; CEG's calls yielding increased turnout in 1984 and 1985, 166; church's missions to defend human dignity, 39; and elections, 10, 46; internal divisions following murder of Grande, 39; Lucas regime as having declared war on Catholicism, 107–8; mediation with Mejia regime via Chapin, 9; opposition to expulsion of priests, 29; pastoral letter on economic and social rights based on CEDAC study, 104; response to Panzós massacre, 49; response to Puebla conference, 60; rift with Casariego, 39, 51, 53, 60, 68–70, 98–99; shift to more aggressive human rights stance, 98. *See also specific time periods' church-state relations*

CEG (Conferencia Episcopal de Guatemala) after Ríos Montt: 1984 pastoral letter calling for new constitution, 154–55; 1985 pastoral letter prior to elections, 160; *Ad Limina Apostolorum* visit to Vatican, 146; denounced for interceding in politics, 143; desire for reform creating conflict with military, 148; shifts after Casariego's death, 141, 143, 147; statement in *El Grafico* on Monasterio's murder, 148; targeted by Serrano, 168. *See also* church-state relations after Ríos Montt; Penados del Barrio, Prospero; Ramírez Monasterio, Augusto

CEH (Comisión para el Esclarecimiento Histórico), documentary value of *vs.* other records, 5

CELAM (Consejo Episcopal Latinoamericano): advocacy for poor praised by USCC, 107; Medellín conference, 23, 58, 165; Puebla conference, 8, 58–60, 165; Santiago seminar on *Populorum Progressio*, 23, 178n62; statement on activism following John Paul II's Mexico visit, 59

Central American Historical Institute, 80

Cerezo Arévalo, Marco Vinicio, election of, 10, 143, *161*, 162–63, 166–67

CERJ (Council of Ethnic Communities), 168

Chapin, Frederic, 9; account of CEG/Mejía clash after Monasterio's murder, 147–48; army/government out of touch with changes in Catholic church, 148; echoing denials of Ríos Montt's massacres, 130–31, 141; as intermediary between Mejia regime

and CEG, 9; monitoring of 1982 election, 119–21; negotiations with Ríos Montt for elections, 124; report on Miller's murder, 111; reports on Ríos Montt's meeting with Reagan, 133–34

Christopher, Warren, 75, 79, 85

Chupina Barahona, Hernán, 54, 121

church-state relations, 1954–1976: impact of Vatican II, 30; and John Paul II, 9; Melville affair and liberation theology as strain on, 23, 30. *See also* CEG; Melville affair; Woods, Bill

church-state relations after Ríos Montt: blessing of National Assembly, 9, 143; relations between CEG and Mejía regime, 143, 148–50; Serrano targeting CEG and activists for investigation, 168; voting as religious obligation, 155, 160. *See also* CEG after Ríos Montt; Penados del Barrio, Prospero

church-state relations under Laugerud regime, 29–31, 33–34, 38, 46, 51. *See also* Casariego; CEG; Panzós massacre; Woods, Bill

church-state relations under Lucas regime, 58–60, 67–69, 72. *See also* CEG

church-state relations under Ríos Montt: evangelicals' disproportionate political and social influence, 124, 142; and John Paul II's visit, 138; Ríos Montt's *discussions*, 138. *See also* CEG; Protestantism (Evangelical); Ríos Montt, Mario Enrique (Bishop)

civil patrols. *See* PACs (Patrullas de Autodefensa Civil)

civil war in Guatemala, summary of impact: death toll, 173n6; survivors' testimonies, 6, 60, 64, 65

Clark, William, 113, 117

Clarke, Maura, 72, 89, 92–93, 106

CNT (Central Nacional de Trabajadores), 57, 63–64

CNUS (Comité Nacional de Unidad Sindical), 63

Coakley, Paul, 170

Collins, John, 14

Colom Argueta, Manuel, 56, 79, 180n91

Committee of Santa Fe, 84–85, 192n49

communism: and Arévalo and Árbenz administrations, 14; CEG statement under Laugerud on suspicions of church as, 38–39; communist groups and the formation of FAR, 16;

and coup attempt against Ydígoras Fuentes, 16; John Paul II's anti-communism, 89; Rossell's call for Catholics to fight, 13. *See also* Marxism; White, Don; *and individual groups*

Concepción, Conrado de la Cruz, 67, 97

Council on Hemispheric Affairs, 80

CUC (Comité de Unidad Campesina), 61–62, 145, 146

Culán, Gaspar, 1, 100, 195n47

DCG (Democracia Cristiana Guatemalteca party), 160, 162

del Barrio Batz, Domingo, 68

de Léon Carpio, Ramiro, 169

Derian, Patricia, 78

DIA (Defense Intelligence Agency), 121, 124, 127, 144, 152–53, 159

diocesan newspapers. *See* US Catholic press

Divini Redemptoris (Pius XI), 19

Dominga, 65

Donovan, Jean, 72, 89, 92–93, 106

Duarte, Jose Napoleón, 92

Echeverría Vielman, José Guillermo, 139

EGP (Ejército Guerrillero de los Pobres): blamed instead of army in Embassy reports, 130; clashes with Laugerud regime in Ixil Triangle (Quiché), 11; formation and coordination with campesinos, 27–29; Frente Luis Turcios Lima and occupation of fincas, 56; murder of José Luis Arenas Barrera, 28; murders after Panzós massacre, 50; persistence under Lucas regime, 55, 60, 109, 110; recruiting in Mayan communities, 61; US fear of extreme left infiltrating priests, 89–90, 98. *See also* García Dávila, Robin Mayro; Marxism; Panzós massacre; URNG

Eisenhower administration, 16, 43, 85, 88

El Calvario church, occupation of, 57

election of 1978, 46–47

election of 1982, 9, 117–21, *120*

election of 1985, 9, 160–61. *See also* Cerezo Arévalo, Marco Vinicio

elections of 1984 and ratification of new constitution, 155

El Gráfico: CEG statement in *El Grafico* on Monasterio's murder, 148; Jesuits accused of subverting pope after statement on Guatemala's violence and inequalities, 68–69; report clergy encouraging voting, 155

El Salvador, 50, 53, 71–75, 92, 186n3, 190n16. *See also* Clarke, Maura; Donovan, Jean; Ford, Ita; Grande, Rutilio; Kazel, Dorothy; Romero, Óscar

EOS (Escuela de Orientación Sindical), 40. *See also* López Larrave, Mario

ESA (Ejército Secreto Anticomunista), 69, 71–72, 171; death list in *Prensa Libre* and murders, 54–55, 121; existence questioned, 41, 55; formation and claimed relationship with MLN, 41; as threat to governments from far right, 44, 71; threat to kill all Guatemalan Jesuits, 69, 72. *See also* García Dávila, Robin Mayro

Escuela Politécnica, 14, 52, 122, 142

Evangelicalism. *See* Protestantism (Evangelical)

FAR (Fuerzas Armadas Rebeldes): decline, 27; formation from other leftists groups, 16; Mein's assassination, 25, 179n79; and Melville affair, 24; offensives against, 26–27; US fear of extreme left infiltrating priests, 98; violent deaths of members, 27, 40, 56, 94. *See also* ORPA

Fischer Sandhoff, Robert, 40–41

Flores Reyes, Gerardo, 49

FMLN (Frente Farabundo Martí para la Liberación Nacional), 190n16

Fontaine, Roger, 84, 95

Ford, Ita, 72, 89, 92–93, 106

Foreign Assistance Act of 1974, 79, 190n25. *See also* Harkin Amendment

Fraser, Donald, 34

Frente Estudiantíl Robin García, 62

FSLN (Frente Sandinista de Liberación Nacional), 33, 72, 75, 190n14. *See also* Nicaragua

Fuentes Mohr, Alberto, 56, 79

FUR (Frente Unido de la Revolución), 56

Gálvez Galindo, Carlos, 97

García, Antonio, 24

García Arredondo, Pedro, 62, 186n11

García Dávila, Robin Mayro, 41–42, 43

Gaudium et Spes, 21–22, 39, 46

genocide, Ríos Montt's acts characterized as, 115–16, 126, 129, 136, 139, 141. *See also* CEH

Gerardi Conedera, Juan José, 96, 169, 170

GHRC (Guatemala Human Rights Commission), 167

Girón Parrone, José, 57

Gleijeses, Piero, 13

GNIB (Guatemala News and Information Bureau), 67. *See also* Aguilar Urizar, Yolanda de la Luz

Goggin, John, 65, 187n47

Gordillo Martínez, Hector Luis, 121, 123

Gran Cirera, José María, 68, 97, 169, 194n36

Grande, Rutilio, 39, 72, 183n31

Guatemala: ¡Nunca Más! (Guatemalan Archdiocese's Human Rights Office), 169

Guevara Rodríguez, Aníbal Angel: 1982 election, *120*, 121; campaign platform, 118–19

Guillermo Spiegeler, Otto, 54

HA (Human Rights and Humanitarian Affairs bureau, US Department of State), 74–75, 78

Haig, Alexander, 89, 91–93, 95–96, 106–7, 193n17

Harkin, Tom, 34, 82–83. *See also* Harkin Amendment

Harkin Amendment, 35, 37, 44, 74

Hehir, Bryan, 90, 92, 114

Hennessey, Ronald, 1, 4, 132–33, 159

Herren, Francesco, 68

Hickey, James, 92

Hombres de Maíz (Miguel Ángel Asturias), 27

House Foreign Affairs Committee, 34, 56–57, 92, 193n17

Huehuetenago (department): atrocities concentrated in, 71, 116, 130–33, 140; Lucas campaign in, 52; testimony of PAC conscript from, 125; Woods and Maryknoll mission in, 28–29. *See also* elections of 1984; La Salle Brothers; Melville affair; Mendoza García, Prudencio

Human Rights and Humanitarian Affairs bureau, State Department (HA) and private munitions sales, 44, *45*

IFIA (International Financial Institutions Act), 34

Iglesia Santiago Apóstol, 1, 2, 101

International Armament Corporation, 44–*45*, 51, 74. *See also* munitions sales, private

International Organizations and Social Movements Subcommittee, 34

Ixil Triangle, 11, 67, 115, 116, 197n1

Jesuits, 39, 61, 68–69, 72, 96

John Paul II (pope): ambiguities in stance on politics and activism, 58–60, 69–70; approach to liberation theology, 58; CELAM Puebla conference, 58–59; denunciation of human rights abuses during Central America visit, 117, 133, 141; meeting with CEG and clash with Mejía, 146

John XXIII (pope), 12–13, 17, 19–20, 22, 58

Joslin, Paul, 110–11

Kazel, Dorothy, 72, 89, 92–93, 106

Kirkpatrick, Jeane, 83, 89, 91

Krol, John, 52

Laghi, Pio, 113

Lamont, Donal, 32

land reform: Árbenz's Decree 900 agrarian reform plan, 13; for campesinos, 28, 49, 119; CEG statement on CEDAC study, 104; and cooperatives sponsored by missions, 11, 28–29, 175n3; discussions of following Panzós massacre, 49; Paul VI advocating for, 22; topic at USAC bookstore, 43. *See also* campesinos; Panzós massacre

La Salle Brothers, 110–11

Latin American Sociology Congress (San Salvador, El Salvador), 24

Laugerud and Lucas regimes and conditional US military aid, 14, 33–38, *45*, 51, 71–73. *See also* munitions sales, private

Laugerud regime: antipathy to mass demonstrations after López's and García's murders, 50; fraudulent election, 122; response to Harkin Amendment, 35–36; statements in support of human rights to US House and UN, 35–36; surge in violence in summer of 1977, 40–44. *See also* CACIF; Laugerud and Lucas regimes and conditional US military aid; Panzós massacre; students/workers/farmers organizing across class lines; Woods, Bill

Leo XIII (pope), 16–17, 19

liberation theology, 12, 23, 30, 39, 58–60, 111–13

Lima Oliva, Byron, 169

224 / Index

Long, Clarence, 131, 144
López Coachita, Hermógenes, 50–51
López Larrave, Mario, 40, 42–43, 185n74. *See also* EOS
Lucas García, Benedicto, 124, 151–53
Lucas García, Fernando Romeo. *See* Lucas regime
Lucas regime: anti-Catholic violence and murder of priests, 96 97; death squads, 60, 69, 71–73, 91, 116; ESA death list and murders, 54–55; explosions in violence, 53–58, 63–64, 67–69, 71, 94, 116; fraudulent election, 46–47, 52, 54; as having declared war on Catholicism, 107–8; initial US assessment of Lucas and contrasts with Villagrán, 53–54, 60–61; Lucas's "siege mentality" fueling violence, 54, 60–61, 97, 188n51; meeting with Sinn about arms sales, 93–94; mistaking priests' political liberalism for Marxism, 97; overthrow of, 121; plots against, 56; response to bus fare strikes, 54–55, 71, 121; vow to improve human rights record, 73. *See also* Casariego y Acevedo, Mario; Catholic activists before Reagan; CEG; church-state relations under Lucas regime; Ortiz Jr., Frank V.; Panzós massacre; Spanish Embassy massacre; US-Guatemalan relations under Lucas regime
Luciani, Alberto (Pope John Paul I), 58
Lucker, Raymond, 144, 156. *See also* New Ulm, Minnesota diocese
Luqueños. *See* San Lucas Tolimán

Mack, James, 78–79, 82
Maldonado Aguirre, Alejandro, 118, 119, *161*
Maldonado Schaad, Horacio Egberto, *120*–121
Manera, Luis, 60
Mano Blanca, 25–26
MAP (Military Assistance Program), 37, *38*
Mariposa, 64–65, 108–9, 171. *See also* San Lucas Tolimán mission
Martinka, Stanley, 20, 178n51
Marxism: Catholic Action as bulwark against in *Ubi Arcano Dei Consilio* (Pius XI), 17–18; Catholic-Mayan-Marxist mélange, 61; church as infiltrated by, 31, 33, 38–39; discussed in papal encyclicals, 17, 19; foreign-born priests in Latin America as susceptible to, 111–12; Nicaragua's Sandinista

Revolution, 53. *See also* communism; *and individual groups*
Maryknoll order, 1. *See also* Melville affair; *and individual missionaries and missions*
Mater et Magistra (John XXIII), 12, 19, 29, 46, 187n36
Mayan population, 50, 61, 128–29, 149, 169. *See also* campesinos; Panzós massacre
McSherry, Thomas, 162
Medellín conference. *See* CELAM; liberation theology
Mein, John, 24, 25, 178n70, 179nn78–80. *See also* Melville affair
Mejía regime: anti-Catholic violence, 145–46, 148; cession of presidency to Cerezo, 143; clash with John Paul II, 146; elections of 1984 resulting in new constitution, 156; human rights abuses abating in some places and persisting in others, 145, 149, 156, 158; increasing public discontent in 1985, 159; threat of coup from Benedicto Lucas García, 151–53; US coverage of rise of, 144. *See also* church-state relations after Ríos Montt; US-Guatemalan relations/policy after Ríos Montt
Melotto, Angelico, 99
Meloy, Francis, 11, 29
Melville, Arthur, 23. *See also* Melville affair
Melville, Thomas, 23, 178n72. *See also* Melville affair
Melville affair, 23–26, 178n72, 178nn69–70, 179n74
Méndez Montenegro, Julio César, 25–26
Méndez Ruíz, Ricardo, 56
Mendoza García, Prudencio, 146, 150
Metropolitan Cathedral (Guatemala City), 15, 67, 154
Miller, James, 2–3, 109–11, 114, 165
mission work, papal perspectives on, 19–20, 22, 177n47
MLN (Movimiento de Liberación Nacional), 26, 33, 40–41. *See also* Sandoval Alarcón, Mario
Molina, Otto Pérez, 169
Molina-Orantes, Adolfo, 36
Monasterio, Augusto Ramírez, 143, 146–47, 149, 150, 157
MR-13 (Movimiento Revolucionario 13 de Noviembre), 16

Index / 225

munitions sales, private: Arms Export Control Act, 74; as disincentive for compliance with US policy, 44, 51, 77–78, 85; Export Administration Act, 74; key US suppliers, 44–45, 51, 74, 78; State Department authorizations of, 45

National Assembly, 9, 26, 126, 143, 155–57, 159

New Ulm, Minnesota diocese: newsletter features on children at mission, 64–66; and San Lucas Tolimán mission, 1, 20, 40, 65, 144. *See also* San Lucas Tolimán mission; Schaffer, Gregory

Nicaragua: Sandinista Revolution, 50, 53, 85, 181n7, 190n14; Somoza family, 33, 53, 66, 75, 80. *See also* FSLN; Obando y Bravo, Miguel; Somoza DeBayle, Anastasio

NISGUA (Network in Solidarity with the People of Guatemala), 106, 112, 114

North American Congress on Latin America, 80

Nueva Organización Anticomunista, 26

Obando y Bravo, Miguel, 7, 53, 96. *See also* Nicaragua

Ojo por Ojo, 27, 71

Oklahoma City, Archdiocese of: Cause for Canonization for Rother, 170. *See also* Rother, Stanley; Salatka, Charles A.; Santiago Atitlán mission

Operation PBSUCCESS, 13, 176n11

ORPA (Organización Revolucionaria del Pueblo en Armas): blamed instead of army in Embassy reports, 130; expansion and recruiting in indigenous communities, 61; formation, 27–28; meeting in Santiago Atitlán, 99; potential to attract priests' assistance, 98; priests suspected by CIA of assisting, 89–90; recruiting in Mayan communities, 61; signaling growing militant left, 60; US fear of extreme left infiltrating priests, 89–90, 98; Woods's denial of association with, 29. *See also* URNG

Ortiz, Dianna, 167, 170

Ortiz Jr., Frank V.: as career diplomat, 75–76, 83; challenge of Carter's foreign policy, 8, 77–78, 118; challenge of State Department policy contradictions, 8, 72, 76–79; criticism and recall of, 51, 70, 82–83; and Lucas, 8, 72, 76; on Lucas and Villagrán, 60–61, 79;

on Lucas's "siege mentality," 54, 60–61, 97, 188n51; personal feelings about Guatemala leaders, 79, 153, 192n47; recommended approach to Guatemala, 77, 81–82, 118, 192n47. *See also* Bushnell, John

Pacem in Terris (John XXIII), 12, 19

PACs (Patrullas de Autodefensa Civil): atrocities in mid 1980s, 145–46, 150; CEG call for dismantling of, 154; human rights abuses between 1978 and 1980, 71; impressment of campesinos, 124–25, 139; Mendoza's murder, 150; Ríos Montt's organization of in Quiché, 124–25, 128

Palacio Nacional (Guatemala), 15, 41, 121, 123

Panzós massacre, 33, 47–51, 48, 128

Partido Unificación Anticomunista, 28

Pastor. *See* Mariposa

Pattee, Richard, 14

Paul VI, 22, 28, 46, 52, 58

Payeras, Mario, 27, 28

peace talks to end Guatemala's civil war, 168–69

Pellecer, Luis, 96–97, 149–50

Peña, Milagros, 17

Penados del Barrio, Prospero, 9, 123–24, 143, 150–51, 154. *See also* CEG after Ríos Montt

Peralta Azurdia, Enrique, 46

Peralta Méndez, Ricardo, 46

Pezzulo, Lawrence, 82

PGT (Partido Guatemalteco del Trabajo), 16, 27, 50, 116

Piedra, Alberto, 158

Pius XI (pope), 17, 19

PN (Policía Nacional): ending bus fare strike, 25, 121; failure to investigate Rother's death, 106–7; lawlessness under Lucas, 55; reaction to Maryknoll affair, 25; Sixth Command Unit, 54, 56, 62; various abuses, 55–56, 71, 78, 94, 155. *See also* Chupina Barahona, Hernán; Valiente, Manuel de Jesus

Populorum Progressio (Paul VI), 12, 22

"*Populorum Progressio* and Latin American Realities" (CELAM), 23

PRC (Presidential Review Committee), 1977, 36–37, 182n22

PRC (Presidential Review Committee), 1979, 75

Prensa Libre: 1984 interview with Penados del Barrio on vision for church in politics,

150–51; Benedicto Lucas García interview attacking Mejía, 151; condemnations of US policy as interventionist or hypocritical, 38, 73, 83; ESA death list, 54–55; Panzós massacre blamed on church and Marxists, 33, *48*, 51; statements on Mendoza's death, 150

priests, population in Guatemala, *20*

Princeps Pastorum (John XXIII), 19

Protestantism (evangelical), 69, 128–29, 138, 149, 167, 171. *See also* Ríos Montt

Quad Cities Religious Task Force, 156

Quadragesimo Anno (Pius XI), 19

Quetzaltenango (department), 41; atrocities, 29, 128, 145–46, 202n14; visit from John Paul II, 137, 139. *See also* elections of 1984; García Dávila, Robin Mayro; Manera, Luis

Quetzaltenango diocese, 29

Quezada Toruño, Rodolfo, 155

Quic Ajuchian, Diego, 101–2

Quiché (department): activists' direct intervention in abuses, 113; atrocities and genocidal campaign under Ríos Montt, 124–30; atrocities under Mejía regime, 145–46; atrocities under Serrano, 167–68; closure of dioceses due to violence, 96; concentration of human rights abuses, 5, 47–50, 94, 140; concentration of Victoria 82 atrocities, 116; diocesan statement on Spanish Embassy massacre, 62; explosion of violence in 1979, 55–57; increasing human rights abuses reported from 1978 to 1980, 49–50, 53, 71, 186n4; Jesuit projects, 61; Lucas's campaign, 52; missionary testimony to US audiences about conditions, 109; parish priest's statement entered into US congressional record, 81; violence and deportations under Arana, 27–29. *See also* Cajal, Máximo; elections of 1984; Gerardi Conedera, Juan José; Gran Cirera, José María; Ixil Triangle; Mariposa; Panzós massacre; San Lucas Tolimán mission; Woods, Bill

Quigley, Thomas E., 81

Quinn, John, 52

Ramírez, Ricardo, 27

Ramírez Cervantes, Elias Osmundo, 27

Ramírez Monasterio, Augusto, 164

Ratzinger, Joseph, 59

Reagan administration foreign policy, 88–93, 95–96; Central America, 91–93; role of Catholic church, 88–90, 95–96. *See also* CEG; Rother, Stanley; Sinn, Melvin; State Department; US Catholic press; USCC

refugees: fleeing to Mexico, 126; murder of, 145; protests of deportations, 158–59; Sanctuary Movement, 132, 156, 158–59

Rerum Novarum (Leo XIII), 17

Rice, Charles Owen, 80, 135–36, 144, 157

Ríos Montt, José Efraín: assuming power from junta, 7, 123, 198n24; as evangelical Protestant, 123–24, 137–38, 140, 148; genocide trial and overturned conviction, 169–70; resignation, 140

Ríos Montt, Mario Enrique (Bishop), 68, 122–23

Ríos Montt regime: atrocities in summer of 1982, 128; background and training, 122; churches as sites of anti-Catholic abuses, 128; Decree Law 45–82, 126–27; dissolution of political structures, 126; Dos Erres, Peten massacre and atrocities, 134–35; Echeverría's letter opening to other calls for civilian rule, 139–40; Frijoles y Fusiles (Beans and Rifles), 126; human rights abuses concentrated in Quiché and Huehuetenango, 140–41; overemphasis of genocidal dictatorship, 6–7; and Reagan administration, 9; targeting Mayan Catholics and Protestants, 128–29; Victoria 82, 127

Rivera y Damas, Arturo, 92, 112

Roach, John, 90, 92, 129, 133, 141

Romero, Carlos Humberto, 66, 75

Romero, Óscar, 7, 33, 39, 53, 72, 183n31

Roncalli, Angelo Giuseppe. *See* John XXIII (pope)

Roney, David, 65–66

Rossell y Arellano, Mariano, 13, *15*, 30, 175n7

Rother, Stanley, *99*; Cause for Canonization, 170; evacuation to Oklahoma, 103–4; first US-born martyr, 170; Iglesia Santiago Apóstol, 1, 2, 101; murder of, 95, 97, 104–7; Saint John the Baptist Church (Edmond, Oklahoma), 103; at Santiago Atitlán mission, 1, 10, 98–104, 195n53. *See also* Brown, Richard; Haig, Alexander; NISGUA; Santiago Atitlán mission; White, Don

Rusk, Dean, 25

Saint James the Apostle Church. *See* Iglesia Santiago Apóstol

Salatka, Charles A., 1–2, 98, 114, 141

Sánchez, Camilo, 25

Sandoval Alarcón, Mario, 33, 38–39, 60, *120–121*, 124. *See also* Lucas regime; MLN

San Lucas Tolimán mission: Casa Feliz, 21, 65, 109, 171; impact of mission, 28; role of Luqueños, 21, 108; Shaffer's funeral, 171. *See also* Mariposa; New Ulm, Minnesota diocese; Schaffer, Gregory

Santiago Atitlán mission: Archdiocese of Oklahoma mission program, 1–2, 4–5, 10, 98, 165–66, 194n42; as center of advocacy, 166; Iglesia Santiago Apóstol, 1, 2, 101; incursion of violence and impacts on mission, 99–104; Rother, Stanley, 10, *97*, 98, 100, 104–6; Tz'utujil dialect, 99, 106, 149; Voz de Atitlán radio station, 1, 100, 194n42, 195n47. *See also* Culán, Gaspar; McSherry, Thomas; Quic Ajuchian, Diego; Rother, Stanley

Schaffer, Gregory: and aftermath of Rother's murder, 105, 107; awarded Order of the Quetzal, 170; concern for safety of Rother and Bocel, 103; death in Minnesota and burial in San Lucas Tolimán, 171; mission in San Lucas Tolimán, 2–4, 20–21, 177n50; as part of coalition of Catholic activists, 2–3, 10, 30; rescue of children to San Lucas Tolimán, 64–65; San Lucas Tolimán cooperative and affordable land ownership, 28–29. *See also* New Ulm, Minnesota diocese; San Lucas Tolimán

schism in Guatemalan Catholic church hierarchy. *See* Casariego y Acevedo, Mario

Second Vatican Council. *See* Vatican II

Serrano Elías, Jorge, *161*, 168

Sinn, Melvin, 93–98, 103, 112–14

Sisniega Otero, Leonel, 83, 140, 152, *161*. *See also* MLN

Smith & Wesson, 44–45, 51, 74, 78. *See also* munitions sales, private

Sololá (department). *See* elections of 1984; New Ulm, Minnesota diocese; Rother, Stanley; San Lucas Tolimán; Santiago Atitlán mission; Welsh, Lawrence

Somoza DeBayle, Anastasio, 11, 33, 66, 72, 75, 85. *See also* Nicaragua

Spanish Embassy massacre, 61–62, *63*, 188n54, 188n56

Spiegler Noriega, Guillermo, *48*, 51, 185n1

Spokane, Dioceses of, 166. *See also* Welsh, Lawrence

State Department: contradictory policies on Guatemala and human rights, 72, 74, 76–79; difficulty understanding intrafactional tensions in Guatemala, 16; false claims of improved human rights conditions under Ríos Montt, 129–31; human rights as Lucas's justification for arms purchase request, 73–74; inability to intercede in mounting violence in 1977, 43–44; mixed policies in 1984, 157–58; optimistic interpretation of Lucas's intentions, 73, 81; personal reactions to Guatemalan dictators coloring US official's views, *153*; reactions to Guatemala's pledge to improve human rights, 54–55; suspension of military assistance for 1991 due to increasing human rights abuses, 167. *See also* Brown, Richard; House Foreign Affairs Committee; Ortiz Jr., Frank V.; PRC (Presidential Review Committee), 1977; PRC (Presidential Review Committee), 1979

students/workers/farmers organizing across class lines, 43–44, 75. *See also* López Larrave, Mario

Survil, Bernard, 3, 80

TAN (Transnational Advocacy Network), 5, 114, 166

Ten Percent Plan, 19–20, 177n47

Torres, Napoleón, 50

Ubi Arcano Dei Consilio (Pius XI), 17

United Fruit Company, 13–14

United Nations, 26

Urizar Leal, Elizardo, 41

URNG (Unidad Revolucionaria Nacional Guatemalteca): on 1982 election, 119–20; on 1985 election, 160; creation of, 116, 119, 131; peace talks, 168–69; rejection of junta, 123; strengthened by frustration with army and Victoria 82, 168; targeted by Serrano, 168

USAC (Universidad de San Carlos), 40–43, 54, 66, 155

US Catholic press: coverage of Central America,

72, 79, 144; coverage of Guatemala after Cerezo's election, 156; coverage of Rother's murder and calls for investigations, 94–95, 114; features linking mission work to spiritual obligation, 156; first hand accounts from missionaries, 61, 165; *vs.* major secular news outlets, 165; wariness of Mejía, 143–44. *See also* refugees; US Catholic press, diocesan newspapers

US Catholic press, diocesan newspapers: on Árbenz's overthrow, 14; carrying Catholic wire services stories, 66–67; children's issues, 40, 95, 157; criticism of Guatemala's dictators and Reagan administration policies, 131–32, 135–36, 144–45; debate over Puebla conference, 59; *vs.* major secular news outlets, 4, 6; *vs.* national Catholic press in highlighting local ties to Guatemala, 6, 66–67, 95, 156–57, 165; reporting on Central America in early 1980s, 9, 94–95; reporting on Laugerud regime's violence, 53; reporting on Ríos Montt regime, 132–33; shift towards criticism of Guatemala's poverty and violence, 30; stories of missionaries returning from Guatemala, 39–40, 61. *See also* US Catholic Press

USCC (United States Catholic Conference): criticism of arms sales restoration, 90, 92; influence on Reagan administration's desire for Catholic cooperation, 166; statements on Central America, 107–8; statements on Ríos Montt's human rights record, 116, 129, 133, 136, 141; suspected of being anti-Reagan Marxist allies, 117

US-Guatemalan relations/policy after Ríos Montt, 143, 148, *153–154. See also* Cerezo

US-Guatemalan relations under Carter administration: Catholic activists' approach of economic instead of military assistance, 34; complicated by contrary assessments of Lucas regime, 34, 55; conditional foreign aid resulting in diplomatic impasse, 7–8, 31, 33, 43–44, 53, 81; House Foreign Affairs Committee, 34, 56–57, 92, 193n17. *See also* Boster, Davis; Ortiz Jr., Frank V.; State Department

US-Guatemalan relations under Lucas regime, 56–57, 71, 108. *See also* Boster, Davis; Harkin, Tom; Harkin Amendment; IFIA; Ortiz Jr., Frank V.; Rother, Stanley; State Department

US-Guatemalan relations under Ríos Montt, 124, 133–43, *135. See also* Chapin, Frederic

Vaky, Viron, 75, 79, 85

Valiente, Manuel de Jesus, 57, 63

Vatican II, 12, 18–19, 21–22, 58, 165, 177n34

Verbo Ministries. *See* Ríos Montt, José Efraín

Victoria 82, 116. *See also* Lucas regime; Ríos Montt regime

Villagrán Kramer, Francisco: compared to Lucas, 60–61; human rights as justification for US arms purchase request, 73–74; as internal threat to Lucas regime, 56; optimistic statements on human rights, 73. *See also* Lucas regime

Villanueva Villanueva, Faustino, 68, 97, 194n36

violence, major shifts in: CEH reflecting change in number and nature of abuses by 1980, 53; demography of, 27, 50–51; towards genocidal campaigns, 50; Wood's murder portending anti-Catholic violence, 30–31

Voordeckers, Walter, 66, 97, 194n36

weapons sales, private. *See* munitions sales, private

Welsh, Lawrence, 4, 87–88, 90, 113

White, Don, 103–4, 195n65

White, Robert, 82

Wilson, William, 89, 113, 192n5

Wojtyla, Karol. *See* John Paul II (pope)

Woods, Bill: letter to Laugerud denying political connections and appealing for help, 29; mission work, 1, 11–12, 29; murder of, 11–12, 13, 29–31, 175n6, 184n50; praised by CEG, 28. *See also* Laugerud regime; Quiché

Wright, Francis W., 39–40

Ydígoras Fuentes, José Miguel Ramón, 16, 44

Yujá Xona, Gregorio, 62. See also CUC

Zelada Carrillo, Ramón, 143